# MASTER DATA STORYTELLING

*Skyrocket Your Business Impact with Data Visualization*

*Rajender Kumar*

This publication is designed to provide accurate and authoritative information in regard to the subject matter covered. All facts and figures are accurate at the time of publishing.

## TRADEMARKS

All product and brand names identified throughout this book are used for their benefit with no intention of infringement of their copyrights.

## SCREENSHOTS

All the screenshots used (if any) in this book are taken with the intention to better explain the tools, technologies, strategies, or the purpose of intended product/ service, with no intention of their copyright's infringement.

## WEBSITE REFERENCES

All website references were current at date of publication.

For more information, contact: support@JambaAcademy.com.

**Published by:**
Jamba Academy

**Printed in the United States of America**
First Printing Edition, 2025

# DISCLAIMER

## Found Typos & Broken Link

We apologize in advance for any typos or broken link that you may find in this book. We take pride in the quality of our content and strive to provide accurate and useful information to our readers. Please let us know where you found the typos and broken links (if any) so that we can fix them as soon as possible. Again, thank you very much in advance for bringing this to our attention and for your patience.

If you found any typos and broken links in this book, please feel free to email us.

support@JambaAcademy.com

## Support

We would love to hear your thoughts and feedback! Could you please take a moment to write a review or share your thoughts on the book? Your feedback helps other readers discover the books and helps authors to improve their work. Thank you for your time and for sharing your thoughts with us!

If there is anything you want to discuss or you have a question about any topic of the book, you can always reach out to us, and we will try to help as much as we can.

support@JambaAcademy.com

*To every reader striving to transform data into impactful stories, your passion for clear, persuasive communication inspires this book's mission to elevate your business influence.*

# TABLE OF CONTENTS

# FOREWORD

In today's global business landscape, data is ubiquitous. From multinational corporations tracking operational efficiency across continents to startups striving to understand customer sentiment in real time, the volume and velocity of data have never been greater. Yet, as organizations amass terabytes of information, a new challenge emerges: The true value of data lies not in its existence, but in our ability to interpret, communicate, and act upon it. This is where the art and science of data storytelling become indispensable.

Having spent over two decades as a data scientist and business consultant—collaborating with Fortune 500 companies, guiding non-profit organizations, and advising entrepreneurial ventures, I have witnessed firsthand the transformative impact of effective data visualization. The ability to distill complex datasets into meaningful stories is, unequivocally, one of the most critical skills for any professional seeking to drive business impact in the digital age.

It is my distinct pleasure to introduce **Master Data Storytelling: Skyrocket Your Business Impact with Data Visualization**, authored by Rajender Kumar, an internationally recognized authority in business analytics and visual communication. Kumar's unique blend of technical mastery and business acumen positions her as a leading voice in this pivotal field.

### The Imperative of Data Storytelling in Business

The business world is awash with dashboards, charts, and reports. Yet, the reality remains: data alone does not drive decisions—stories do. Decision-makers gravitate toward narratives that illuminate the "why" behind the numbers and the "so what" that compels action. In the absence of a coherent story, even the most sophisticated analysis risks being overlooked or misunderstood.

Consider the case of a global retail chain that, despite investing millions in data infrastructure, struggled to improve customer retention. Their quarterly reports overflowed with bar charts and line graphs, but executives lamented a lack of actionable insight. It wasn't until a data analyst visualized customer churn as a journey—mapping touchpoints, highlighting moments of friction, and pairing data with customer testimonials—that leadership grasped the root causes and rallied behind a targeted strategy. Within a year, the company saw a measurable uptick in loyalty and revenue.

This example underscores a universal truth: Data storytelling bridges the gap between analysis and action. It transforms abstract metrics into tangible narratives that resonate with stakeholders at every level—from the marketing team in São Paulo to the C-suite in Tokyo.

## A Timely and Transformative Guide

*Master Data Storytelling* stands apart in a crowded field of business books. Rather than treating data visualization as a technical afterthought, Rajender elevates it to a central business discipline. The book demystifies the process of transforming raw numbers into compelling stories, blending foundational theory with practical application.

What differentiates this work is its holistic approach. Kumar deftly guides readers through the essentials—chart selection, color theory, and design principles—before advancing into the nuanced world of narrative construction, emotional resonance, and cultural sensitivity in data presentation. Each chapter is enriched with real-world business examples, from an African fintech startup leveraging infographics to secure investor confidence, to a European pharmaceutical company using interactive dashboards to streamline clinical decision-making.

In a world where remote collaboration and cross-cultural teams are the norm, the ability to communicate insights clearly and inclusively is more vital than ever. The author recognizes that data stories must transcend borders, integrating global perspectives and adapting to varied business contexts. The book's diverse case studies, actionable frameworks, and emphasis on ethical data representation make it an invaluable resource for professionals everywhere.

## Empowering Business Professionals at Every Level

Whether you are a novice analyst eager to make your first presentation or a seasoned executive tasked with steering organizational strategy, this book meets you where you are. Author's approachable style and step-by-step guidance empower readers to:

- Decode complex data sets with confidence
- Select and design visuals that clarify, not confuse
- Weave numbers into narratives that inspire and persuade
- Avoid common pitfalls that undermine credibility

For the marketing manager in Mumbai seeking to demonstrate campaign ROI, the HR director in Toronto presenting workforce analytics, or the product lead in Nairobi pitching a new solution, the tools and techniques in this book will prove indispensable.

### A Timely Example: Data Storytelling in Crisis Response

The COVID-19 pandemic illuminated the profound need for clear data communication. Governments, businesses, and communities around the world relied on data visualizations to inform critical decisions—be it resource allocation, supply chain adjustments, or public health messaging. Companies that excelled in data storytelling were able to respond with agility and transparency, building trust and securing stakeholder buy-in during unprecedented uncertainty.

One striking example comes from a logistics company operating across Southeast Asia. By visualizing shipment delays alongside changing government regulations, the company enabled its partners to anticipate disruptions and adapt routes proactively. The result was not only operational resilience but also strengthened client relationships, demonstrating that effective data storytelling can drive both tactical and strategic success.

### Endorsement of the Author

Author brings a wealth of experience to this subject, blending academic rigor with pragmatic insight. His work has empowered leaders across five continents to harness the power of data storytelling, and his training sessions are renowned for their clarity, relevance, and impact. Readers of this book will benefit from his deep expertise, thoughtful guidance, and passion for making data accessible to all.

### An Invitation to Transform Your Business Impact

As you prepare to embark on this journey, I encourage you to approach these pages with curiosity and ambition. The ability to master data storytelling will not only enhance your professional toolkit but also position you as a catalyst for innovation, influence, and growth within your organization.

Whether you are seeking to persuade a skeptical stakeholder, inspire a team, or chart a new strategic direction, the art of data storytelling is your greatest ally. Let the author be your guide to unlocking this essential business skill.

Dive in, embrace the practice, and prepare to transform how you—and your organizations see and shape the world through data.

**— Dr. Marcus Lee, PhD**
Senior Data Scientist and Business Consultant
Global Advisor in Data-Driven Strategy

# PREFACE

In a world where data is both abundant and indispensable, the ability to transform streams of numbers into meaningful insights has never been more critical. As a business professional, I have witnessed firsthand the dramatic impact that effective data storytelling can have—not only on decision-making but on the very trajectory of organizations. The journey that led to this book, *Master Data Storytelling: Skyrocket Your Business Impact with Data Visualization*, is both deeply personal and universally relevant. It is driven by a passion to bridge the gap between raw data and actionable business wisdom, empowering professionals from all walks of life to communicate with clarity, confidence, and conviction.

My fascination with data visualization began early in my career, when I was tasked with presenting quarterly sales figures to a diverse board of directors at a multinational company. The dataset was robust, the numbers promising, yet my initial presentation—filled with dense tables and jargon-heavy charts—elicited more confusion than excitement. A seasoned executive approached me afterward and said, "Rajender, the numbers are impressive, but what's the real story? How does this change what we do next?" That moment was a turning point. I realized that the true power of data lies not in the numbers themselves, but in the stories they can tell and the actions they can inspire.

This book is the culmination of years spent at the intersection of analysis, design, and business strategy. Through collaborations with marketers driving brand growth, analysts uncovering market trends, and executives steering organizations through uncertainty, I have observed a common challenge: the struggle to convey complex data in ways that resonate with both logic and emotion. Too often, vital insights are lost in translation, buried beneath technical details, or presented in ways that fail to engage decision-makers. The result? Opportunities missed, innovations stalled, and potential left unrealized.

*Master Data Storytelling* is my response to this challenge. It is designed for those who recognize that data alone is not enough. Whether you are a marketer seeking to justify campaign investments, an analyst striving to highlight emerging patterns, or an executive aiming to align teams around a shared vision, this book provides a roadmap for making your insights both understandable and unforgettable.

What sets this book apart is its focus on practical, real-world application. Data visualization is often treated as a technical skill, reserved for specialists or relegated to the domain of "pretty charts." I take a different approach. Here, visualization is not just about aesthetics, it is a strategic business tool. By demystifying the principles behind effective visuals and grounding them in business contexts, I aim to make data storytelling accessible to everyone, regardless of technical background. The techniques, frameworks, and examples presented are drawn from diverse industries and geographies, reflecting the global nature of today's business landscape.

One experience that particularly shaped my perspective occurred during a consulting engagement with a retail company expanding into Southeast Asia. The leadership team was overwhelmed by data: sales trends, customer feedback, market forecasts. Each department spoke its own "data language," resulting in siloed decisions and missed synergies. Working together, we developed a unified visualization strategy—one that distilled complex datasets into intuitive dashboards and compelling narratives. The transformation was remarkable. Teams found common ground, strategies were refined, and the company achieved its most successful product launch to date. It was a vivid demonstration of how data storytelling can break down barriers, foster collaboration, and drive tangible business results.

Throughout this book, you will find a blend of foundational concepts and advanced techniques, always anchored in business relevance. You will learn how to choose the right charts for your message, harness the psychology of color and design, and structure narratives that appeal to both the analytical and the intuitive. Real-world examples—from a North American tech company's product pitch, to a European NGO's fundraising campaign, to an Asian manufacturer's operational review—illustrate how organizations around the world are using data storytelling to spark innovation and influence outcomes.

The need for effective data storytelling has never been greater. As organizations grapple with ever-expanding datasets, remote collaboration, and rapidly shifting markets, the ability to communicate insights clearly and persuasively is a competitive advantage. Yet, common pitfalls persist: overcrowded dashboards, misleading visualizations, and narratives that fall flat. This book addresses these challenges head-on, offering actionable guidance to avoid mistakes and achieve clarity.

Ultimately, my goal is to empower you, the reader, to become a catalyst for change within your organization. By mastering the art of data storytelling, you will not only elevate your professional impact but also contribute to a culture of evidence-based decision-making, innovation, and shared understanding. Whether you are presenting to a boardroom of executives, collaborating with global partners, or engaging with clients, the skills you develop here will help you turn insight into action.

As you embark on this journey, I invite you to approach data visualization not as a technical hurdle, but as a creative and strategic endeavor. Embrace the opportunity to connect with your audience, to illuminate possibilities, and to inspire meaningful action. The tools and perspectives shared in these pages are designed to grow with you, adapting to new challenges and opportunities as your career evolves.

Thank you for joining me in this exploration of data storytelling. I am confident that, together, we can unlock the full potential of your data—and in doing so, help your business not just compete, but lead and thrive in a data-driven world.

**Rajender Kumar**

# ACKNOWLEDGEMENTS

The journey of writing *Master Data Storytelling: Skyrocket Your Business Impact with Data Visualization* has been an extraordinary tapestry woven from the insights, encouragement, and expertise of many remarkable individuals. As I reflect on the path from initial concept to final manuscript, I am deeply grateful for the collective wisdom and support that made this book possible.

First, my heartfelt thanks go to the editorial team at Jamba Academy, whose keen eyes and commitment to clarity elevated every chapter. Special appreciation is due to my lead editor, Priya Shah, whose meticulous attention to detail and constructive feedback helped transform technical drafts into engaging narratives. Her guidance ensured that the content remained accessible, relevant, and compelling for business professionals across industries.

I am indebted to a global network of data professionals who contributed generously throughout the writing process. Dr. Ahmed El-Gamal, a data scientist based in Cairo, offered invaluable feedback on visual analytics and shared practical perspectives on the evolving landscape of data storytelling in emerging markets. Meanwhile, Mei Lin, a visualization specialist from Singapore, provided detailed critiques on early drafts of the visual case studies, helping to sharpen the book's focus on cross-cultural communication and inclusivity in design. Their diverse viewpoints enriched the book's examples and reinforced its relevance for an international audience.

My gratitude extends to mentors and colleagues who encouraged me to pursue this project and challenged me to think bigger. Professor Evelyn Carter, whose pioneering research on narrative and cognition shaped my understanding of storytelling's power, served as an intellectual sounding board from the outset. My colleagues at Bridge Group Analytics, especially Akash Sharma and Tanwir Khan, offered both technical insights and real-world business scenarios, bridging the gap between abstract concepts and practical application.

Research assistance from Anika Patel, a graduate student at the Florida International University, proved indispensable. Her diligent sourcing of global business case studies and her knack for distilling complex research into actionable insights kept the book grounded in current, real-world challenges.

On a personal note, I am profoundly grateful to my family and friends. My partner, provided unwavering emotional support and patience throughout countless late nights and early mornings. Their encouragement, humor, and understanding kept me focused and inspired.

Collaboration has been the heart of this book's development. Each contributor, whether through critical feedback, technical expertise, or steadfast encouragement—has shaped its voice, depth, and reach. The process underscored the very principles at the core of data storytelling: that the clearest, most impactful stories emerge when diverse perspectives come together in pursuit of a common goal.

To all who shared their time, knowledge, and encouragement: thank you. This book stands as a testament to your contributions and to the power of community in making complex ideas accessible, actionable, and truly transformative for business professionals everywhere.

## ABOUT THE AUTHOR

Rajender Kumar is a distinguished data professional with over a decade of hands-on experience at the intersection of data science, visualization, and business analytics. Renowned for his expertise in transforming raw data into compelling business narratives, Rajender has partnered with industry frontrunners such as Walgreens Boots Alliance, Healthcare Retroactive Audits, NEBA, and Loxia Technologies. His career spans a diverse array of sectors, providing him with a uniquely global perspective on how data-driven storytelling can spark innovation and drive impactful decision-making.

Rajender's journey into the world of data storytelling began early in his career, when he was tasked with presenting complex healthcare analytics to a non-technical executive team. Faced with blank stares and disengagement, he realized that simply sharing numbers, even the most critical ones, was not enough. This pivotal moment ignited his passion for bridging the gap between technical data insights and clear, actionable business stories. Since then, Rajender has dedicated himself to perfecting the art and science of Master Data Storytelling, helping organizations turn information overload into strategic clarity.

Known for his meticulous approach, Rajender excels at designing tailored data visualization solutions that resonate with both startups seeking agility and established enterprises aiming for operational excellence. His methodology goes beyond aesthetics; he delves deep into understanding organizational goals, audience needs, and cultural contexts to ensure every visualization serves a distinct business purpose. Whether building dashboards for healthcare compliance audits, visualizing retail performance trends, or guiding digital transformation initiatives, Rajender consistently empowers stakeholders to see the story behind the numbers.

A hallmark of Rajender's work is his commitment to inclusivity and accessibility in data communication. He has led cross-functional teams spanning North America, Europe, and Asia, always adapting his storytelling techniques to suit diverse audiences. One of his proudest achievements includes mentoring a team of young analysts in India, guiding them as they developed a real-time data visualization suite that drove a 20 percent increase in customer satisfaction for a global client.

Rajender is a champion of continuous learning and mentorship. He regularly conducts workshops and webinars on Master Data Storytelling, sharing best practices and emerging trends with aspiring data professionals and business leaders alike. His contributions extend beyond corporate walls, as he volunteers time to mentor students and early-career professionals, nurturing the next generation of data storytellers.

His philosophy is simple yet powerful: effective data visualization is not just about making data "look good"—it's about making data matter. Through his work, Rajender Kumar has helped organizations across the globe transform their approach to data, ensuring that every insight is both seen and understood. His unwavering dedication to education, innovation, and impactful communication cements his reputation as a leading authority in the field of Master Data Storytelling.

# INTRODUCTION: FROM NUMBERS TO NARRATIVE

It began with a single chart. In 2014, Airbnb's growth had stagnated in New York City, and the leadership team was searching for answers. Analysts pored over spreadsheets, but the insights were hidden in columns and rows—obscured by noise and complexity. Then, a data scientist visualized user behavior on a city map, revealing clusters where hosts struggled with bookings. The story didn't stop at the visualization; it sparked a narrative about trust, neighborhood perceptions, and local regulations. Armed with this story, Airbnb recalibrated its marketing and outreach, leading to a surge in bookings and a new understanding of its customer base. This wasn't just a business win—it was a triumph of **data storytelling**.

In today's fast-paced business landscape, data is everywhere. Organizations collect more information than ever before, from customer preferences and sales figures to supply chain metrics and social media sentiment. Yet, amid this deluge, one truth stands out: **Data alone doesn't drive decisions—stories do**.

## The Rise of Data Storytelling in Business

Data's role in decision-making has evolved dramatically. In the early days of business analytics, companies relied on static report-printed tables, basic bar charts, and dense presentations. These documents served their purpose but rarely inspired action. Over time, as technology advanced, so did our ability to collect, analyze, and present data. Tools like Tableau, Power BI, and Python's data visualization libraries made it possible to create dynamic, interactive visuals.

However, even the most beautiful chart can fall flat if it lacks context or emotional resonance. The world's most successful organizations have realized that true impact comes not just from showing data, but from **weaving it into compelling stories**. This approach transforms raw numbers into narratives that clarify, persuade, and motivate.

Consider the 2018 campaign by a global consumer products company seeking to rebrand after a series of lackluster quarters. Traditional reports failed to move skeptical board members. But when the marketing team crafted a narrative—supported by clear, evocative visuals—showing how shifting consumer demographics were driving new trends, the conversation changed. The board was no longer reviewing numbers; they were seeing a future unfold, supported by data. The rebranding effort gained traction, and the company's market share rebounded.

### Why Data Storytelling Matters Now More Than Ever

The world's leading firms understand that the ability to **tell stories with data** is a game-changer. It bridges the gap between technical analysis and business action, making insights accessible and memorable for diverse audiences. This is particularly crucial for business professionals across roles:

- **Marketers** need to communicate campaign results, market trends, and consumer insights in a way that resonates with creative teams and executives alike.
- **Analysts** must translate complex data sets into clear recommendations, ensuring that stakeholders understand both the 'what' and the 'why.'
- **Executives** rely on concise, persuasive data stories to guide strategy, inspire teams, and align stakeholders.

In a global context, data storytelling transcends language and cultural barriers. For example, a multinational telecommunications firm in Singapore leveraged data-driven narratives to illustrate customer pain points across different regions. By visualizing these patterns and sharing them in story form, they united cross-cultural teams around shared objectives and innovative solutions.

### The Objectives and Scope of This Book

**Master Data Storytelling: Skyrocket Your Business Impact with Data Visualization** is designed to be your practical, accessible guide to transforming business data into powerful stories. Whether you are new to data visualization or a seasoned professional seeking to refine your storytelling skills, this book will provide you with:

- **A clear understanding of the principles** behind effective data storytelling
- **Step-by-step strategies** to craft visuals that not only inform but inspire
- **Techniques for selecting the right charts and design elements** for your audience and objectives
- **Real-world examples and case studies** from diverse industries and cultural contexts
- **Actionable tips** for overcoming common pitfalls and ensuring your message lands with impact

Unlike technical manuals that focus solely on data tools, this book bridges the gap between **data literacy** and **business communication**. It emphasizes both the art and science of storytelling, equipping you to make data-driven insights not just understandable, but unforgettable.

### Three Real-World Milestones in Data Storytelling

To underscore the transformative power of data storytelling, let's briefly explore three business milestones:

**Starbucks' Global Expansion (2010s):** Starbucks used geospatial data visualization to identify untapped markets worldwide. By mapping consumer trends, population growth, and purchasing behaviors, they crafted a narrative that convinced stakeholders to invest in new regions. The result? Successful entries into markets from China to India, driven by data stories tailored to local cultures.

**UNICEF's Polio Eradication Campaign:** In partnership with data scientists, UNICEF visualized vaccination coverage and outbreak risks across Africa. Their narrative, supported by maps and infographics, galvanized donor support and government action, directly contributing to a historic reduction in polio cases.

**Netflix's Content Strategy:** Netflix famously leverages data storytelling to inform its content investments. By visualizing viewer engagement patterns and weaving these insights into presentations, Netflix's leadership justifies multi-million-dollar programming decisions, ensuring buy-in across creative and financial teams.

Each of these successes shares a common thread: leaders who could not just analyze data, but **communicate its meaning through story**.

### What Makes This Book Different?

While many resources teach the mechanics of creating charts or dashboards, few address the critical question: **How do you turn data into stories that move people to action?** This book is built on three pillars:

**Business-first perspective:** Every concept is grounded in real-world business challenges, ensuring that techniques are immediately applicable in boardrooms, marketing reviews, and client meetings.

**Inclusive, global approach:** Examples span industries and cultures, with attention to how data storytelling adapts to different audiences and business contexts.

**Balance of theory and practice:** You'll gain foundational knowledge, learn how to avoid common pitfalls, and get hands-on guidance for crafting your own data stories, regardless of your technical background.

### A Global Perspective: Data Storytelling Without Borders

In an era of globalization, business professionals increasingly work in diverse, multicultural environments. Data storytelling is a universal language—when done thoughtfully, it can unite teams across continents and backgrounds. For instance, a large pharmaceutical company headquartered in Germany used data visualizations to communicate clinical trial results across its Asian and African divisions, adapting colors, symbols, and narrative cues to local preferences. The initiative accelerated regulatory approvals and built trust with both internal and external stakeholders.

Similarly, a digital marketing agency in Brazil leverages data storytelling to bridge gaps between creative teams and analysts. By visualizing campaign results and customer journeys in engaging story formats, they foster collaboration and innovation, ensuring that data drives both creativity and strategy.

These examples illustrate that while tools and data sources may vary, the core principles of effective data storytelling are universal. This book reflects that truth, offering approaches and insights relevant for professionals in any industry or geography.

### Your Journey Begins Here

You are not just a consumer of data, you are its interpreter, translator, and advocate. The ability to turn raw information into persuasive, actionable stories is one of the most valuable skills in business today. Whether you're persuading a skeptical board, inspiring a creative team, or guiding customers through complex choices, your mastery of data storytelling will set you apart.

As you move through the chapters of this book, you'll gain not only technical know-how, but also the confidence to communicate insights with clarity, empathy, and impact. You'll learn how to avoid information overload, sidestep common pitfalls, and create visuals that resonate—no matter your audience.

**Now, let's embark on this journey together. Unlock the power of your data, harness the art of storytelling, and watch your business impact soar.** The future belongs to those who can see the story behind the numbers—and tell it with skill and conviction. Let's begin.

*"Numbers have an important story to tell. They rely on you to give them a clear and convincing voice."*

— Stephen Few, Data Visualization Expert & Author

# PREREQUISITES: BUILDING YOUR FOUNDATION

Before embarking on the journey to master data storytelling and transform your business impact with visualization, it's crucial to assess and build the foundational skills and knowledge that will maximize your success with this book. Data storytelling sits at the intersection of business acumen, analytical thinking, visual design, and effective communication. Whether you are a beginner eager to unlock the power of data, an intermediate professional seeking to refine your skills, or an advanced leader aiming to drive strategic impact, understanding your starting point and addressing potential knowledge gaps will set you up for meaningful progress.

This section outlines the essential prerequisites tailored for various experience levels. For each, practical business scenarios demonstrate the importance of these skills, along with recommended resources to support your development. No matter what your background, you'll find encouragement and guidance to help you engage fully with the content ahead.

## For Beginners: Laying the Groundwork

If you're new to data visualization or analytics, you may wonder whether you have what it takes to tell compelling stories with data. The good news is that anyone with curiosity and a willingness to learn can master these skills. However, a basic understanding of data concepts and business context will help you get the most from this book.

### *Essential Knowledge and Skills*

- **Basic Numeracy:** Comfort with reading charts, interpreting percentages, and understanding simple calculations.
- **Familiarity with Microsoft Excel or Google Sheets:** Ability to create basic tables, simple charts (like bar or pie charts), and perform elementary data sorting.
- **Business Context Awareness:** Understanding of your organization's goals, key metrics, and what constitutes success in your role or industry.

### *Practical Example*

Imagine you are a marketing assistant tasked with reporting last quarter's campaign performance. Without the ability to create a simple bar chart showing leads by channel, your findings may be lost in a sea of numbers. Grasping visualization basics lets you turn raw data into an instant snapshot that your manager can act on.

*Recommended Resources*

**Online Course:** "Data Visualization with Excel" by Coursera (offered by PwC)

**Website:** [Microsoft's Excel Training Center](https://support.microsoft.com/excel)

*Addressing Barriers*

You may feel intimidated by the prospect of working with data if you lack a technical background. Rest assured, this book is designed to guide you step by step, starting from visual and conceptual basics. Leverage the resources above to build confidence and familiarity before diving into more advanced storytelling techniques.

### For Intermediate Learners: Deepening Analytical and Visual Skills

Business professionals with some experience in data analysis or reporting are well-positioned to take their skills to the next level. At this stage, you may be comfortable generating reports and basic charts but want to create more insightful, persuasive, and visually compelling stories.

*Essential Knowledge and Skills*

- **Analytical Thinking:** Ability to interpret trends, patterns, and outliers in data.
- **Intermediate Charting Skills:** Familiarity with line charts, scatter plots, and the use of filters or pivot tables in Excel or Google Sheets.
- **Basic Data Cleaning:** Understanding how to prepare and restructure raw data for analysis (e.g., removing duplicates, handling missing values).
- **Audience Awareness:** Recognizing the differing needs of stakeholders such as executives, clients, or team members.

*Practical Example*

Consider a sales analyst preparing a quarterly performance review for a regional manager. Beyond basic totals, the analyst needs to highlight trends, identify underperforming territories, and recommend actions. Selecting the right charts and focusing on key insights makes the report actionable, not just informative.

*Recommended Resources*

**Book:** "Good Charts: The HBR Guide to Making Smarter, More Persuasive Data Visualizations" by Scott Berinato

**Online Course:** "Data Visualization: Storytelling" by LinkedIn Learning

**Website:** [FlowingData](https://flowingdata.com) by Nathan Yau for inspiration and practical tips

**Free Tool:** [Tableau Public](https://public.tableau.com/) for hands-on experience with interactive visualizations

*Addressing Barriers*

A common challenge at this stage is moving from "making charts" to "telling stories." It's easy to fall into the habit of producing busy dashboards or overwhelming stakeholders with data. This book will help you focus on clarity, relevance, and narrative structure. Use the resources above to expand your analytical toolkit and practice designing with purpose.

### For Advanced Learners: Driving Strategic Impact

Executives, senior analysts, and data-driven leaders often operate at the intersection of strategy, insight, and influence. You likely have strong analytical and communication skills, but may be seeking to refine your ability to inspire action, align teams, or drive innovation through data storytelling.

*Essential Knowledge and Skills*

- **Strategic Framing:** Ability to connect data insights to broader business objectives and outcomes.
- **Advanced Visualization Tools:** Experience with platforms like Tableau, Power BI, or Google Data Studio, including interactive dashboards and custom visualizations.
- **Change Management:** Understanding how to use data stories to influence organizational culture, drive adoption of new initiatives, or shape strategic decisions.
- **Cultural Sensitivity:** Recognizing that stories and visuals may resonate differently across global audiences, and adapting accordingly.

*Practical Example*

A regional executive at a multinational company may use data storytelling to secure buy-in for a new market entry strategy. By tailoring data visuals to illustrate both global trends and local nuances, the executive bridges cultural gaps and aligns diverse stakeholders behind a common vision.

*Recommended Resources*

**Book:** "The Big Data-Driven Business: How to Use Big Data to Win Customers, Beat Competitors, and Boost Profits" by Russell Glass and Sean Callahan

**Online Course:** "Data-Driven Decision Making" by Coursera (offered by PwC)

**Website:** [Harvard Business Review's Data & Visuals Section](https://hbr.org/data-visualization) for strategic case studies and best practices

**Community:** [Data Visualization Society](https://www.datavisualizationsociety.com/) for global perspectives and professional networking

### *Addressing Barriers*

Advanced professionals may struggle with balancing detail and simplicity or adapting data stories for culturally diverse or cross-functional audiences. This book's later chapters provide frameworks for strategic storytelling and inclusive communication, helping you maximize your influence at the highest levels.

## Overcoming Common Barriers: Encouragement for Every Learner

Regardless of your starting point, it's normal to encounter obstacles such as lack of confidence, unfamiliarity with visualization tools, or uncertainty about audience expectations. The key is to approach learning with curiosity and persistence. Remember, the skills needed for data storytelling are learnable and grow with practice. As you progress through this book, you'll find guidance, examples, and practical exercises designed to meet you where you are and propel you forward.

## Reflection and Next Steps

By identifying your current level and bridging any knowledge gaps now, you'll be better equipped to master the art of data storytelling for business impact. Use the recommended resources to strengthen your foundation, and approach each chapter with an open mind, ready to engage, practice, and apply new techniques. No matter your background, you are poised to unlock the power of data visualization and lead your organization to new heights through the stories you tell.

# ESSENTIAL TOOLS, RESOURCES, AND MINDSET

Data visualization is no longer an exclusive domain reserved for data scientists or graphic designers with years of specialized training. In today's business landscape, the ability to turn raw data into compelling, actionable stories is accessible to anyone with the right tools, resources, and mindset. This section will demystify the essentials you need—and, just as importantly, what you do **not** need—to master data storytelling and drive business results.

### Rethinking the Barriers: What You Don't Need

Before diving into the practical tools and resources, it's important to dispel some of the most common myths that can discourage business professionals from embracing data visualization:

- **You do not need an advanced degree in statistics or computer science.** While understanding the basics of data is helpful, you don't need to be a mathematician to tell powerful stories with data.
- **You do not need expensive, enterprise-grade software.** There are numerous affordable—and even free—tools that are more than sufficient for creating impactful visualizations.
- **You do not need to be a professional designer.** Mastery of aesthetics helps, but most tools now offer intuitive interfaces and design templates that allow anyone to create polished, visually appealing charts and graphics.

By eliminating these perceived barriers, you free yourself to focus on what truly matters: clarity, relevance, and the ability to spark action through your insights.

### The Right Mindset: Curiosity, Empathy, and Clarity

The most essential "tool" in your data storytelling toolkit is your mindset. Effective data storytellers are not just translators of numbers, they are curious explorers, empathetic communicators, and relentless simplifiers.

**Curiosity:** A willingness to dig deeper into data, ask questions, and uncover meaningful patterns.

**Empathy:** Understanding your audience's needs, backgrounds, and concerns so you can tailor your message for maximum impact.

**Clarity:** Striving to remove clutter, jargon, and unnecessary complexity, focusing instead on messages that are both clear and actionable.

Adopting this mindset will help you approach data visualization as a process of communication, not just analysis.

## Affordable and Accessible Data Visualization Tools

The modern business environment offers a wealth of tools designed to make data visualization approachable and effective for everyone. Here are a few standout options that balance power, user-friendliness, and affordability:

### *Microsoft Excel and Google Sheets*

These ubiquitous spreadsheet tools are often underestimated, but they offer robust charting capabilities that are more than adequate for most business scenarios. With built-in templates for bar charts, line graphs, pie charts, and more, both Excel and Google Sheets allow users to create professional visualizations with just a few clicks.

- **Excel:** Particularly strong for advanced chart types and integration with other Microsoft Office tools.
- **Google Sheets:** Cloud-based, collaborative, and ideal for teams working remotely or across geographies.

### *Tableau Public*

Tableau has become an industry standard for interactive data visualization, and its free version, Tableau Public, is a powerful option for business professionals. It allows you to create interactive dashboards and publish them online, making it easy to share insights within your organization or with clients.

### *Datawrapper*

Designed for simplicity and speed, Datawrapper is a free online tool that enables users to create interactive charts, maps, and tables without any coding or design expertise. Its focus on accessibility and clean design makes it a favorite among journalists and business professionals alike.

### *Power BI*

Microsoft Power BI offers a free version that integrates seamlessly with Excel and other Microsoft products, making it ideal for businesses already embedded in the Microsoft ecosystem. Power BI's drag-and-drop interface enables users to build dynamic dashboards and share them effortlessly.

### *Canva*

While Canva is primarily known as a graphic design tool, its data visualization features are increasingly robust. Canva's intuitive interface, along with a vast library of templates, makes it easy for non-designers to produce attractive infographics and reports.

## Real-World Applications: Turning Tools into Business Impact

To illustrate how these tools and resources come to life in business, consider the following real-world examples from diverse industries and cultural contexts.

### *Example 1: Retail Sales Analysis (Excel & Power BI, United States)*

A regional retail manager in the United States used Excel to track monthly sales data across multiple store locations. By creating simple bar and line charts, she identified patterns in seasonal sales and product performance. To present these insights to senior management, she imported the data into Power BI, building an interactive dashboard that allowed executives to drill down by region, product, and time period. This clear, visual storytelling empowered the team to optimize inventory and promotional strategies, resulting in a 15% increase in quarterly sales.

### *Example 2: Social Impact Reporting (Datawrapper, Nonprofit, India)*

A nonprofit organization in India wanted to communicate the results of its clean water initiatives to international donors. Using Datawrapper, the communications team transformed survey results and field data into interactive maps and charts that highlighted the number of wells built, communities reached, and health outcomes improved. These visuals were embedded in digital reports and shared via social media, dramatically increasing donor engagement and attracting new funding.

### *Example 3: Marketing Campaign Performance (Google Sheets & Canva, Brazil)*

A marketing team in Brazil needed to report on the success of a national advertising campaign. They used Google Sheets to aggregate data from various channels, then leveraged built-in charts to visualize key metrics like reach, engagement, and conversion rates. For internal presentations, they exported these visuals to Canva, combining them with photos and narrative text to create a visually compelling summary. The result was a report that not only communicated ROI but also inspired creative discussions for future campaigns.

## Making the Most of What You Have

These examples underscore a crucial point: the true power of data storytelling does not reside in the sophistication of your software or the complexity of your analysis. Instead, it lies in your ability to connect the dots, deliver insights that matter, and engage your audience with clarity and purpose. Whether you’re a small business owner, a nonprofit leader, or a global executive, you can achieve world-class results using accessible tools and a thoughtful approach.

### Key Takeaways and Next Steps

To unlock the full potential of data visualization in your business, remember:

- Start with curiosity and empathy for your audience, not with the tools.
- Use affordable, readily available software—Excel, Google Sheets, Tableau Public, Datawrapper, Power BI, or Canva—to bring your stories to life.
- Focus on clarity, relevance, and simplicity; your goal is to illuminate, not to impress with complexity.
- Practice with real data from your business environment, learning by doing and iterating as you go.

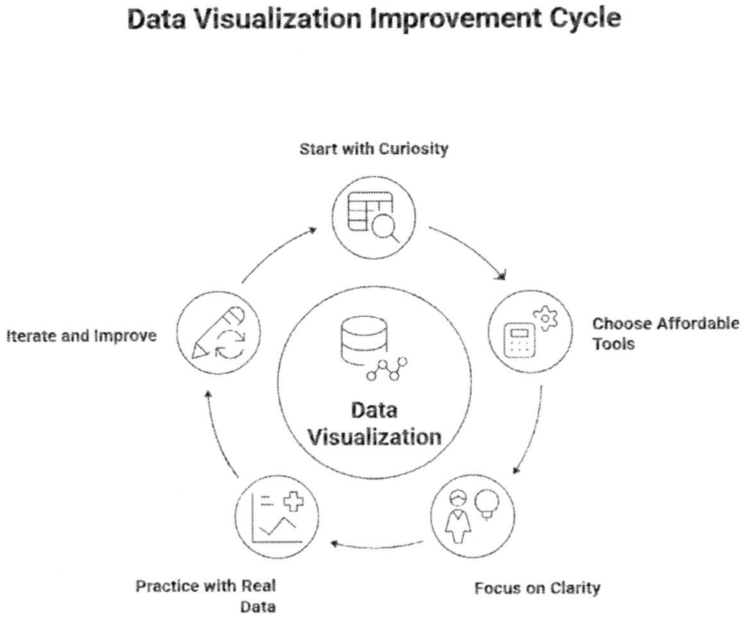


By embracing these principles and leveraging the right tools, you'll find that data storytelling is not only achievable, but transformative. As you progress through this book, you'll discover even more strategies and techniques to make your insights unforgettable, ensuring your business impact continues to grow.

## WHAT YOU WILL GAIN FROM THIS BOOK

In today's business world, data is everywhere, streaming in from digital campaigns, customer transactions, supply chains, and beyond. Yet, most organizations struggle to turn that raw information into actionable insight. The true value of data emerges not just in its collection, but in its communication. This book, **Master Data Storytelling: Skyrocket Your Business Impact with Data Visualization**, is designed to bridge that critical gap. Whether you're a marketer seeking to justify campaign ROI, an analyst aiming to influence strategic decisions, or an executive determined to align teams around a shared vision, this guide will equip you with the skills to transform numbers into compelling stories that drive meaningful business results.

As you progress through the chapters, you will develop a robust toolkit of data visualization and storytelling skills applicable across business functions and industries. Specifically, you will learn to:

- **Decode complex data** and distill it into clear, persuasive messages.
- **Select the right visualization types** for your audience and objectives, moving beyond generic bar charts to tailored visual narratives.
- **Apply core design principles**—such as color theory, hierarchy, and layout—to create visuals that are both aesthetically pleasing and instantly comprehensible.
- **Craft data-driven stories** that resonate emotionally and intellectually, blending quantitative analysis with qualitative context.
- **Communicate insights effectively** to diverse stakeholders, anticipating their needs and adapting your approach accordingly.
- **Avoid common pitfalls** in data visualization, such as misleading scales or cluttered graphics, ensuring your presentations are both ethical and impactful.
- **Leverage modern tools and platforms** for visualization, including emerging trends like interactive dashboards and real-time data storytelling.

Each of these outcomes is supported by hands-on exercises, practical frameworks, and real-world business examples, ensuring you can immediately apply your new skills to your daily work.

### Practical Applications in Business Contexts

The art of data storytelling is not just a technical exercise—it's a strategic business capability. Let's explore how these skills translate into tangible values in professional settings.

***Example 1: Marketing Campaign Optimization***

Consider a marketing manager at a multinational consumer goods company. Faced with declining engagement rates, she needs to convince the executive team to invest in a new digital ad strategy. Rather than presenting a dense spreadsheet of click-through rates and demographic breakdowns, she uses a series of annotated line graphs and heatmaps to illustrate how engagement shifts by channel and region. By weaving in customer testimonials and market trends, she creates a narrative that not only clarifies the problem but also inspires confidence in her proposed solution. The result? Approval for her budget request and a renewed focus on high-impact channels.

***Example 2: Operational Efficiency in Manufacturing***

Now, imagine a data analyst in a Japanese manufacturing firm tasked with improving supply chain efficiency. Armed with months of sensor data, he constructs an interactive dashboard highlighting bottlenecks and their downstream effects on delivery times. By combining process flow diagrams with real-time data visualizations, he enables plant managers—many of whom lack technical backgrounds—to instantly identify and prioritize areas for intervention. This approach leads to a 15 percent reduction in downtime within a single quarter, demonstrating the real-world power of clear storytelling.

***Example 3: Financial Services and Regulatory Reporting***

In the financial sector, a compliance officer at a London-based bank faces the daunting task of presenting risk exposure metrics to both internal executives and external regulators. By employing layered dashboards that allow users to drill down from high-level summaries to granular transaction details, she ensures that each stakeholder receives the precise information they need. Her transparent, visually-driven approach not only simplifies complex regulations but also builds trust with both colleagues and authorities.

These examples underscore a common truth: **effective data storytelling turns analysis into action**. It empowers decision-makers, accelerates consensus, and ultimately drives better business outcomes.

### For Every Professional: Supporting All Experience Levels

One of the strengths of this book is its accessibility. Whether you are just beginning your journey with data or are a seasoned expert seeking to hone your craft, you will find value here.

**Beginners** will benefit from foundational chapters that demystify key concepts—such as data literacy, chart selection, and the basics of visual perception—using jargon-free language and step-by-step guides. Practical exercises and checklists help solidify learning and build confidence with real datasets.

**Intermediate professionals** will discover advanced techniques for storytelling, including narrative arcs, audience analysis, and the responsible use of persuasive visuals. Case studies and sidebars offer perspectives from diverse industries and cultures, highlighting global best practices.

**Advanced practitioners** can dive into cutting-edge topics, such as interactive dashboards, real-time visualizations, and the ethical implications of data presentation. In-depth explorations of topics like data bias, accessibility, and cross-cultural communication ensure that even experts will expand their toolkit and stay ahead of trends.

Throughout, the book acknowledges the different challenges faced by various roles—from marketers and analysts to executives and consultants—ensuring that each reader can tailor their learning journey to their unique context.

### Meeting Today's Challenges: Trends and Relevance

The business landscape is evolving rapidly, driven by an explosion of data, increased competition, and heightened stakeholder expectations. Mastery of data storytelling is no longer optional; it is a core competency for leaders and organizations alike. This book is attuned to several key trends shaping the future of business communication:

**Data democratization:** As more employees gain access to analytics tools, clear communication becomes vital to prevent misinterpretation and ensure that data-driven decisions align with strategic goals.

**Remote and global teams:** With teams operating across borders and time zones, visuals and stories serve as universal languages, bridging cultural and linguistic gaps.

**Interactive and real-time insights:** Stakeholders now expect dynamic dashboards and on-demand analysis. You'll learn how to create and present these effectively, keeping pace with technological advances.

**Ethical data use:** As concerns about privacy and transparency grow, responsible storytelling is crucial. This book guides you in building trust by presenting data honestly and inclusively.

By aligning with these trends, the content remains both forward-looking and grounded in practical reality.

### Your Transformation Starts Here

Mastering data storytelling is not just about making prettier charts—it's about unlocking your full potential as a communicator, influencer, and leader. The skills you gain from this book will help you cut through noise, articulate your vision, and elevate your organization's impact in a crowded market. Whether you are navigating your first dashboard or orchestrating cross-functional strategy sessions, you will emerge with a new confidence in your ability to turn data into decisions and insights into outcomes.

Embrace the journey ahead. The tools, techniques, and stories within these pages are your blueprint for transforming data from an afterthought into your most powerful asset. Let's begin the journey to making your insights unforgettable—and your business unstoppable.

RAJENDER KUMAR

# Master Data Storytelling: Skyrocket Your Business Impact with Data Visualization

# 1. THE POWER OF DATA STORYTELLING IN MODERN BUSINESS

In today's hyper-competitive business world, information flows faster and in greater volume than ever before. Yet, amid terabytes of spreadsheets and dashboards, the real challenge isn't accessing data—it's making that data meaningful. The ability to translate raw numbers into clear, persuasive narratives is what separates those who merely report from those who truly influence. This chapter lays the groundwork for mastering data storytelling, revealing how visual communication can elevate your insights, drive better decisions, and ultimately set your business apart.

We begin by examining why data storytelling has become essential in modern business, exploring how human brains are naturally wired to process stories and visuals far more effectively than isolated facts or figures. By understanding the science behind visual communication, you'll discover why even the most complex datasets can—and should—be transformed into stories that resonate. We'll clarify what data storytelling actually means, moving beyond buzzwords to a practical definition that you can apply across roles and industries.

Throughout this chapter, you'll see how compelling data stories have driven strategic shifts in global organizations, from marketing campaigns that captured new markets to operations initiatives that streamlined processes. We'll address common misconceptions, such as the belief that data visualization is just about making charts look attractive, and highlight the true business impact of well-crafted stories.

Whether you're a marketer, analyst, or executive, you'll gain a fresh perspective on how data storytelling can empower your function and amplify your influence. As we embark on this journey, prepare to unlock the skills and mindset needed to transform data into your most persuasive business asset, setting the stage for deeper learning in the chapters ahead.

## 1.1. Why Data Storytelling Matters Today

In today's fast-paced business landscape, data is everywhere. Companies collect information from sales transactions, customer feedback, website analytics, and even social media interactions. However, the sheer volume of data can overwhelm teams, making it difficult to extract actionable meaning. This is where data storytelling becomes a crucial skill. Transforming numbers into compelling stories bridges the gap between raw data and impactful decision-making, empowering professionals to drive change, communicate value, and foster innovation.

*The Evolution from Data Reporting to Data Storytelling*

Traditional business reporting has often relied on static charts and dense tables to present information. While these methods provide facts, they rarely inspire action or forge emotional connections. Data storytelling takes reporting a step further. By combining visualizations with narrative context, it enables audiences to grasp not just what is happening, but why it matters and what should be done next.

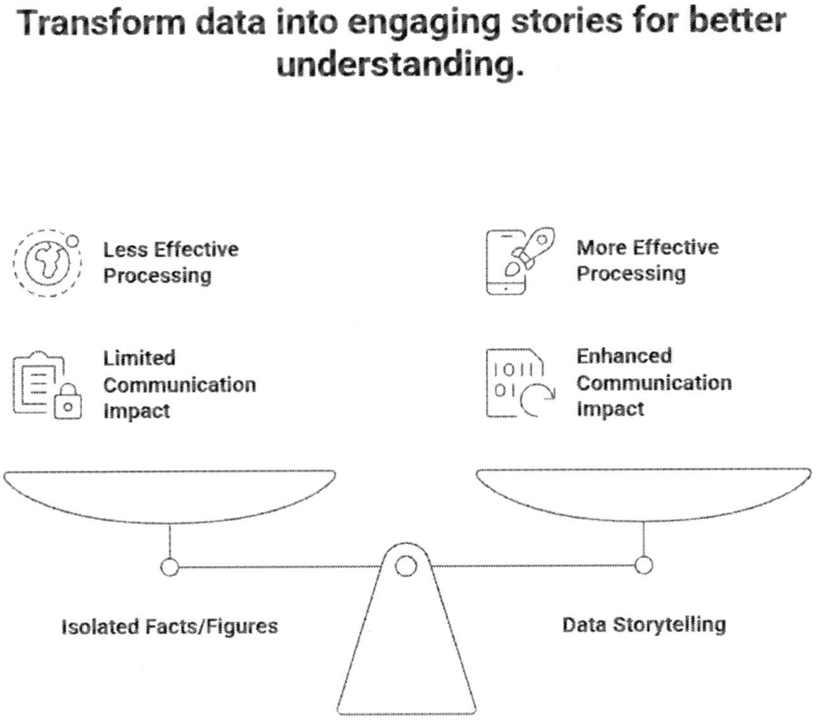


For example, when a marketing manager presents quarterly sales data, simply displaying a line graph may show trends, but weaving that trend into a story—such as highlighting how a targeted campaign in Southeast Asia led to a notable uptick in sales—makes the insight memorable and actionable.

*The Business Case for Data Storytelling*

Data storytelling matters today because organizations face several key challenges:

- **Information Overload:** With so much data available, it's easy for critical insights to get lost unless they are presented clearly and persuasively.

- **Diverse Audiences:** Stakeholders come from varied backgrounds, each with different levels of data literacy. Storytelling makes complex data accessible to everyone.
- **Decision Fatigue:** Decision-makers are bombarded with choices. Stories help them focus on what's important and prompt decisive action.
- **Global Collaboration:** Teams often work across borders and cultures. A well-crafted data story can cut through language barriers and resonate universally.

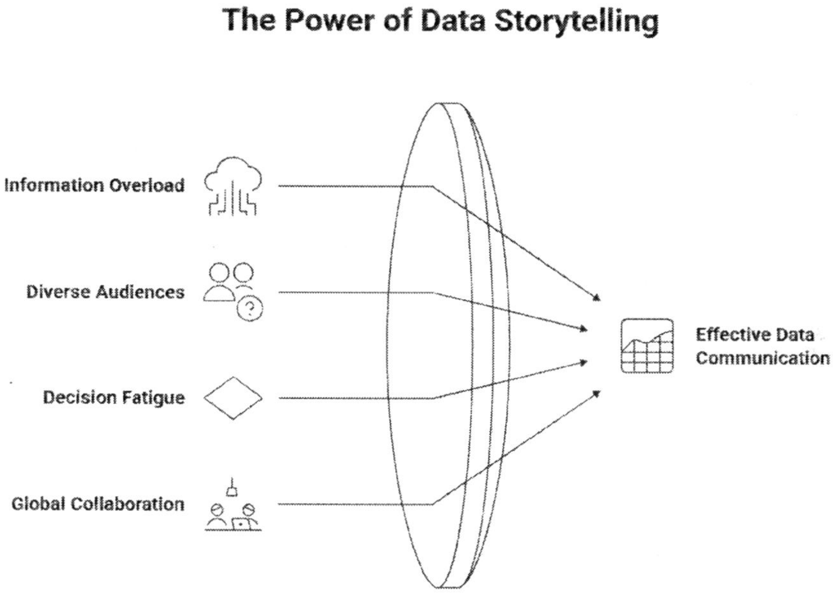


***Real-World Scenarios: Data Storytelling in Action***

To appreciate the impact of data storytelling, consider these scenarios drawn from real-world business contexts:

### 1. Retail Dashboard Drives Global Strategy

A global retail brand uses Tableau, a leading data visualization tool, to consolidate sales, inventory, and customer feedback across its regions. Instead of inundating executives with spreadsheets, the analytics team designs an interactive dashboard that tells a story. The dashboard highlights a sudden dip in customer satisfaction scores in Latin America, correlating it with delayed shipments. The narrative, supported by concise visuals and annotations, prompts the executive team to prioritize logistics improvements in that region, leading to a rapid recovery in both customer sentiment and sales.

**2. Healthcare Insights Transform Patient Care**

A hospital in Singapore leverages Microsoft Power BI to track patient outcomes and resource utilization. By visualizing the patient journey—using flowcharts and heatmaps—the data team uncovers a bottleneck in the emergency department during weekends. Sharing this story through an interactive report, complete with patient testimonials and key statistics, motivates hospital leadership to adjust staffing schedules. The result is improved patient wait times and higher satisfaction ratings.

***Visualization Tools: Enabling Effective Storytelling***

Modern data visualization tools such as Tableau, Power BI, and Google Data Studio are instrumental in building compelling data stories. These platforms allow users to:

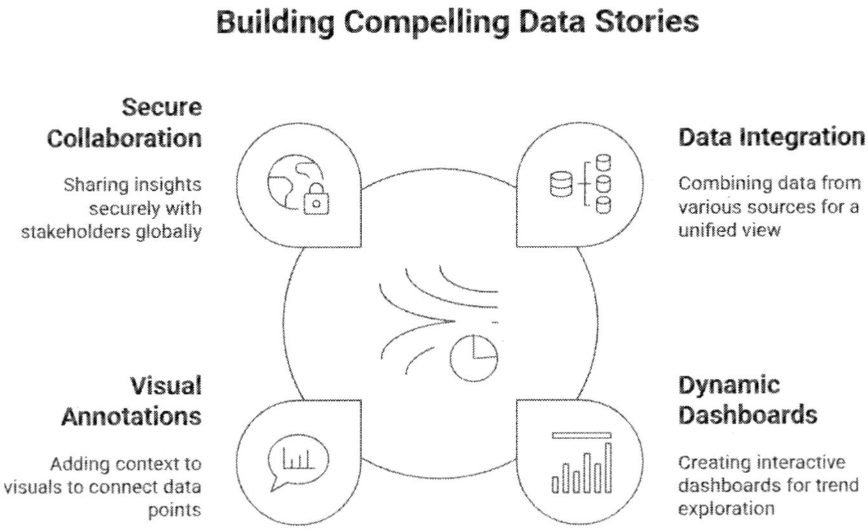


- Integrate data from multiple sources for a holistic view
- Create dynamic dashboards that invite exploration and reveal trends
- Annotate visuals to connect data points with business context
- Collaborate and share insights securely with stakeholders worldwide

For instance, a well-designed dashboard might combine bar charts, line graphs, and geographic maps, each serving a purpose in the overarching narrative. A sales dashboard may start with a big-picture revenue trend, then allow users to drill down into product categories or regions, highlighting where opportunities or challenges lie (an illustrative example shown below).

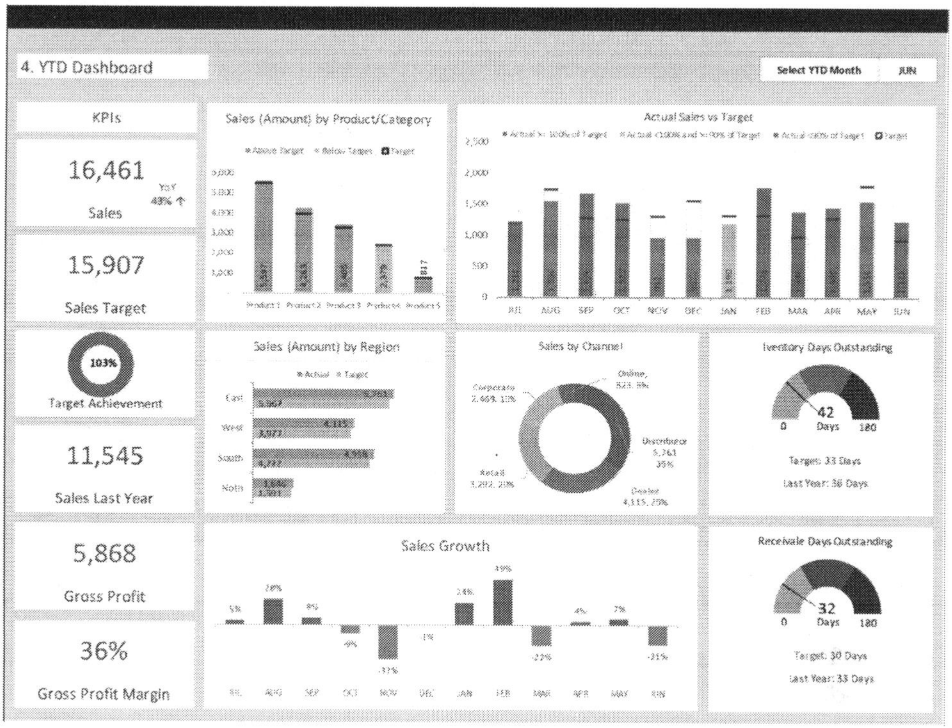


In summary, data storytelling is more than a technical skill; it's a business imperative in today's data-rich world. By transforming raw figures into accessible and engaging stories, professionals can unlock deeper insights, rally teams around priorities, and drive strategic outcomes. As we move forward, we'll explore the foundational elements of effective data visualization—the building blocks that turn everyday data into extraordinary stories.

## 1.2. The Human Brain and Visual Communication

Understanding why data visualization is so powerful begins with our own biology. The human brain is naturally wired to process visual information rapidly and intuitively. While we may spend years learning to interpret words and numbers, our ancestors depended on visual cues for survival—spotting ripe fruit, detecting predators, or navigating terrain. This evolutionary legacy makes visual communication uniquely effective in today's data-driven business environment.

### *How the Brain Processes Visual Information*

When you glance at a chart or dashboard, your brain doesn't just see colors and shapes; it instantly begins to recognize patterns, detect anomalies, and form judgments. This process, called **pre-attentive processing**, allows us to absorb complex information in milliseconds, often before we're fully conscious of it.

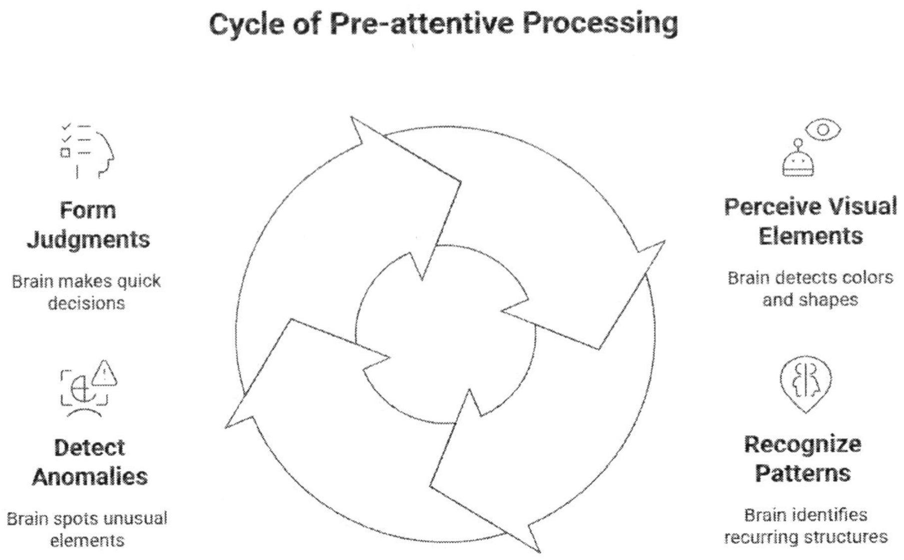


Key aspects of visual processing include:

- **Pattern Recognition**: The brain excels at identifying trends, outliers, and relationships in visual data. This makes charts and graphs far more effective than tables of raw numbers for conveying meaning.
- **Memory Retention**: Information delivered visually is easier to recall. Studies show people remember up to 65% of visual content after three days, compared to just 10% for verbal information.
- **Emotional Resonance**: Images and colors can evoke emotions, making data stories more compelling and memorable.

By harnessing these innate strengths, data visualization allows business professionals to communicate more efficiently and persuasively.

### *Visual Communication in Business: Real-World Scenarios*

Consider a global retail company launching a new product line. The marketing team gathers vast datasets from customer feedback, sales channels, and regional performance. Presenting this information in lengthy spreadsheets would likely overwhelm executives. Instead, a well-designed dashboard in **Power BI** displays sales trends, regional hotspots, and customer sentiment in a single, interactive view. Executives can instantly identify which markets are outperforming and where adjustments are needed.

Similarly, in the pharmaceutical sector, a European analytics team uses **Tableau** to visualize clinical trial outcomes across different demographics. By representing results with heat maps and trend lines, they quickly spot where a new drug is most effective and communicate these insights to diverse stakeholders—regulatory agencies, healthcare providers, and global partners—without language barriers or technical misunderstandings.

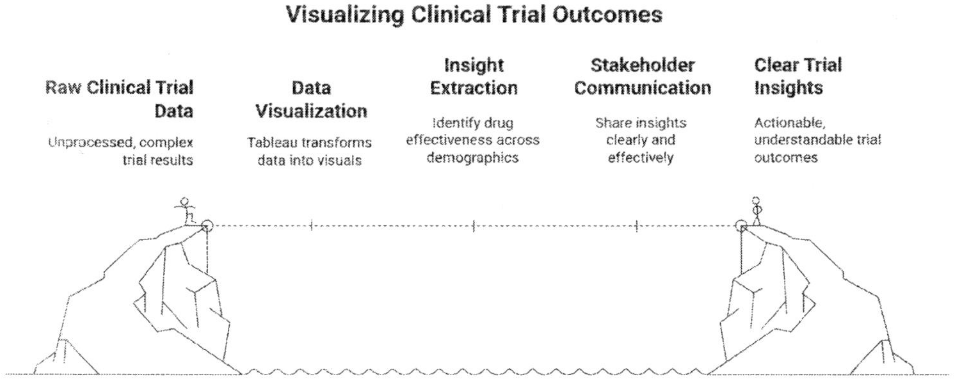


These examples highlight how visual communication helps bridge the gap between complex data and actionable business decisions. Visualization tools do not simply make data attractive; they make it accessible, understandable, and actionable.

***Business Dashboards: Bridging Data and Decision-Making***

One of the most impactful applications of visual communication is the **business dashboard**. Dashboards consolidate multiple data streams into a unified, interactive visual interface. By leveraging the brain's visual acuity, dashboards help users track key performance indicators (KPIs), diagnose issues, and forecast trends efficiently.

A typical dashboard might include:

- **Line charts** to visualize sales growth over time
- **Bar graphs** comparing product performance by region
- **Heat maps** revealing geographical sales concentrations
- **Pie charts** illustrating market share distribution

These elements are not chosen at random. Each visual is carefully selected to match the type of data and the business question at hand, maximizing clarity and impact.

For instance, a financial analyst at a multinational conglomerate might use Tableau to create a real-time dashboard that monitors currency fluctuations and their impact on overseas revenue. With color-coded alerts and historical trend lines, decision-makers can react instantly to emerging risks or opportunities, something that would be almost impossible with static reports.

### *Visualization Tools: Turning Data into Visual Stories*

Modern visualization tools like Tableau, Power BI, and Google Data Studio empower professionals to translate raw data into meaningful visuals without extensive programming knowledge. These platforms offer intuitive drag-and-drop interfaces, built-in templates, and advanced analytics capabilities.

A simple example in Python, using the popular Matplotlib library, might look like:

```
import matplotlib.pyplot as plt

sales = [200, 340, 300, 420, 500]
months = [ 'Jan', 'Feb', 'Mar', 'Apr', 'May']

plt.plot(months, sales)
plt.title( 'Monthly Sales Trend')
plt.xlabel( 'Month')
plt.ylabel( 'Sales')
plt.show()
```

While business dashboards developed in Tableau or Power BI provide interactive, shareable, and dynamic views, even basic coding tools can help visualize patterns for smaller teams or quick analyses.

Visual communication taps into the brain's natural strengths, transforming overwhelming data into clear, memorable, and actionable business insights. By leveraging dashboards and modern visualization tools, professionals can present their ideas with clarity and confidence, ensuring their insights resonate across cultures and organizational levels. Next, we'll dive deeper into the core principles of effective data visualization, exploring the design choices that make stories not only seen, but truly understood.

## 1.3. Defining Data Storytelling

Data storytelling is more than just presenting facts and figures—it is the deliberate craft of transforming raw data into narratives that inform, persuade, and inspire action. In the business world, where information overload is the norm, having the ability to weave data into compelling stories empowers professionals to cut through the noise and make an undeniable impact.

To understand data storytelling, imagine standing in front of a room of executives, tasked with explaining last quarter's sales performance. A spreadsheet brimming with numbers may contain all the answers, but without context or a clear storyline, those insights remain lost. Data storytelling bridges this gap, guiding the audience through the data landscape with clarity, relevance, and purpose.

### *The Anatomy of Data Storytelling*

At its core, data storytelling fuses three essential elements:

- **Data:** The foundation, representing facts, metrics, and evidence collected from business activities.
- **Visualization:** The medium, using charts, graphs, and dashboards to present data in visually digestible forms.
- **Narrative:** The connective tissue, providing context, sequence, and emotional resonance to the information.

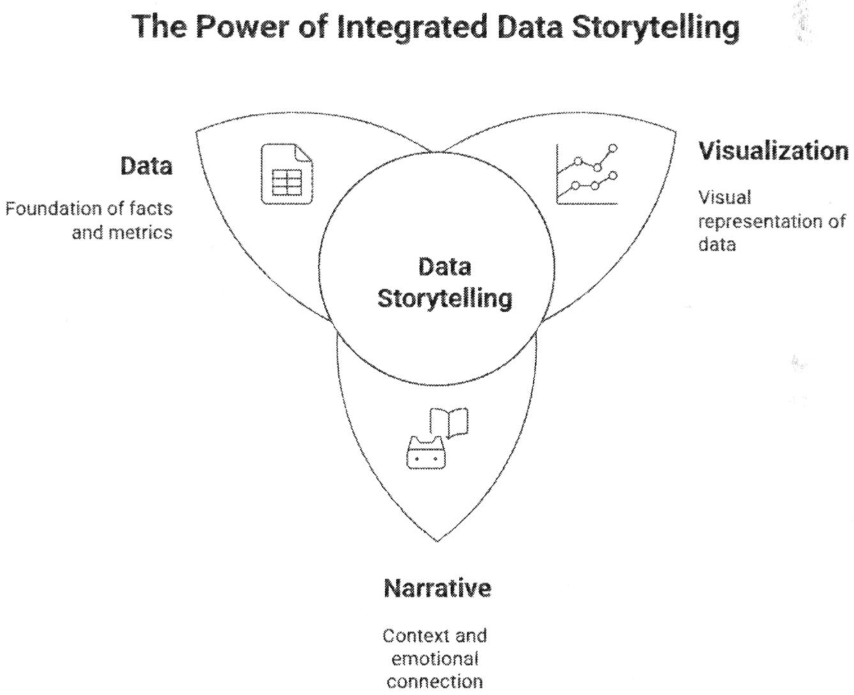


When these elements come together, the result is a story that not only communicates what happened, but also why it matters and what should be done next.

### *Why Data Storytelling Matters in Business*

Businesses today rely on data-driven decisions at every level, from strategic planning to day-to-day operations. However, data alone rarely drives action. It's the interpretation and communication—how the data is framed and shared—that makes the difference.

Consider the following benefits of mastering data storytelling:

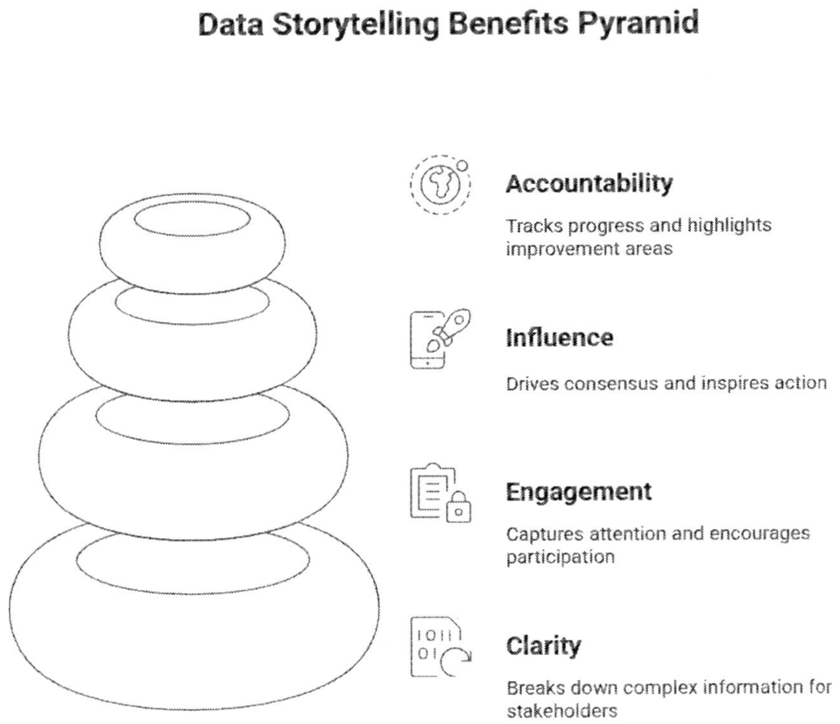


- **Clarity:** Breaks down complex information, making it accessible to all stakeholders.
- **Engagement:** Captures attention and encourages participation, whether in small team meetings or large-scale presentations.
- **Influence:** Drives consensus and inspires action by aligning stakeholders around a shared understanding.
- **Accountability:** Tracks progress and highlights areas for improvement using transparent, well-communicated data.

### *Real-World Business Scenarios*

To ground these concepts, let's examine two scenarios where data storytelling transformed business outcomes.

### Scenario 1: Retail Expansion Decisions Using Power BI

A global retail chain was evaluating which new markets to enter. Analysts assembled vast amounts of demographic, sales, and competitor data. But the executive team struggled to see the full picture until the data was visualized in a Power BI dashboard. The dashboard combined interactive maps and trend lines, all anchored by a narrative highlighting consumer behavior patterns and regional opportunities. The clear story enabled leaders to confidently select two new markets, leading to successful launches and increased revenue.

### Scenario 2: Improving Employee Engagement with Tableau Dashboards

An HR department at a multinational technology firm faced declining employee engagement scores. Raw survey data alone failed to reveal actionable insights. Using Tableau, the HR team created a series of dashboards illustrating engagement trends by department, tenure, and geography. Accompanied by a concise narrative, these visuals pinpointed specific challenges for remote teams in Asia and highlighted successful practices in European branches. Leadership used the story to launch targeted interventions, improving morale and productivity across the company.

#### *Visualization Tools and Dashboard Illustrations*

Effective data storytelling often hinges on the right tools. Popular platforms like **Tableau** and **Power BI** enable users to create interactive dashboards, blending data and visual elements seamlessly. For example:

**Tableau:** Allows intuitive drag-and-drop visualizations, ideal for crafting dynamic stories that update in real time.

**Power BI:** Integrates business analytics and visual storytelling, offering customizable dashboards with narrative annotations.

A well-designed dashboard might include:

Key metrics (e.g., sales growth, customer retention) presented as clear, concise visuals.

Filters and interactive elements that let users explore data from multiple angles.

Annotation features to highlight trends, anomalies, or recommendations within the broader story.

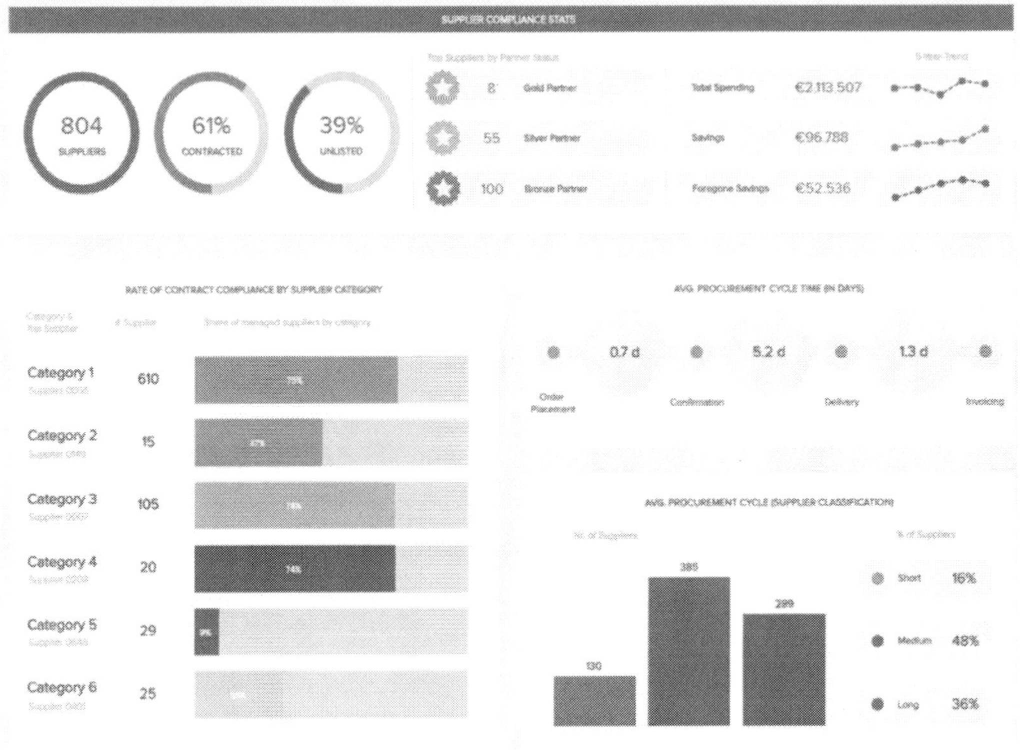


This simple code snippet mimics how sales data might be visualized as part of a broader business dashboard, turning raw numbers into a story about growth and opportunity.

```
# Example: Highlighting sales trends with Power BI

import matplotlib.pyplot as plt

months = [ 'Jan', 'Feb', 'Mar', 'Apr', 'May']
sales = [200, 250, 300, 280, 350]

plt.plot(months, sales, marker= 'o')
plt.title( "Monthly Sales Trend")
plt.xlabel( "Month")
plt.ylabel( "Sales (in thousands)")
plt.grid(True)
plt.show()
```

Defining data storytelling sets the stage for mastering the art of impactful communication in modern business. By combining data, visuals, and narrative, professionals create stories that resonate and drive results. Up next, we'll delve into the foundational principles of effective data visualization, ensuring your stories are not only compelling but also crystal clear to every audience.

## 1.4. Business Impact: Driving Decisions with Stories

Effective data storytelling has rapidly become an essential business skill, bridging the gap between raw data and actionable business decisions. In today's dynamic market, organizations generate and collect vast amounts of information, yet the true value lies in how this data is translated into meaningful narratives. When done right, data stories have the power to clarify priorities, motivate action, and unify teams around strategic goals.

### *Moving Beyond the Numbers: Why Stories Drive Action*

While data provides evidence, stories provide context and emotion. Numbers alone, no matter how precise, rarely inspire change. However, when those numbers are woven into a narrative that illustrates a problem, opportunity, or trend, decision-makers are more likely to engage and act. This is because stories help audiences:

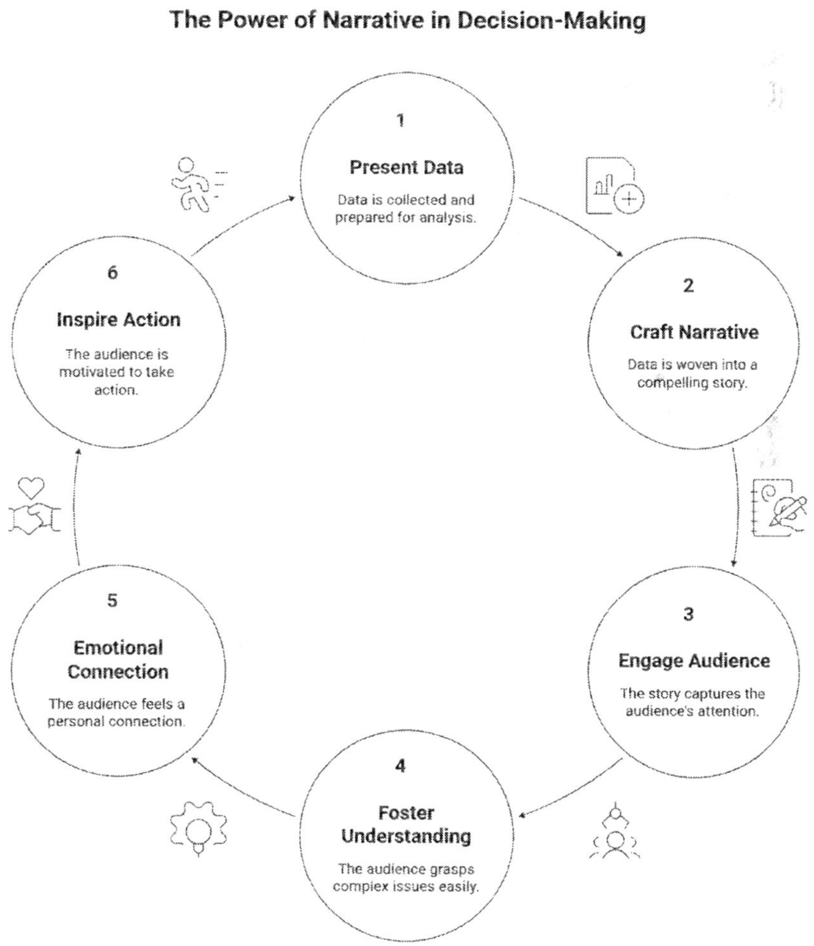

- Understand complex issues through relatable scenarios
- See themselves or their customers reflected in the data
- Remember and recall key insights more easily
- Connect emotionally to business challenges or successes

This approach is especially important in multicultural or global organizations, where stakeholders may have diverse backgrounds and perspectives. By grounding data in storytelling, communicators can foster a shared understanding regardless of technical expertise or cultural context.

***Real-World Use Case: Retail Expansion Decision***

Consider a retail chain evaluating potential markets for expansion. The analytics team gathers data on sales trends, demographic shifts, and competitor presence. Instead of presenting a dense spreadsheet, the team builds an interactive dashboard using **Power BI**. The dashboard visually maps sales growth alongside population changes and highlights areas with rising customer demand.

To tell the story, the team creates a narrative that follows "Sofia," a typical customer persona in a rapidly growing city. Through visualizations, stakeholders see Sofia's shopping patterns, the convenience of a new store location, and projected revenue impacts. This story, supported by clear visuals, enables executives to make a confident, data-backed decision to expand into that city.

***Real-World Use Case: Healthcare Service Improvement***

A global healthcare provider wants to improve patient wait times across its clinics. Using **Tableau**, analysts build a dashboard that tracks average wait times by location, time of day, and patient demographics. Instead of just displaying numbers, they craft a story around "Mr. Lee," an elderly patient experiencing delays.

The narrative follows Mr. Lee's journey, supported by timeline visualizations and heatmaps. This approach highlights bottlenecks, such as understaffed hours, and demonstrates how targeted staffing changes could reduce wait times. The story motivates clinic managers to implement new scheduling practices, resulting in measurable improvements in patient satisfaction.

***Business Dashboards: The Storytelling Canvas***

A well-designed business dashboard is more than a collection of charts—it's the canvas for your data story. To maximize impact, consider the following when building a dashboard:

**Define the Narrative Arc:** Identify the key message or decision your story supports.

**Prioritize Clarity:** Use clean layouts, consistent color schemes, and straightforward labels.

**Guide the Audience:** Highlight critical data points, use callouts, and arrange visuals in a logical flow.

**Encourage Exploration:** Enable interactive elements so stakeholders can dig deeper into areas of interest.

A global logistics company, for example, used Power BI dashboards to narrate the success of its new shipping routes. By visually comparing delivery times and costs before and after the changes, the story became clear: the new strategy delivered tangible business value.

As we move forward, we'll lay the groundwork for your own data storytelling journey by exploring the essential principles of effective data visualization. This foundation will help ensure your stories are not only engaging but also clear and credible to every audience.

## 1.5. Overcoming Common Misconceptions

Before diving into visualization techniques, it's crucial to dispel some persistent myths about data storytelling. Many business professionals, especially those new to the field, approach data visualization with assumptions that can limit their effectiveness. Addressing these misconceptions early on will empower you to craft more persuasive, accessible, and impactful stories with your data.

### *Misconception 1: "Data Visualization Is Just About Making Pretty Charts"*

A common pitfall is believing that data visualization is synonymous with aesthetic design. While visual appeal matters, the primary goal is **clarity and communication**. A visually stunning dashboard that confuses or misleads the audience is less valuable than a simple, clear chart that reveals actionable insights. Tools like Tableau and Power BI provide a range of design options, but their true power lies in helping users distill complex information into understandable visuals.

Consider a global marketing team preparing a quarterly report. Using Tableau, they initially focus on vibrant color palettes and intricate chart types to impress executives. However, the excessive detail and color distract from the main message: which regions are underperforming. After refocusing on clear bar charts and concise annotations, the team successfully highlights key trends, prompting decisive action and resource reallocation.

### *Misconception 2: "Only Data Scientists or Analysts Can Tell Data Stories"*

Another prevalent belief is that data storytelling is the exclusive territory of technical experts. In reality, **any business professional**—from marketers to C-suite executives—can harness data storytelling with the right approach. Modern visualization tools like Power BI offer user-friendly interfaces and templates, enabling anyone to create dashboards that communicate insights, regardless of their technical background.

For example, a sales manager in an Australian retail chain uses Power BI to monitor store performance across regions. Without writing a single line of code, she builds a dashboard highlighting sales dips during local holidays. This insight allows her to adjust promotional campaigns, demonstrating that impactful data stories can come from anyone equipped with the right tools and mindset.

### *Misconception 3: "More Data Means More Value"*

It's easy to assume that including more data will make your story stronger. However, **information overload** can overwhelm audiences and obscure your message. Effective data storytelling requires careful selection and curation of relevant data points.

Imagine an executive dashboard designed for a South American logistics company. Initially, the dashboard displays dozens of metrics: delivery times, vehicle mileage, customer ratings, fuel usage, and more. Stakeholders struggle to identify priorities. By narrowing the focus to on-time delivery rates and customer satisfaction, the team creates a concise, actionable dashboard that drives targeted improvement initiatives.

### *Misconception 4: "Visualizations Speak for Themselves"*

Some believe that once a visualization is created, its meaning is self-evident. In practice, **context and narrative are essential**. Without clear explanations or annotations, even the best-designed visual can be misinterpreted or ignored.

For instance, a European fintech startup presents a line graph showing user growth. Without context, stakeholders interpret a plateau as stagnation. However, by adding a narrative about seasonal trends and recent product launches directly onto the dashboard, the team clarifies the story: growth is cyclical and aligns with historical patterns, shifting the conversation from concern to strategy.

### *Visual Tools and Dashboard Illustrations*

Modern business visualization platforms like Tableau and Power BI make it easier than ever to address these misconceptions. Both tools offer features such as:

- **Pre-built dashboard templates** that prioritize clarity and best practices.

- **Story points and annotation features** that allow you to weave narrative into your visuals.
- **Data selection and filtering tools** that help focus attention on what matters most.

A well-designed business dashboard, for example, might combine a simple bar chart highlighting quarterly sales with a brief text box explaining the underlying drivers. This blend of visual and narrative elements ensures the audience understands both the "what" and the "why."

By recognizing and overcoming these common misconceptions, you lay the groundwork for effective data storytelling. Remember, the best data stories are those that balance clarity, relevance, and narrative. In the next section, we'll explore the essential principles of effective data visualization—empowering you to transform your raw data into meaningful stories that resonate across your organization and beyond.

## 1.6. The Role of Data Storytelling Across Functions

In today's data-driven business landscape, the need for clear, persuasive communication is universal. Data storytelling is not limited to analysts or data scientists; it is a vital skill that transcends departments, industries, and organizational roles. By weaving numbers into narratives, professionals across functions can drive better decisions, align teams, and inspire action. To fully appreciate the reach and importance of masterful data storytelling, let's explore how it transforms some of the most critical business functions.

### *Marketing: Turning Campaign Data into Actionable Insights*

Marketing teams handle vast amounts of data, from website traffic to social media engagement and campaign performance. Yet raw metrics alone rarely spark change. Through data storytelling, marketers can craft narratives that explain not just *what* happened, but *why* it matters and *what* to do next.

Consider a global cosmetics company launching a new product line. The marketing team uses Tableau to create a dashboard visualizing sales by region, customer demographics, and campaign touchpoints. By integrating these visuals with a narrative that connects a surge in sales among younger consumers to a particular social media strategy, the marketing lead can recommend reallocating resources to high-performing channels. This story-driven approach ensures that insights are not lost in translation and that decisions are both data-backed and actionable.

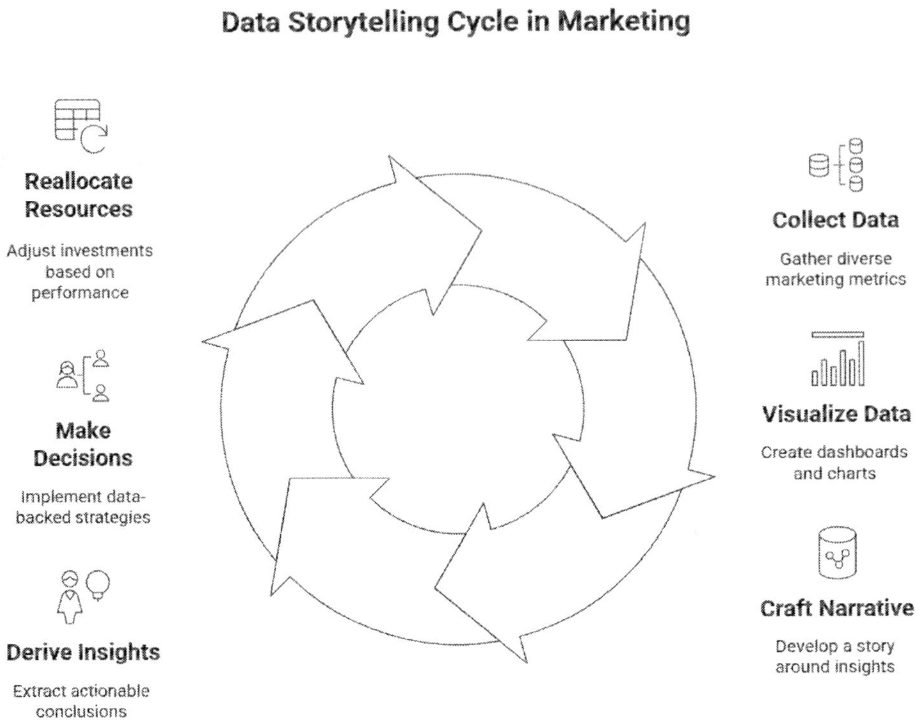


***Finance: Clarifying Complex Trends for Strategic Decisions***

Finance professionals regularly present budget forecasts, revenue projections, and risk analyses. However, financial data can quickly become overwhelming and opaque without a clear story. Effective data storytelling transforms spreadsheets into narratives that clarify trends, highlight risks, and outline opportunities.

Imagine a multinational manufacturing company reviewing quarterly financial performance. Using Power BI, the finance team creates interactive dashboards that visualize cost trends, profit margins, and cash flow across regions. By combining these visuals with a concise narrative that explains the impact of currency fluctuations on profitability in Asia, the team empowers executives to make informed decisions on pricing strategies and resource allocation. The result is a more engaged audience and a clearer path forward.

***Human Resources: Unveiling Patterns in People Data***

HR departments are increasingly relying on data to improve recruitment, retention, and employee satisfaction. Yet people data often contains subtle patterns that are easily missed without effective visualization and storytelling.

For example, a technology startup's HR team uses Google Data Studio to visualize employee engagement survey results. By mapping satisfaction scores across departments and overlaying them with turnover rates, the team identifies a correlation between low engagement and high attrition in a specific division. They present this story to leadership, recommending targeted interventions. This approach not only highlights the issue but also proposes a data-backed solution, ensuring HR has a seat at the strategic table.

***Sales: Driving Performance with Clear Visual Narratives***

Sales leaders rely on data to motivate teams, set targets, and optimize pipelines. However, sales data is most powerful when it tells a story that resonates with both individual contributors and leadership.

A regional sales manager at an international logistics firm creates a Power BI dashboard tracking quarterly performance, pipeline health, and win/loss ratios. By narrating the story behind the numbers—such as how a new lead qualification process led to higher win rates in Latin America—the manager energizes the team and secures buy-in for further process improvements.

***Bringing It All Together: Cross-Functional Dashboards and Collaboration***

Business impact is greatest when data storytelling bridges functional silos. Many organizations now deploy integrated dashboards that provide a unified view of key metrics across departments. These dashboards, built with tools like Tableau, Power BI, or Qlik, allow teams to collaborate around a shared narrative, aligning on goals and strategies.

For instance, a retail chain's executive dashboard may combine sales, supply chain, and customer satisfaction metrics. By weaving these together into a cohesive story during leadership meetings, executives gain a holistic understanding of business health and can make more informed, strategic decisions.

In summary, data storytelling is a universal language that empowers every business function—from marketing and finance to HR and sales—to communicate insights, drive alignment, and inspire action. By mastering the art of translating data into meaningful stories, professionals at all levels can maximize their business impact.

Next, we'll dive into the core principles of effective data visualization, laying the groundwork for transforming your data into stories that captivate and persuade.

## 1.7. Summary

As we close this opening chapter, it is clear that the ability to transform data into compelling stories is a critical differentiator in today's business landscape. Data storytelling bridges the gap between raw numbers and actionable insights, not only clarifying complex information but also engaging stakeholders on an intellectual and emotional level. By mastering this skill, professionals can drive decisions, inspire innovation, and set themselves apart in an increasingly data-driven world.

Throughout this chapter, we have explored how data storytelling is much more than simply presenting data in charts and tables. It is about crafting a narrative that resonates with your audience, whether you are a marketing manager justifying a campaign, an analyst presenting quarterly results, or an executive outlining a strategic vision. Let's reinforce these ideas with a couple of real-world scenarios that highlight the transformative power of data storytelling in business environments.

***Visualization Tools and Business Dashboards in Action***

Modern data visualization tools such as Tableau and Power BI are indispensable for turning raw data into compelling stories. These platforms offer intuitive drag-and-drop interfaces, a wide range of chart types, and capabilities for interactive dashboards. For instance, a business dashboard illustrating monthly sales performance might feature:

- A line chart visualizing sales growth over time, annotated to highlight major marketing campaigns.
- A pie chart showing market share by product category, color-coded for clarity.
- A map dashboard displaying regional sales performance, with hotspots indicating areas of opportunity.

```
# Example: Creating a simple sales trend line chart in Tableau#
(Pseudocode for illustrative purposes)Data: Monthly_Sales (Date,
Sales_Amount)
Visualization:
    - Drag 'Date'to Columns
    - Drag 'Sales_Amount'to Rows
    - Add 'Campaign'as annotation
    - Format with corporate color palette
```

By combining these visualizations with clear storytelling—such as narrative captions and interactive filters—business professionals can guide their audience's attention, emphasize key messages, and foster deeper understanding.

### *Key Takeaways*

- Data storytelling transforms complex information into narratives that drive business impact.
- Visualization tools like Tableau and Power BI enable the creation of interactive, insightful dashboards.
- Successful data stories connect analytical insights with human experiences, fostering engagement and action.
- Real-world scenarios highlight the role of data storytelling in decision-making, strategy, and securing stakeholder buy-in.

### *Looking Ahead*

With the foundation now set, you are prepared to move from understanding the "why" behind data storytelling to mastering the "how." In the next chapter, we will explore the core principles of effective data visualization. You will learn how to select the right charts, apply design best practices, and structure your data for maximum clarity and persuasion.

By building on this chapter's insights, you will be well-equipped to transform your data into visual stories that captivate, persuade, and drive results. Let's embark on the next stage of your journey toward data storytelling mastery.

# 2. FOUNDATIONS OF EFFECTIVE DATA VISUALIZATION

In today's data-driven business landscape, the difference between information overload and actionable insight often comes down to how data is visualized. A powerful data visualization can transform abstract numbers into clear, persuasive narratives that accelerate decision-making and drive impact. But crafting visuals that truly resonate requires more than just picking the right chart—it demands an understanding of the foundational principles that underpin effective visual communication.

This chapter lays the groundwork for mastering data storytelling by exploring the essential building blocks of successful visualization. You will learn how to harness the core principles of visual communication to make your data clear, engaging, and memorable. We will unravel the "language" of charts and graphs, equipping you with the skills to choose and design the most effective visuals for your message. Key elements such as clarity, relevance, and integrity will be discussed to ensure your visualizations not only look compelling but also tell an honest and accurate story.

Recognizing the importance of data quality and integrity, this chapter provides guidance on presenting trustworthy insights that inspire confidence among stakeholders. We also address the critical topics of accessibility and inclusivity, making sure your visualizations connect with diverse audiences across cultures, abilities, and organizational roles.

To ground these concepts in reality, you'll see how leading organizations in finance and operations leverage visualization to solve complex challenges and create business value. By the end of this chapter, you will have a robust foundation to build impactful, inclusive, and trustworthy data stories—setting the stage for more advanced techniques in your data storytelling journey.

## 2.1. Principles of Visual Communication

Effective data visualization begins with a strong grasp of visual communication principles. These principles serve as the bridge between raw data and meaningful insights, ensuring that your message is not just seen, but understood and acted upon. By thoughtfully applying visual communication techniques, you can elevate your data presentations from mere charts to persuasive, memorable stories that resonate with diverse audiences.

***Understanding How People Perceive Visual Information***

Human brains are hardwired to process visual information rapidly. Color, shape, and spatial arrangement can all guide attention, reveal patterns, or highlight outliers. Recognizing these tendencies is fundamental to designing impactful data visuals.

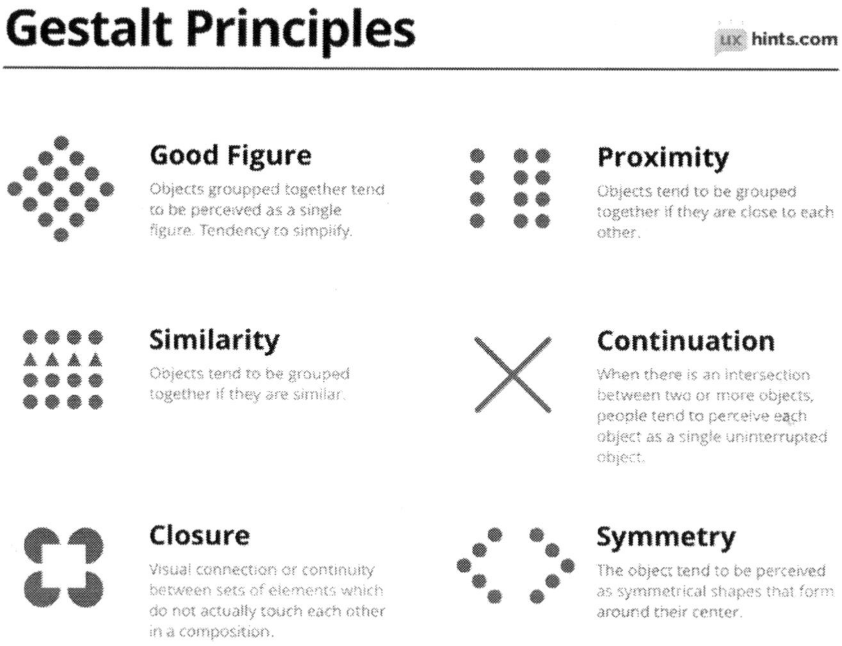


For example, using contrasting colors can direct viewers to the most critical part of a dashboard, while grouping related metrics with proximity and alignment helps audiences make sense of complex information at a glance. The principle of **pre-attentive attributes**—such as color, size, and orientation—enables viewers to quickly spot trends or anomalies before they consciously process the details.

***Key Principles of Visual Communication***

To ensure your data visuals communicate effectively, consider these foundational principles:

- **Clarity:** The visualization must be easy to read and interpret. Avoid clutter, unnecessary decoration, and overly complex chart types.
- **Hierarchy:** Establish a clear order of importance so viewers know where to focus first. This can be achieved through size, color, and layout.

- **Consistency:** Use similar visual elements for similar data types. This helps users recognize patterns and reduces cognitive load.
- **Context:** Provide enough information (such as labels, legends, and time frames) so viewers understand what they're seeing and why it matters.
- **Accuracy:** Visuals should reflect the data truthfully. Beware of misleading axes, distorted proportions, or omitted data.
- **Relevance:** Every visual element should support the story you're telling. Remove anything that distracts from your main message.

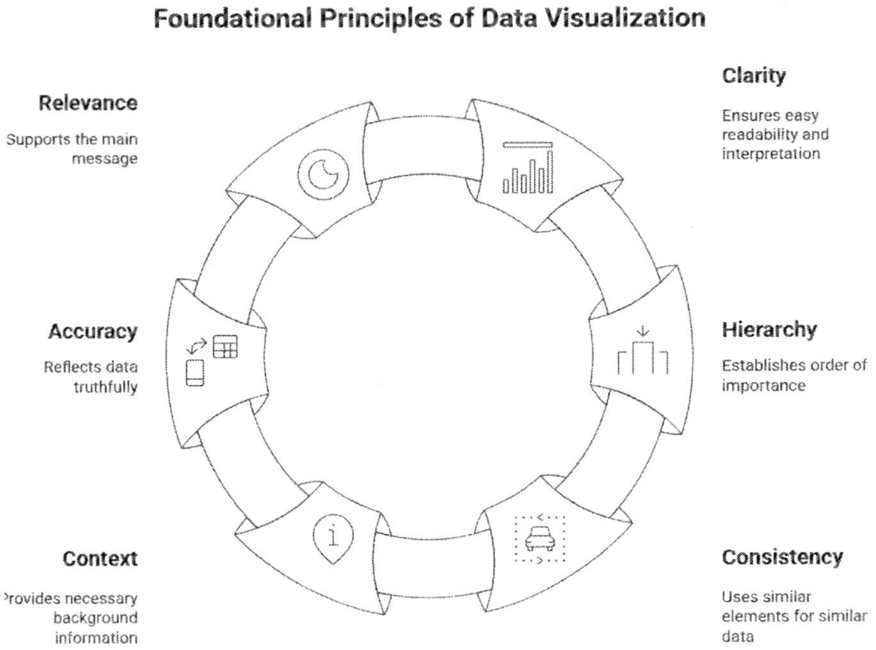


*Visual Communication in Action: Business Use-Cases*

To illustrate these principles, let's explore two real-world business scenarios where visual communication made a measurable difference.

**Scenario 1: Sales Performance Dashboard — North America & Asia-Pacific**

A multinational company wanted to compare sales performance across its key regions. Using Microsoft Power BI, the analytics team developed a dashboard with:

A color-coded map to highlight top-performing countries in blue and underperformers in red.

Bar charts showing monthly sales trends, with a consistent color scheme between regions for easy comparison.

A clear title and concise filter options, ensuring that executives could immediately focus on the most relevant segment.

By following visual communication principles, the dashboard enabled leadership to quickly spot growth opportunities in Asia-Pacific, guiding strategic decisions for resource allocation.

**Scenario 2: Marketing Campaign Insights — Global FMCG Brand**

A marketing analyst at a leading fast-moving consumer goods (FMCG) company used Tableau to present campaign effectiveness across different cultural markets:

Interactive visuals allowed stakeholders to filter results by country, with consistent icons and color palettes reflecting brand guidelines.

A heatmap highlighted customer engagement rates, making high and low-performing regions instantly recognizable.

Contextual tooltips provided additional details without cluttering the main view, supporting both high-level and deep-dive analysis.

This approach ensured global marketing managers could compare performance while respecting regional differences, ultimately leading to more tailored and successful campaigns.

Mastering the principles of visual communication is essential for transforming data into actionable business stories. By prioritizing clarity, hierarchy, consistency, context, accuracy, and relevance, you ensure your visuals capture attention and drive informed decisions across cultures and markets. In the next section, we'll delve deeper into choosing the right chart types for your data—empowering you to further tailor your storytelling for maximum business impact.

## 2.2. The Language of Charts and Graphs

Charts and graphs are the visual vocabulary of data storytelling. Just as language enables us to communicate ideas clearly, the right chart transforms data from raw numbers into insights that can be quickly understood, discussed, and acted upon. To harness the true power of data visualization, it's crucial to become fluent in the basic types of charts, understand their unique strengths, and recognize the specific business questions each one helps answer.

### *Understanding Basic Chart Types*

At their core, charts are tools for comparison, trend analysis, distribution, or composition. Choosing the right visual form is the first step in ensuring your message is not just seen but understood.

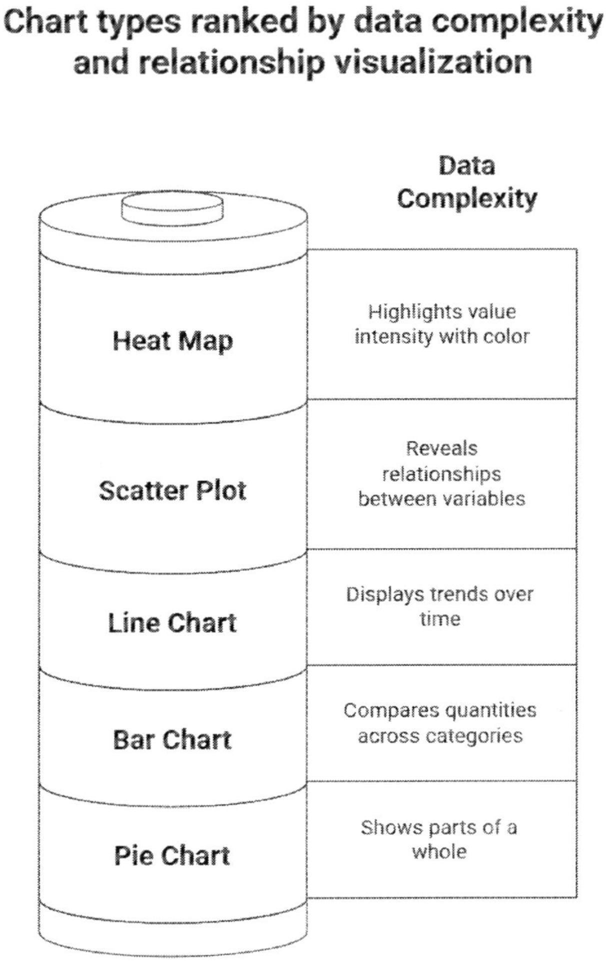


**Bar Charts**: Best for comparing quantities across categories. For example, a sales team might use a bar chart in Tableau to compare quarterly revenue by product line, quickly highlighting outperformers.

**Line Charts**: Ideal for showing trends over time. An executive dashboard in Power BI might display monthly website traffic as a line chart, making it easy to spot upward or downward trends.

**Pie Charts**: Useful for illustrating proportions or parts of a whole. Marketing professionals often use pie charts to show market share distribution, but it's important to limit the number of slices for clarity.

**Scatter Plots**: Reveal relationships between two numeric variables. Analysts may use scatter plots to visualize the correlation between advertising spend and sales performance.

**Heat Maps**: Highlight intensity of values using color. For instance, an operations manager in Tokyo might use a heat map to identify peak hours in customer service call volumes.

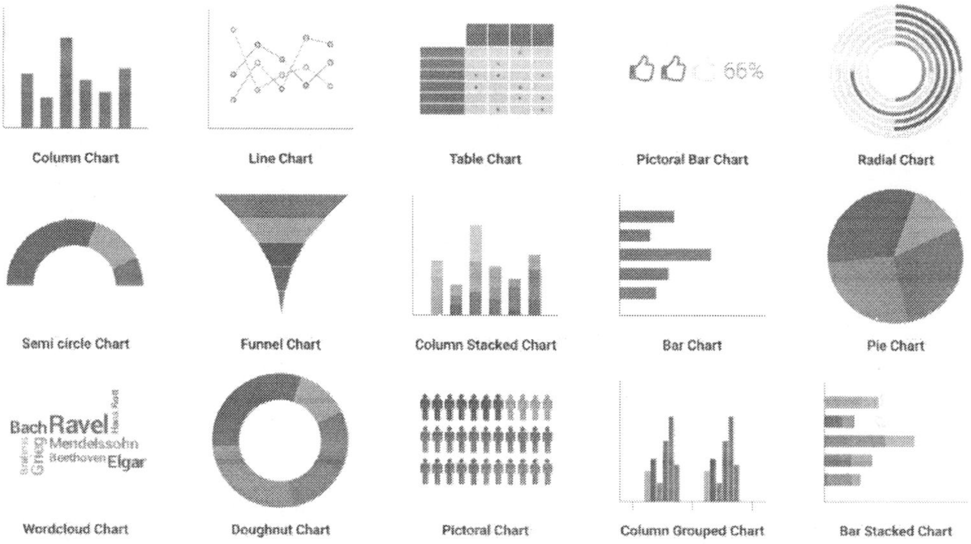


Each chart type serves a specific narrative purpose, and selecting the wrong one can easily confuse or mislead your audience.

#### *Choosing the Right Chart: Business Use-Cases*

To illustrate, let's consider two scenarios:

### Scenario 1: Retail Sales Performance

A regional sales manager in Brazil needs to present quarterly performance to stakeholders. Using Power BI, she builds a dashboard featuring:

- A bar chart showing total sales by region
- A line chart tracking monthly sales growth over the year
- A pie chart breaking down product categories

This combination allows her audience to compare performance, track trends, and understand category contributions at a glance.

### Scenario 2: Marketing Campaign Analysis

A digital marketing team in Germany wants to analyze the effectiveness of recent campaigns. In Tableau, they create:

- A scatter plot mapping ad spend against lead generation
- A heat map indicating which demographics respond best to each campaign

By choosing appropriate chart types, the team draws direct connections between their investments and results, enabling data-driven decisions for future campaigns.

#### *Visualization Tools and Dashboard Examples*

Modern visualization tools such as Tableau and Power BI have democratized chart creation, allowing users to build interactive dashboards that support real-time business decision-making. These platforms offer intuitive interfaces for selecting chart types, customizing visuals, and embedding them into reports.

For example, a global logistics company might use a Tableau dashboard to show:

- A world map highlighting shipment volumes by country (geographical heat map)
- Bar charts ranking top-performing routes
- Trend lines for on-time deliveries over several quarters

The dashboard becomes a living story, updating as new data arrives, and empowering managers across continents to collaborate using a common visual language.

#### *Interpreting Chart Elements*

Beyond selecting the right chart, it's essential to understand and communicate the meaning behind axes, legends, scales, and labels (shown below). Clear labeling, appropriate scaling, and thoughtful use of color prevent misinterpretation and ensure that business audiences, regardless of their technical background, can engage with the data confidently.

For instance, a misleading scale on a bar chart could exaggerate minor differences, leading to poor business decisions. Good practice in tools like Power BI includes setting axis minimums and maximums intentionally, using color to draw attention to key values, and providing clear legends.

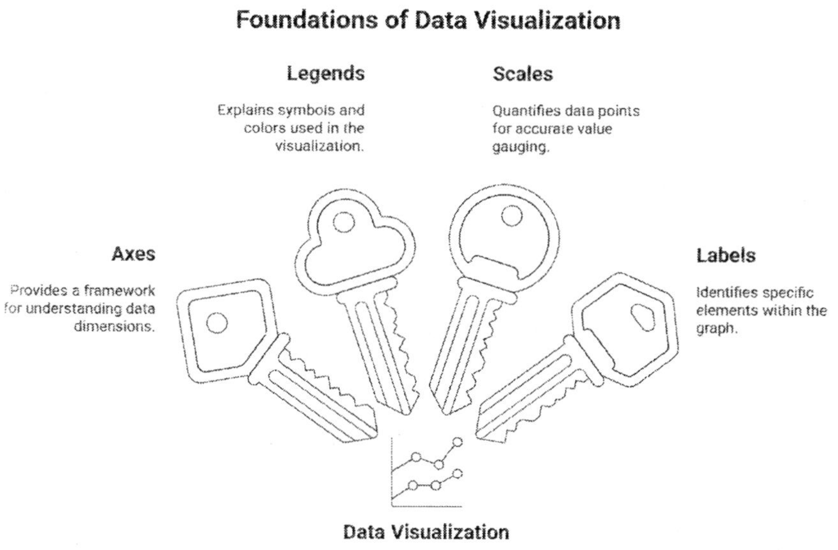


The chart below shows the use of all these elements:

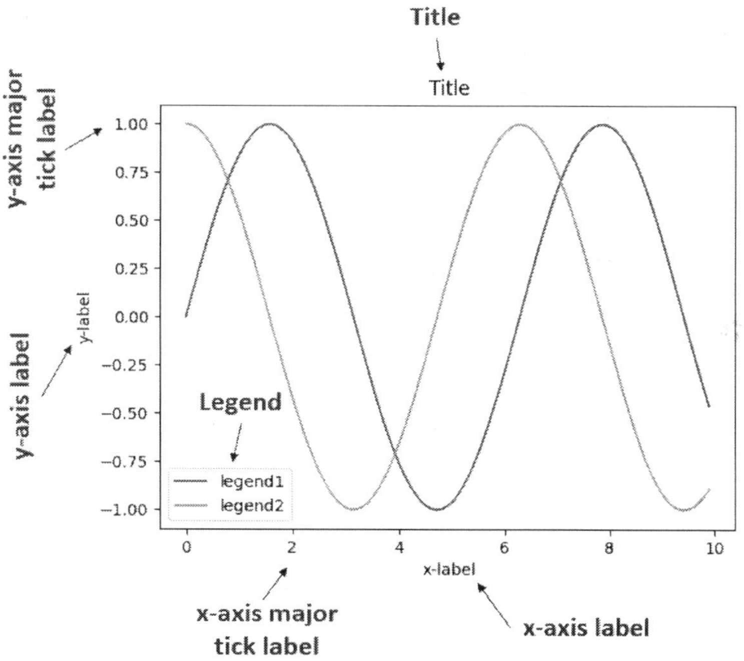


***Bringing It All Together***

Mastery of the language of charts and graphs is foundational to effective data storytelling. By matching your data and message to the right chart type, and leveraging modern visualization tools, you transform numbers into actionable business insights that resonate across teams and cultures.

As you gain fluency in this visual language, you'll be prepared to make smart chart choices that clarify your message and support confident decision-making. In the next section, we'll dive deeper into the art and science of selecting the most impactful chart for each business scenario, ensuring your data stories are as compelling as they are clear.

## 2.3. Elements of a Successful Visualization

A successful data visualization is much more than a visually appealing chart or dashboard. It's a carefully crafted bridge between raw data and actionable business insight. To master data storytelling, it's essential to understand the fundamental elements that underpin every effective visualization. These elements ensure your visuals not only inform but also engage and persuade your audience, regardless of their technical background.

### *Clarity: Making Data Understandable*

At the heart of every successful visualization is clarity. Your audience should be able to grasp the main message at a glance, without deciphering confusing labels or cluttered displays. Clarity involves:

- **Simplifying complex data** so the story emerges naturally.
- **Using straightforward language** in titles, labels, and annotations.
- **Avoiding unnecessary elements** that distract from the core message.

For instance, a sales dashboard built in Tableau for a retail chain should highlight key performance metrics such as total sales, year-over-year growth, and top-performing regions. Clear labeling and logical grouping make it easy for executives to spot trends and take action.

### *Relevance: Tailoring Content to Audience Needs*

Not every stakeholder needs the same information. A successful visualization is tailored to its audience, presenting the most relevant data in context. This means:

- **Identifying the decision-makers** and their priorities.
- **Selecting data points** that answer specific business questions.
- **Providing context** through comparisons or benchmarks.

Consider a scenario where a marketing analyst uses Power BI to report on campaign performance. For a board presentation, the visualization focuses on ROI, reach, and conversion rates, while a team-level dashboard might dive deeper into channel performance or demographic breakdowns.

#### *Accuracy: Representing Data Honestly*

Trust is built on accuracy. Your visualization must reflect the underlying data truthfully, without distortion or cherry-picking. To ensure accuracy:

- **Use appropriate scales** that don't exaggerate or minimize results.
- **Represent proportions correctly** (e.g., pie charts should total 100%).
- **Double-check data sources** and calculations.

In financial reporting, a misrepresented trend line or manipulated axis can lead to misinformed decisions. Using built-in validation features in tools like Tableau helps maintain integrity and transparency.

#### *Design: Enhancing Engagement and Comprehension*

Effective design doesn't just make data look good; it makes it easier to interpret. Good design principles include:

- **Consistent color schemes** to group related data or highlight key areas.
- **Judicious use of white space** to prevent overcrowding.
- **Readable fonts and clear hierarchies** for textual elements.

A global logistics company might use Power BI's dashboard features to visualize supply chain efficiency. By using color-coded regions and clear icons, they help regional managers quickly discern bottlenecks and prioritize interventions.

#### *Interactivity: Empowering Exploration*

Modern business dashboards often benefit from interactivity. Interactive features allow users to explore data, drill down into specifics, and customize their view. Useful interactive elements include:

- **Filters and slicers** for time periods, regions, or product lines.
- **Hover-over tooltips** that provide additional context.
- **Clickable drilldowns** for deeper analysis.

In a multinational marketing organization, a Tableau dashboard with interactive filters lets country managers view campaign effectiveness in their own region, supporting localized decision-making.

#### *Real-World Business Scenarios*

**Global Retail Case:**

A European retail chain implemented a real-time sales dashboard in Power BI. By emphasizing clarity and relevance, the dashboard streamlined over 50 regional reports into one unified view. Executives could instantly compare performance across countries, leading to a 15% faster response time to underperforming locations.

**Healthcare Analytics Example:**

In the US, a healthcare provider used Tableau to visualize patient wait times by department. Accurate and interactive visualizations allowed administrators to identify bottlenecks and reallocate resources, resulting in a measurable improvement in patient satisfaction scores.

Mastering these elements—clarity, relevance, accuracy, design, and interactivity—ensures your visualizations become powerful tools for business impact. By thoughtfully applying these principles, you transform static numbers into compelling stories that inform, persuade, and drive change. In the next section, we will explore the strategic process of choosing the right chart or graph to match your business objective, further strengthening your data storytelling toolkit.

## 2.4. Data Quality and Integrity

Before diving into specific chart types and visualization techniques, it is essential to understand that even the most beautifully designed visuals can mislead or lose credibility if the underlying data is unreliable. Data quality and integrity are foundational pillars that support every effective data visualization and ensure your story is both persuasive and trustworthy.

### *What is Data Quality and Integrity?*

**Data quality** refers to the accuracy, completeness, consistency, and reliability of your data. High-quality data is free from errors, up to date, and relevant to your business questions. **Data integrity** goes further, encompassing the processes and protocols that maintain and protect the accuracy and consistency of data throughout its lifecycle.

When you build visualizations on solid data, you empower your audience to make informed decisions. Conversely, poor data quality can distort insights, erode stakeholder trust, and lead to costly business mistakes.

### *Why Data Quality Matters in Storytelling*

A compelling data story is only as strong as the facts it is built upon. For example, imagine presenting a sales dashboard to your executive team using Power BI, only to realize later that half of the regional sales figures were outdated or duplicated. Not only does this undercut your credibility, but it can also drive misguided strategies.

In business, **data integrity** is not just about technical accuracy—it's about maintaining the trust between you and your audience. Executives, marketers, and analysts all rely on data-driven stories to inform their next steps. If your numbers are questionable, so too is your message.

### *Key Dimensions of Data Quality*

To ensure your visualizations rest on a firm foundation, consider the following dimensions:

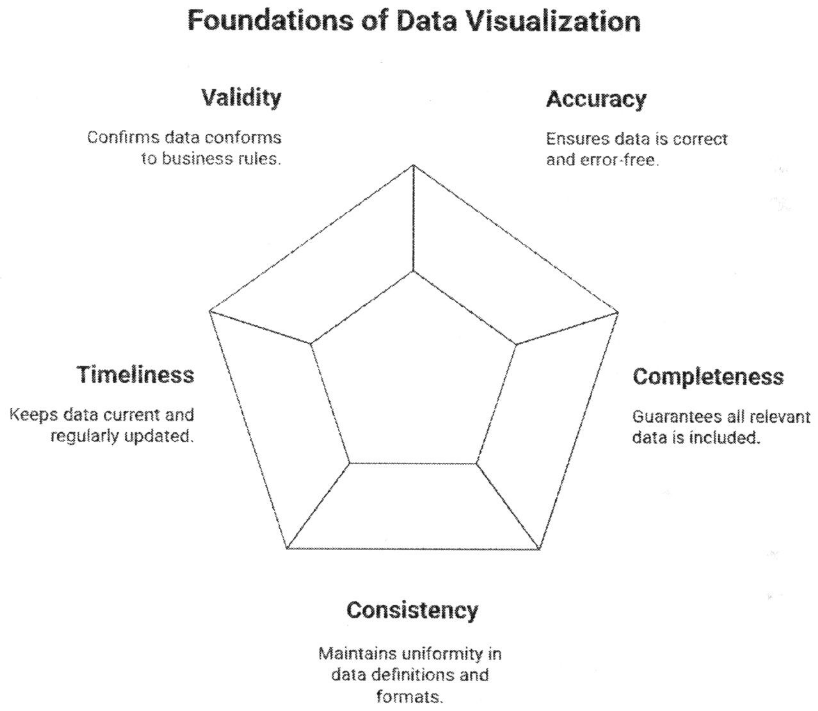


- **Accuracy**: Are your numbers correct and free from errors?
- **Completeness**: Is all relevant data included, or are there gaps?
- **Consistency**: Are definitions, formats, and calculations uniform across datasets?
- **Timeliness**: Is your data current and updated regularly?
- **Validity**: Does your data conform to business rules or constraints?

Neglecting any of these aspects may result in misleading visuals, undermining your entire data storytelling effort.

***Real-World Scenario: Global Retail Dashboard***

Consider a global retail company using Tableau to visualize sales performance across continents. The marketing team pulls data from multiple sources—point-of-sale systems, e-commerce platforms, and regional warehouses. If product categories are labeled differently or time zones are not standardized, the resulting dashboard could show misleading trends or false comparisons.

For instance, a spike in sales during a "quarter" might be exaggerated if one region's data is still being uploaded while others are finalized. By instituting data validation checks and automated data cleaning routines, the company ensures consistency and accuracy, creating a dashboard that truly reflects global performance. Stakeholders can then trust the insights and act with confidence.

***Ensuring Data Integrity: Best Practices***

Maintaining data integrity is an ongoing process, not a one-time task. Here are some practical steps to uphold data quality:

- **Automate Data Cleaning**: Use tools like Tableau Prep or Power BI Dataflows to identify and correct errors, remove duplicates, and standardize formats before visualizing.
- **Establish Clear Data Governance**: Define who is responsible for data entry, updates, and validation. This ensures accountability and minimizes human error.
- **Regular Audits and Quality Checks**: Schedule periodic reviews to catch inconsistencies or outdated information. Many dashboard tools allow you to set up alerts for anomalies.
- **Document Data Sources and Assumptions**: Clearly annotate dashboards with the origin of your data, any filters applied, and the date of the last update.

```
# Example: Simple data cleaning in Python using pandas

import pandas as pd

df = pd.read_csv( 'sales_data.csv')
df.drop_duplicates(inplace=True)
df[ 'date'] = pd.to_datetime(df[ 'date'])
df = df[df[ 'sales_amount'] >= 0] # Remove negative sales
```

***Business Dashboard Illustration: Manufacturing KPI Dashboard***

A manufacturing company uses Power BI to track equipment downtime and production output. The dashboard draws from real-time sensor readings and manual logs. If sensor data is intermittently missing or log entries are inconsistent, the downtime calculations may be inaccurate. By integrating automated data validation routines and flagging incomplete records, the company ensures that dashboard metrics reflect true operational performance. As a result, managers can pinpoint bottlenecks and allocate resources efficiently.

Strong data quality and integrity are the bedrock of persuasive data storytelling. By ensuring your data is accurate, complete, and consistent, you protect your credibility and empower stakeholders to make informed decisions. In the next section, we'll build on this foundation by exploring how to select the most effective charts and graphs to communicate your key business messages, maximizing the impact of your insights.

## 2.5. Accessibility and Inclusivity in Visualization

As you begin to master the basics of data visualization, it's essential to recognize that effective visuals are not just about clarity or aesthetics, they must also be **accessible** and **inclusive**. In today's global business landscape, your audience is likely to be diverse, spanning different abilities, cultures, and levels of data literacy. Ensuring your visualizations can be understood and used by everyone is both a strategic advantage and a professional responsibility.

### *Why Accessibility Matters in Business Visualization*

Accessibility in data visualization means creating visuals that all users, including those with disabilities, can interpret and act upon. This includes colleagues with color vision deficiencies, clients who rely on screen readers, and stakeholders who may have limited English proficiency or differing cultural interpretations of color and symbols.

An accessible dashboard or report not only broadens your reach but also signals your commitment to inclusivity, which can enhance brand reputation, improve decision-making, and foster innovation. In many regions, accessibility is also a legal requirement for digital content, making it a non-negotiable standard for business communication.

### *Key Principles of Inclusive Visualization*

To make your visualizations accessible and inclusive, consider the following foundational principles:

- **Use Sufficient Color Contrast:** Ensure that text and critical data points stand out clearly from backgrounds. Tools like Tableau and Power BI offer built-in color contrast checks.
- **Avoid Reliance on Color Alone:** Combine color with patterns, shapes, or labels so that colorblind users or those viewing in grayscale can still interpret your visuals.

- **Provide Text Alternatives:** Use descriptive titles, labels, and tooltips. Alt text for images and charts helps users of assistive technologies.
- **Choose Clear Fonts and Sizes:** Select readable fonts and avoid small font sizes, especially for dashboards viewed on different devices.
- **Design for Simplicity:** Minimize clutter and prioritize information hierarchy so that essential insights are immediately apparent to all users.

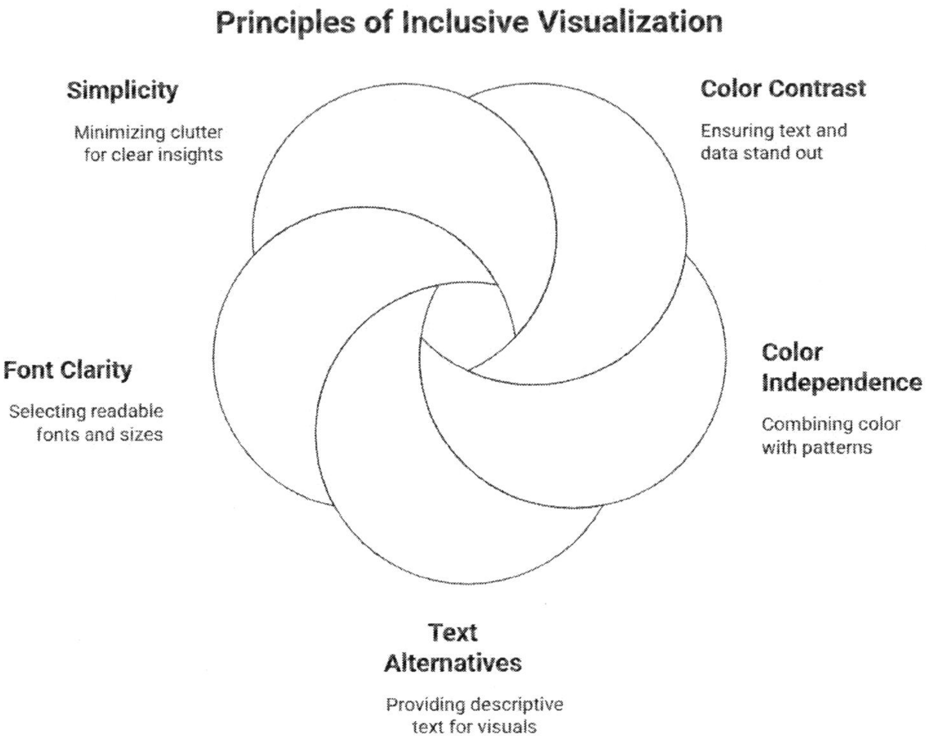


***Business Scenario: Global Sales Dashboard***

Consider a multinational retail company using Power BI to create a sales performance dashboard. Employees across Asia, Europe, and the Americas access this dashboard in multiple languages and on various devices.

To ensure accessibility and inclusivity:

- The dashboard uses high-contrast color palettes and patterns to differentiate between product categories.
- All charts include clear axis titles and data labels, avoiding abbreviations that might confuse non-native English speakers.
- Interactive elements, such as filters and buttons, are keyboard-navigable and have descriptive tooltips.

- A "text view" toggle allows users with screen readers to access the same insights in a tabular format.

This approach not only increases engagement but also enables geographically and culturally diverse teams to make informed decisions quickly, driving unified action across regions.

***Case Study: Financial Services and Colorblind Accessibility***

A European bank's analytics team discovered that a significant number of its stakeholders were colorblind. In response, they revised their Tableau dashboards to:

Replace red-green status indicators with icons and labels.
Use blue and orange, a colorblind-friendly palette, for profit and loss charts.
Add dynamic descriptions that explain trends in plain language, accessible via screen readers.

This shift improved report comprehension scores across the organization and reinforced the company's commitment to inclusive excellence.

***Making the Most of Visualization Tools***

Modern visualization platforms like Tableau and Power BI support accessibility in several ways:

**Tableau:** Built-in color palette checks, customizable tooltips, and options to add alt text to images and dashboards.
**Power BI:** Accessibility checker, keyboard shortcuts, and high-contrast themes designed for low-vision users.

To illustrate, here's how you might configure a Power BI dashboard for accessibility:

```
1. Select a high-contrast theme from the View menu.
2. Use the 'Alt Text' field in the Visualizations pane to provide
descriptions for each chart.
3. Test keyboard navigation with the Tab key to ensure all interactive
elements are accessible.
4. Preview dashboard using Power BI's accessibility checker before
publishing.
```

Prioritizing accessibility and inclusivity in your data storytelling ensures that your insights reach the broadest possible audience and drive meaningful, equitable business outcomes. By leveraging the strengths of modern visualization tools and following best practices, you create visuals that empower everyone to participate in data-driven decision-making.

Next, we'll apply these inclusive principles as we explore how to select the most effective charts and graphs for your business narrative, ensuring that every insight is both impactful and accessible.

## 2.6. Real-World Application: Finance and Operations

Building on the foundational principles of clarity and inclusivity, let's now ground our understanding of effective data visualization in practical, high-stakes business environments: finance and operations. These domains thrive on the ability to transform vast quantities of data into actionable insights, and visualization sits at the heart of that transformation. Whether you are a financial analyst seeking to communicate trends to executives or an operations manager aiming to streamline logistics, mastering data storytelling can dramatically enhance your impact.

### *Financial Performance Dashboards: Driving Executive Decisions*

Finance departments are inundated with numbers—revenues, expenses, forecasts, and key ratios. The challenge is distilling these figures into a narrative that guides strategic decisions. Modern visualization tools like **Tableau** and **Power BI** have become indispensable for this task, enabling users to create interactive dashboards that bring financial stories to life.

Imagine a multinational corporation preparing for its quarterly board meeting. The finance team assembles a dashboard illustrating:

Monthly revenue trends as a line chart, highlighting growth patterns and seasonal dips.
An interactive bar chart comparing actual versus budgeted expenses across departments.
A pie chart breaking down revenue by region, with filter options for North America, Europe, and Asia-Pacific.

Such a dashboard enables executives to drill down into specific data points, identify underperforming segments, and make informed decisions about resource allocation. The visualization does more than report numbers; it tells a story about financial health and future opportunities.

### *Operations Dashboards: Uncovering Efficiency*

Operational excellence depends on visibility into processes and performance metrics. For example, a logistics company operating across continents needs real-time insight into shipment status, delivery times, and bottlenecks.

Consider a scenario in which an operations manager uses Tableau to monitor supply chain efficiency. The dashboard might include:

A map visualization showing delayed shipments, color-coded by severity, across global hubs.
A stacked bar chart comparing on-time deliveries by carrier or route.
A scatter plot analyzing the relationship between shipment volume and average delivery time.

These visualizations empower teams to spot inefficiencies quickly and respond proactively. In one global logistics organization, transitioning from static spreadsheets to interactive dashboards reduced response times to supply chain disruptions by 30 percent, directly improving customer satisfaction and operational cost savings.

### Tableau Dashboard Example:

```
# Example Tableau dashboard worksheet elements
- Map: Shipment Status by Hub (Color: On-Time, Delayed, Critical)
- Bar Chart: Delivery Performance by Carrier (Stacked by Region)
- Filters: Date Range, Route, Carrier
```

By integrating real-time data feeds, these dashboards become living documents that support continuous improvement and agile decision-making.

#### *Global and Cross-Cultural Perspectives*

It's important to recognize that data storytelling in finance and operations is not one-size-fits-all. For instance, a Japanese manufacturing firm may prioritize visualizations that emphasize efficiency and waste reduction (lean metrics), while a European retailer may focus on cross-border sales and local market performance. Understanding the cultural context ensures that visuals are designed to resonate with diverse audiences, taking into account color preferences, data literacy, and decision-making styles.

## 2.7. Summary and Reflection

Building on the foundational elements we have explored—clarity, simplicity, context, and accessibility—it's evident that effective data visualization is much more than a technical skill. It is an essential business communication strategy. When done right, data visualization bridges the gap between raw data and actionable insights, transforming numbers into narratives that drive business impact.

Throughout this chapter, we highlighted the core principles that underpin successful visual storytelling. These are not merely academic ideals; they have real, measurable consequences in diverse business settings. To demonstrate the practical effect of mastering these foundations, let's look at a few real-world scenarios.

***Visualization Tools: Bringing Principles to Life***

The technologies available today make it easier than ever to apply these principles. Tools like **Tableau** and **Power BI** offer drag-and-drop interfaces, built-in templates, and accessibility features that support the creation of clear, compelling visuals. For example:

```
# Example: Creating a simple bar chart in Power BI

# 1. Load your dataset (e.g., sales by region).

# 2. Select the 'Bar Chart' visualization.

# 3. Drag 'Region' to the Axis and 'Sales' to the Value field.

# 4. Apply color coding to highlight underperforming areas.

# 5. Add a filter for time period selection.

# The result: A clear, interactive chart illustrating sales performance
at a glance.
```

By using these tools, business professionals can focus on storytelling rather than wrestling with code or complex design decisions. The dashboards produced not only synthesize large volumes of data but also guide viewers toward the most important insights.

# 3. UNDERSTANDING YOUR AUDIENCE

Every great data story begins not with numbers, but with people. No matter how compelling your data or how striking your visuals, the true measure of success lies in how your message resonates with your audience. In today's interconnected and diverse business landscape, understanding who you're speaking to is just as vital as what you're saying. Whether you're presenting to a board of directors in London, a marketing team in Mumbai, or a cross-functional project group in São Paulo, your ability to adapt your narrative for different audiences can mean the difference between insight and indifference.

This chapter delves into the art and science of audience-centric data storytelling. You'll discover practical strategies for segmenting your audience, uncovering their key questions and decision-making needs, and communicating complex information in ways that engage and inspire. We'll explore the importance of cultural sensitivity—ensuring your visuals and narratives are inclusive, respectful, and relevant across geographies and backgrounds. Alongside this, you'll learn how to tailor your charts, colors, and messaging to maximize business impact, and how to leverage stakeholder feedback to continuously refine your approach.

By the end of this chapter, you'll be equipped to move beyond generic presentations and craft data stories that truly connect—turning passive listeners into active champions of your ideas. This foundation is pivotal to mastering data storytelling, setting the stage for advanced techniques that drive business impact throughout the rest of this book.

## 3.1. Audience Segmentation for Data Stories

Understanding your audience is a crucial foundation for effective data storytelling. Once you identify who will consume your data story, you can tailor not only the content but also the presentation, tone, and level of technical detail, ensuring the message resonates and drives action. Audience segmentation is the process of dividing your potential viewers into distinct groups based on their roles, interests, data literacy, and decision-making authority. This approach helps you craft stories that connect and inspire, rather than overwhelm or confuse.

### *Why Segment Your Audience?*

Not all stakeholders approach data with the same background or objectives. Executives typically need high-level insights to guide strategy, while analysts may seek granular details to inform their recommendations. Marketers could be focused on campaign performance, while product managers might prioritize user behavior trends. By recognizing these differences, you can avoid the common pitfall of a "one-size-fits-all" data presentation.

Segmenting your audience allows you to:

- Speak directly to what matters most for each group.
- Avoid unnecessary technical jargon or excess detail.
- Increase engagement and comprehension.
- Drive relevant action based on the audience's unique needs.

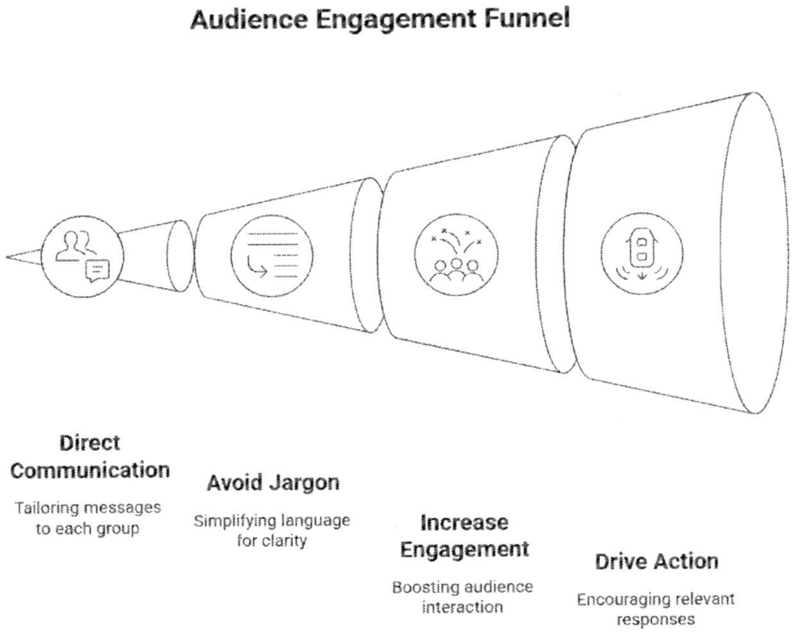


***Common Audience Segments in Business Data Storytelling***

Let's explore several typical business audiences, noting their priorities and preferred data formats:

### Executives and Senior Leaders

Executives are focused on strategic outcomes, KPIs, and big-picture trends. They value:

- High-level dashboards
- Visual summaries (charts, infographics)

- Clear, action-oriented recommendations

**Managers and Department Heads**

This group balances strategic oversight with operational detail. They often prefer:

- Drill-down dashboards
- Comparative visualizations (e.g., period-over-period)
- Focused explanations of drivers behind performance

**Technical Teams (Data Analysts, IT, Developers)**

Technical audiences are comfortable with data complexity. They seek:

- Detailed tables and interactive visualizations
- Access to raw data and methodology
- Annotations for anomalies or outliers

**Front-Line Staff or Field Teams**

Operational teams benefit from simple, actionable insights. They appreciate:

- Quick-glance performance gauges
- Geographic or task-specific visuals
- Alerts or thresholds for immediate action

***Real-World Scenario: Marketing Campaign Performance***

Consider a multinational retail company launching a global marketing campaign. The marketing analyst must report results to three different groups:

**The CMO (Chief Marketing Officer)** needs a concise dashboard that highlights ROI, overall sales uplift, and campaign reach. The data story here uses bold visuals, color-coded KPIs, and a narrative focused on strategic impact.

**Regional Marketing Managers** require more granular visuals: performance by country, channel, and demographic. An interactive dashboard in Tableau or Power BI allows them to filter and drill down, focusing on actionable areas for their teams.

**The Digital Marketing Team** wants to explore click-through rates, conversion funnels, and A/B test results. They need detailed heatmaps and trend analyses, perhaps with the ability to export raw data for further examination.

By segmenting the audience, the analyst ensures each group receives the right level of detail and visual format, maximizing understanding and buy-in.

***Practical Application: Using Visualization Tools for Segmented Audiences***

Modern visualization tools such as **Tableau** and **Power BI** offer robust features to create audience-specific dashboards and reports. Here's how these tools can support segmentation:

**Dashboard Customization:** Create separate views or tabs for different audience segments. For instance, a summary tab for executives, and detailed analytics for operational teams.

**Interactive Filters:** Empower users to explore data relevant to their needs. Regional managers can filter by location, while executives might view only key metrics.

**Role-Based Access:** Control who sees sensitive or complex data, ensuring that each audience engages only with what is relevant.

```
# Example: Using Power BI to create role-specific dashboards

if user_role == "Executive":
    show_dashboard( "StrategicOverview")
elif user_role == "Manager":
    show_dashboard( "OperationalDrilldown")
elif user_role == "Analyst":
    show_dashboard( "DetailedAnalytics")
```

***Global Perspective: Financial Services in Asia-Pacific***

A leading bank in Singapore implemented segmented dashboards for its annual performance review. Executives accessed a high-level Power BI dashboard with profit margins, customer growth, and compliance trends, using color-coded visuals for instant clarity. Relationship managers, meanwhile, used Tableau dashboards to examine client portfolios, transaction histories, and regional opportunities. This segmentation improved the quality of decision-making at every level, demonstrating the value of targeted data storytelling in a multicultural, layered organization.

Audience segmentation is not just a technical step but a strategic one, enabling you to craft data stories that resonate, inform, and empower. By considering the unique needs and preferences of each stakeholder group, you ensure your insights are not lost in translation but spark real business impact.

## 3.2. Identifying Key Questions and Needs

Effective data storytelling begins not with charts or dashboards, but with a deep understanding of your audience's key questions and needs. By identifying what matters most to your stakeholders, you ensure that every visual and narrative choice is purposeful, relevant, and actionable. This section guides you through the process of uncovering those pivotal questions, illustrating how this foundational step elevates your data storytelling and maximizes business impact.

***Why Audience Questions Matter***

Before you build a single visualization, it's crucial to clarify what your audience genuinely wants to know. Data is most powerful when it answers specific questions, addresses business pain points, or uncovers opportunities. When you align your story with these needs, you foster engagement, build trust, and drive meaningful decisions.

Consider a marketing manager looking to optimize campaign spending. Their key questions might be, "Which channels deliver the highest ROI?" or "Where are we overspending without sufficient return?" In contrast, a C-suite executive may focus on broader outcomes: "Are we hitting quarterly growth targets?" or "How do our results compare to industry benchmarks?" Recognizing these distinct priorities ensures your data story resonates.

***Techniques for Uncovering Key Questions***

Identifying the right questions is both an art and a science. Successful data storytellers use a blend of discovery techniques to surface what truly matters to stakeholders.

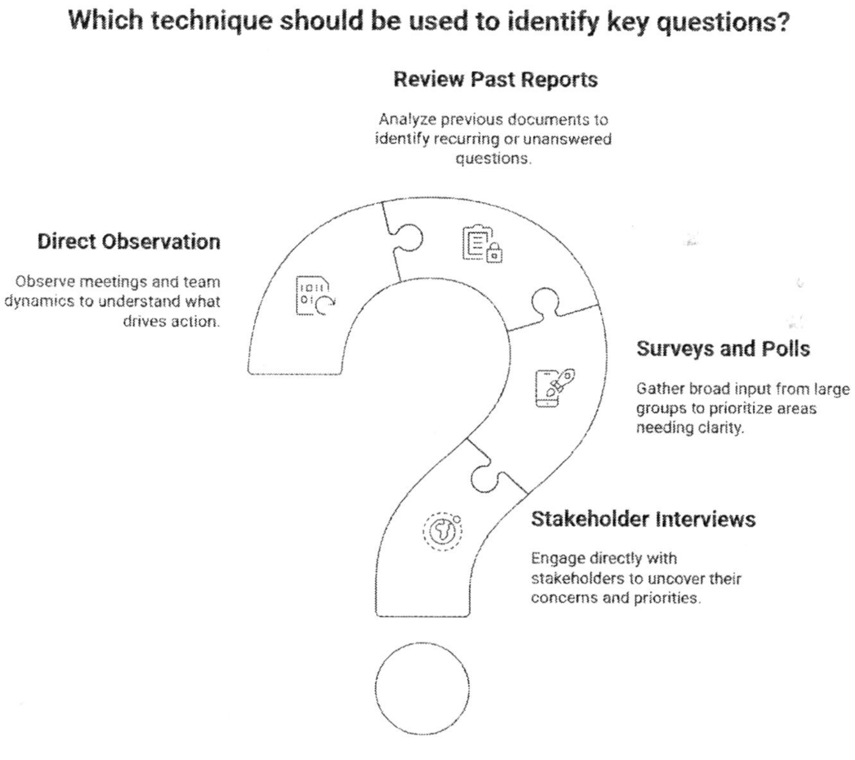


- **Stakeholder Interviews:** Engage with your audience through informal conversations or structured interviews. Ask open-ended questions such as,

"What keeps you up at night?" or "If you could have one metric at your fingertips, what would it be?"

- **Surveys and Polls:** Distribute brief surveys to capture broader input, especially in large organizations or remote teams. Use these to prioritize which areas need the most clarity.
- **Reviewing Past Reports and Meetings:** Analyze previous presentations, dashboards, or meeting minutes to see which questions were frequently raised or left unanswered.
- **Direct Observation:** Attend meetings or shadow teams to observe what information sparks debate or drives action.

By combining these approaches, you create a well-rounded understanding of both explicit and unspoken needs. You also position yourself as a proactive partner rather than just a data provider.

*From Questions to Data Stories: Real-World Scenarios*

To illustrate how identifying key questions can dramatically reshape your data storytelling, let's look at two business scenarios from different cultural and industry contexts.

### 1. Sales Performance in a Global Retail Chain

A European-based retail company operates stores across multiple continents. The regional managers in Asia are concerned about declining sales in urban locations, while the headquarters in Paris focuses on overall profit margins. By interviewing both groups and reviewing last quarter's dashboards, you learn:

- Regional managers want to know: "Which product categories are underperforming in urban stores, and why?"
- Headquarters asks: "How do these regional trends affect yearly profit projections?"

Using tools like **Power BI** or **Tableau**, you craft dashboards tailored to each group. For the regional team, a heat map highlights sales by category and store location, quickly revealing underperformers. For the headquarters, a line chart compares projected and actual profit margins by region, emphasizing the larger business impact.

### 2. Customer Churn Analysis for a SaaS Startup

A North American SaaS startup is experiencing higher-than-expected customer churn. Customer success managers wonder, "Which user segments are most likely to churn, and what are their common characteristics?" Meanwhile, the CEO wants to know, "What is the forecasted churn rate, and how will it affect revenue targets?"

By hosting a cross-functional workshop, you gather insights from both groups. You then use Tableau to build interactive dashboards:

- A cohort analysis visualizes churn rates by user segment, allowing customer success teams to target interventions.
- A revenue impact chart projects how different churn scenarios will influence quarterly goals, giving the CEO a clear decision framework.

In both cases, identifying key questions enables you to build targeted, actionable stories that speak directly to stakeholder priorities.

#### *Visualization Tools and Dashboard Strategies*

Selecting the right tools and designing effective dashboards are essential for making key questions visible and actionable.

**Tableau:** Excellent for interactive dashboards that allow users to drill down into specifics, such as filtering by store, region, or segment.
**Power BI:** Integrates seamlessly with Microsoft products and supports real-time data visualizations for operational dashboards.
**Google Data Studio:** Useful for quick, collaborative dashboard creation, especially when sharing insights with distributed teams.

When designing dashboards, always start with the core questions in mind. Place the most important metrics front and center, use clear labels, and limit distractions. For example, if executives care most about year-over-year growth, make that the focal point of your dashboard, with supporting details available via tooltips or secondary visuals.

```
# Example: Using Python to filter sales data for a key metric
visualization

import pandas as pd
import matplotlib.pyplot as plt

sales_data = pd.read_csv( 'sales_by_category.csv')
urban_stores = sales_data[sales_data[ 'location_type'] == 'urban']
category_sales = urban_stores.groupby( 'product_category')[
'sales'].sum()
category_sales.plot(kind= 'bar', title= "Urban Store Sales by
Category")
plt.show()
```

This code snippet demonstrates how you might quickly isolate and visualize a key question—urban store category sales—before refining it for your final dashboard.

***Common Pitfalls and How to Avoid Them***

It's easy to fall into the trap of answering the questions you find interesting, rather than those your audience cares about most. Another common pitfall is overwhelming stakeholders with data that lacks context or relevance.

To avoid these mistakes:

- Validate your understanding of key questions by sharing draft visuals early and soliciting feedback.
- Prioritize clarity over comprehensiveness; a focused dashboard is more effective than a cluttered one.

Identifying your audience's key questions and needs is the cornerstone of impactful data storytelling. By taking the time to understand what truly matters to stakeholders, you set the stage for compelling, relevant, and actionable visual narratives. In the next section, we'll explore how to match these identified needs with the most effective visual representations, ensuring your insights are not just seen, but truly understood and acted upon.

## 3.3. Cultural Sensitivity in Data Communication

As we tailor our data stories to the needs of our audience, it is essential to recognize that cultural context shapes how information is received, interpreted, and acted upon. **Cultural sensitivity** in data communication means not only respecting cultural norms but also actively designing your data visuals and narratives to resonate with diverse backgrounds, experiences, and expectations. In a globalized business environment, overlooking these nuances can lead to misinterpretations, missed opportunities, or even unintended offense.

***Why Cultural Sensitivity Matters in Data Storytelling***

Culture influences everything from color interpretation and reading direction to preferred communication styles and decision-making processes. For instance, a red color in financial dashboards might signal loss or danger in Western cultures, but could symbolize prosperity in parts of Asia. Similarly, some cultures value detailed, context-rich reports, while others prefer concise, high-level summaries.

Ignoring these differences can result in:

- Miscommunication of key insights

- Decreased stakeholder trust and engagement
- Reduced effectiveness of data-driven recommendations

A culturally sensitive approach ensures your data story is clear, accessible, and compelling—no matter who is in the room.

### *Key Elements of Culturally Sensitive Data Visualizations*

To communicate data effectively across cultures, consider these foundational elements:

#### 1. Color Choices

Colors carry distinct meanings in different cultures. When designing dashboards or data visuals in tools like **Tableau** or **Power BI**, use color palettes that avoid ambiguity or negative associations for your audience.

For example:

- Avoid using red to represent positive outcomes in East Asian business reports.
- Use neutral tones for global audiences, or customize dashboards based on regional deployments.

#### 2. Language and Symbols

Language barriers and unfamiliar symbols can hinder understanding. Ensure that labels, legends, and annotations are clear and, where possible, localized. Many visualization tools allow multilingual support or custom text fields.

#### 3. Data Formats and Numeracy

Date formats, time conventions, and even the units of measurement vary globally. For example, 05/06/2024 can mean May 6 or June 5, depending on the audience. Always clarify or adapt formats within your visuals.

#### 4. Narrative Structure

Some cultures prefer direct, bottom-line conclusions, while others appreciate background, evidence, and context before recommendations. Structure your data stories accordingly, balancing narrative flow with audience expectations.

### *Real-World Use Cases*

To illustrate the importance of cultural sensitivity, let's look at two scenarios where attention to cultural context transformed business outcomes.

### Global Sales Dashboard for a Multinational Retailer

A European retailer rolled out a Tableau dashboard to regional managers across Asia, Europe, and North America. The initial dashboard used red for declining sales and green for growth, with English-only labels and European date formats. Asian managers reported confusion and discomfort—red, for them, was not a negative color, and the unfamiliar date format hampered quick decision-making.

The retailer's analytics team responded by:

- Allowing users to toggle between color themes suitable for their region
- Localizing language and numerical formats
- Providing context-sensitive tooltips in multiple languages

The result was better engagement, fewer misinterpretations, and improved regional performance tracking.

### Healthcare Analytics in the Middle East

A health analytics company used Power BI to present public health data to stakeholders in the Middle East. The team initially left dashboards in left-to-right orientation, included Western-centric icons, and used US date and currency formats. Feedback indicated that right-to-left (RTL) layouts, region-specific icons, and Arabic numerals would make the visuals more intuitive.

By adapting their dashboards:

- Power BI's RTL support was enabled
- Icons were switched to culturally appropriate alternatives
- All text was translated, and numbers reformatted

This led to more productive meetings and greater buy-in for data-driven health initiatives.

#### *Practical Tips for Applying Cultural Sensitivity in Visualization Tools*

Modern business intelligence platforms offer features that support culturally sensitive data storytelling:

**Tableau**: Use the "Workbook Locale" setting to adjust date and number formats, and design color palettes that suit your audience. Tableau's "Workbook Language" can be changed to localize dashboards.

**Power BI**: Leverage language packs, customize report themes, and enable RTL layouts when needed. Use "Conditional Formatting" to adapt colors for different user groups.

**Dashboard Design**: Include user-selectable settings for language, color scheme, and data format. Provide legends or explanations for icons and symbols.

#### *Business Dashboards: Illustrative Example*

Imagine a global sales dashboard with the following features:

```
- Region selector: Customizes language, color palette, and number
formats
- Color-coded charts: Green for positive change in Western regions,
gold in Asian markets
- Date format toggler: MM/DD/YYYY or DD/MM/YYYY based on user
preference
- Dual language labels: English and local language side-by-side
- Icon library: Swappable icons based on cultural relevance
```

These simple additions can make a world of difference in how your insights are received and acted upon.

Being attuned to cultural differences is not just a mark of respect; it is a strategic business advantage. By leveraging the customization capabilities of modern data visualization tools and maintaining cultural awareness, you ensure your data stories are meaningful and actionable across borders.

### 3.4. Tailoring Visuals for Impact

Before diving into the creation of any data visual, it's crucial to recognize that the ultimate power of your work lies not just in the numbers, but in how those numbers resonate with your audience. Tailoring your visuals for impact means aligning your design choices with the unique needs, expectations, and cultural backgrounds of the people you're communicating with. This section explores actionable strategies for customizing data visuals, illustrates these principles through real-world business scenarios, and introduces practical tools that help bring impactful visual storytelling to life.

#### *Knowing Your Audience: The First Step to Relevance*

Every audience brings a different level of data literacy, business context, and decision-making responsibility. A visualization that captivates a technical analytics team might overwhelm a group of senior executives focused on high-level trends, or confuse stakeholders from different cultural backgrounds who interpret colors and symbols differently.

To tailor visuals effectively, start by asking:

- Who are your primary viewers? Executives, marketers, analysts, clients, or a cross-functional team?
- What are their goals and pain points? Are they seeking strategic direction, operational detail, or a quick snapshot?
- How familiar are they with the data or subject matter?
- What cultural factors might influence their interpretation of visuals (such as color meanings or reading direction)?

This foundational understanding guides every decision, from chart selection to color palette.

***Customizing Visuals for Stakeholder Needs***

Once you've mapped out your audience profile, you can adapt your visuals for maximum impact. Let's break this down through practical business scenarios.

**Scenario 1: Executive Dashboard for Global Retail Performance**

Imagine you are a data analyst at a multinational retail company tasked with presenting quarterly performance to the executive board. Executives typically prefer concise, high-level overviews that highlight key performance indicators (KPIs) and strategic trends.

In this context, your dashboard in **Power BI** or **Tableau** might include:

- A **summary scorecard** displaying top-line metrics like revenue, profit margin, and year-over-year growth.
- A **simple line chart** showing sales trends across regions.
- A **color-coded map** illustrating performance by country, using blues and greens for positive growth (universally perceived as positive in most cultures) and muted tones for neutral or negative areas.

To further enhance clarity, use minimal text and avoid technical jargon. Interactive tooltips in Tableau or slicers in Power BI allow executives to drill down on demand, without cluttering the main view.

**Scenario 2: Marketing Campaign Analysis in a Culturally Diverse Team**

Now, consider a marketing manager in an Asia-Pacific division, preparing a campaign performance report for a culturally diverse team spread across Singapore, Australia, and India. Here, color choices and iconography are particularly important.

In **Tableau**, the manager might:

- Use **bar charts** to compare campaign conversions by country, ensuring that colors are accessible to those with color vision deficiencies (using blue and orange, for example, instead of red and green).
- Incorporate **custom icons** that are culturally neutral, steering clear of symbols that may carry unintended connotations in certain regions.
- Add **text annotations** to highlight key findings, keeping language concise and avoiding idioms that might not translate well.

This approach ensures that the story behind the data is clear and respectful of the audience's diverse backgrounds.

Below is a simple example of how you might configure an executive dashboard in Power BI:

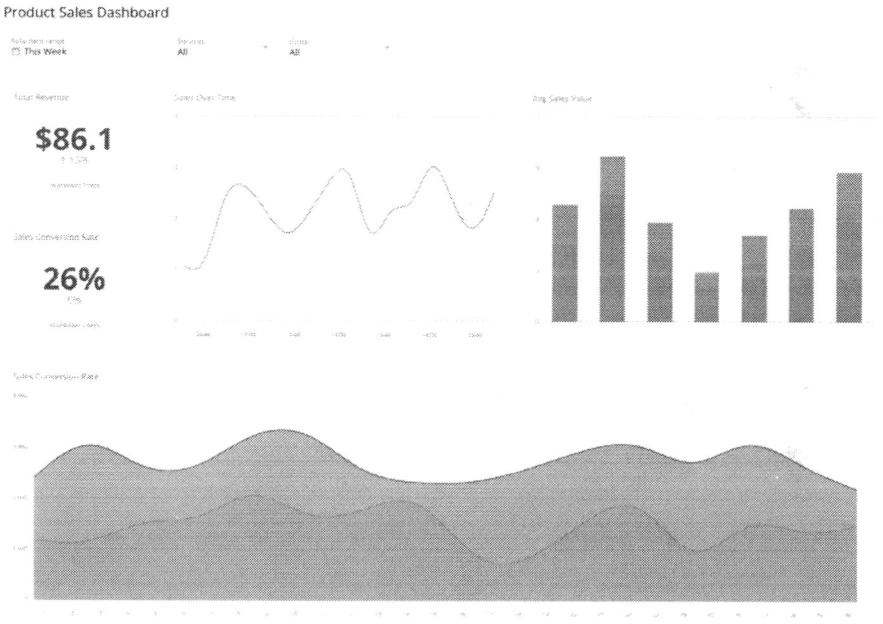


This layout prioritizes high-level metrics and visual clarity, with interactivity for deeper exploration.

Customizing your data visuals ensures that your message doesn't just inform, but influences and inspires. By understanding your audience's needs and context, choosing appropriate visuals, and leveraging the right tools, you elevate your data storytelling from functional to unforgettable.

## 3.5. Leveraging Feedback for Continuous Improvement

No matter how compelling your data visuals or how thoroughly you tailor your narrative to your audience, your work is never truly finished after a single presentation. In the dynamic environment of business communication, feedback is essential for refining your approach, deepening your understanding of your audience, and achieving greater impact with each iteration. Leveraging feedback is not just a post-presentation activity—it's a mindset that transforms your data storytelling into a living, evolving practice.

### *The Value of Feedback in Data Storytelling*

Feedback is more than a thumbs-up or a simple critique. When approached thoughtfully, it becomes a powerful tool for continuous improvement. It helps you uncover blind spots, validate assumptions, and adapt your storytelling techniques to different stakeholders. Most importantly, feedback closes the communication loop, ensuring your visuals are not just seen, but understood and acted upon.

- **Clarity:** Assess whether your audience grasped the main message.
- **Engagement:** Determine if your visuals held attention or caused confusion.
- **Actionability:** Understand if your data inspired decisions or changes in behavior.

This ongoing dialogue between presenter and audience is fundamental for anyone aiming to master data storytelling.

### *Gathering Feedback: Approaches and Best Practices*

To harness feedback effectively, you need structured processes that go beyond casual conversations. Consider these practical strategies:

- **Direct Questions During and After Presentations**
    - Ask open-ended questions, such as "Which part of this visualization was most helpful for your decision-making?"
    - Use live polling tools or digital surveys (e.g., through Microsoft Forms or Google Forms) to collect immediate reactions.

- **Observing Audience Behavior**
    - Watch for signs of confusion, disengagement, or excitement during your presentation. This can be particularly insightful when presenting dashboards in tools like Tableau or Power BI, where interactivity can reveal what draws attention.

- Record virtual sessions (with consent) to review questions asked or points of friction.

- **Feedback Forms and Follow-Up Interviews**
  - After a presentation, distribute a feedback form focused on the clarity, design, and relevance of your visuals.
  - Conduct brief interviews with key stakeholders to probe deeper into their experience and gather nuanced suggestions.

- **Digital Analytics for Dashboards**
  - Many business intelligence tools offer built-in analytics. For example, Power BI's usage metrics or Tableau's dashboard engagement data can reveal which visuals are most or least viewed, and where users interact most.

***Real-World Use Cases: Feedback in Action***

Let's explore how organizations worldwide are using feedback to elevate their data storytelling.

**Scenario 1: Marketing Dashboard Optimization in a Global Retailer**

A multinational retail company uses Tableau dashboards to track campaign performance across regions. After the initial rollout, the marketing team noticed regional managers in Asia rarely interacted with certain charts. Through follow-up interviews and dashboard usage analytics, they discovered the color schemes and terminology used were less intuitive for these managers due to cultural differences. By gathering this feedback, the team redesigned the dashboards with more universally recognized icons and localized terminology. Engagement improved, and regional managers began using the dashboards to inform weekly strategy meetings.

**Scenario 2: Financial Reporting Enhancement in a U.S. Healthcare Provider**

A healthcare provider's finance department presented quarterly results using Power BI dashboards. Initially, executives found the visualizations too granular and struggled to identify actionable insights. The department implemented a feedback loop, distributing digital surveys post-presentation and inviting executives to highlight confusing elements. Guided by this feedback, the team simplified the dashboards, added narrative context, and used color more purposefully to emphasize key metrics.

The result was a marked increase in executive satisfaction, and more importantly, faster consensus on budgetary decisions.

*Making Iteration Part of Your Process*

Feedback is only valuable if it leads to tangible improvements. Here's how to embed continuous improvement into your workflow:

- **Review and Analyze Feedback**
  - Categorize input into themes (e.g., clarity, engagement, design).
  - Prioritize changes based on frequency and potential impact.
- **Implement Iterative Updates**
  - Update your visuals or narrative in your dashboarding tool.
  - Test revised versions with a small group before a broader rollout.
- **Communicate Changes**
  - Let your audience know you've acted on their feedback. This closes the loop and fosters trust.
- **Repeat the Cycle**
  - Each iteration brings you closer to data storytelling mastery. Continuous feedback ensures your approach remains audience-centric and effective.

```
# Example: Using Tableau to monitor dashboard engagement

# (Assume you have access to Tableau's built-in usage metrics)

# Steps:

# 1. Open Tableau Server or Tableau Online

# 2. Navigate to your dashboard

# 3. Click on 'Usage' tab to view engagement analytics

# 4. Analyze metrics such as 'Views by User', 'Time Spent',
'Interactions'

# 5. Use findings to identify which visuals need improvement
```

## 3.6. Summary and Key Takeaways

Throughout this chapter, we have explored the foundational principle that effective data storytelling begins not with charts or numbers, but with a deep understanding of your audience. Recognizing who your stakeholders are, what they value, and how they prefer to receive information shapes every decision in the storytelling process, from the data you select to the visuals you create. By focusing first on audience needs, you set the stage for communication that is not only clear and relevant, but also persuasive and actionable.

### *Recapping Audience-Centric Storytelling*

Before diving into new data or visualization techniques, it's crucial to remember the importance of audience segmentation and empathy. Identifying your audience's roles—whether they are executives seeking strategic insights, marketers needing customer trends, or analysts desiring granular data—allows you to tailor your narrative and visuals accordingly.

- **Executives** often require high-level dashboards with KPIs and trend analysis to make strategic decisions quickly.
- **Marketers** benefit from visualizations that highlight customer behavior and campaign performance, focusing on actionable insights.
- **Analysts** look for detailed, interactive charts that allow for data exploration and hypothesis testing.

This segmentation supports the creation of data stories that resonate, minimizing confusion and maximizing engagement.

### *Visualization Tool Strategies*

Selecting the right visualization tool is a critical component of audience-centric storytelling. Tools like Tableau and Power BI offer templates and customization options that make it easier to design with your audience in mind. For example:

- **Tableau** excels at building interactive dashboards for executive overviews or regional comparisons.
- **Power BI** is powerful for integrating multiple data sources, enabling marketers to explore campaign results with drill-down capabilities.

When using these tools, consider:

- **Clarity over complexity:** Avoid overwhelming your audience with unnecessary detail. Use summary cards, clean layouts, and concise narratives.
- **Customization:** Tailor dashboards to each audience segment. A single "one-size-fits-all" dashboard is rarely effective.
- **Iterative design:** Gather feedback from your audience and refine your visuals and stories continuously.

### *Key Takeaways*

As you reflect on this chapter, keep in mind these core principles:

- **Know your audience:** Invest time in understanding their roles, goals, and information preferences.
- **Tailor your message:** Adapt the depth of information, visualization types, and narrative style to your audience's needs.
- **Use the right tools:** Leverage visualization platforms such as Tableau and Power BI to create impactful, audience-specific dashboards.
- **Seek feedback:** Treat data storytelling as an iterative process, inviting feedback and making improvements to ensure clarity and relevance.

By focusing on your audience, you set the groundwork for data stories that connect, persuade, and drive action. Mastering this element ensures your future visualizations are not just seen, but understood and acted upon.

# 4. CRAFTING THE NARRATIVE: FROM DATA TO STORY

Imagine standing before a room full of decision-makers. Your data is robust, your analysis impeccable, yet eyes glaze over as you present your findings. What's missing? The answer is often not more data, but a compelling story that transforms raw numbers into meaningful business insight. This chapter unlocks the secrets to bridging that gap, showing you how to shape data into narratives that resonate, persuade, and drive meaningful action.

As you progress through these pages, you'll discover the core elements that make up a powerful data story. We'll explore how to find the narrative thread hidden within complex datasets, moving beyond charts and spreadsheets to uncover the central message that matters most for your audience. You'll learn proven techniques for storyboarding and outlining, ensuring your data-driven presentations unfold with clarity and purpose. We'll discuss how to strike the right balance between data, visuals, and text, weaving them together to create cohesive, engaging stories.

Real-world business scenarios will illustrate how these skills translate into measurable impact, from clarifying a marketing strategy in Singapore to guiding executive decisions in a European tech firm. Along the way, we'll highlight common narrative missteps and provide practical guidance for avoiding them. By the end of this chapter, you'll be equipped to craft data stories that not only inform but inspire, turning insight into influence and making your business voice unforgettable. Let's begin the journey from data to story—where true business impact begins.

## 4.1. The Anatomy of a Data Story

A compelling data story is more than just a collection of charts or numbers—it's a structured narrative that guides your audience from initial curiosity to clear understanding and actionable insight. For beginners, understanding the anatomy of a data story is crucial. This structure provides a roadmap, ensuring your message is coherent, persuasive, and relevant to business objectives.

### *The Core Elements of a Data Story*

Every effective data story consists of several interconnected parts. These components work together to move your audience from raw data to a meaningful conclusion.

- **Context:** The background or situation that frames your data, answering why the analysis matters.

- **Characters:** The stakeholders or entities affected by the data, such as customers, sales teams, or departments.
- **Conflict or Challenge:** The problem, opportunity, or question being addressed.
- **Evidence:** The data itself—presented through charts, tables, or dashboards.
- **Resolution:** The insights, recommendations, or decisions that follow from the evidence.
- **Call to Action:** The next steps or desired outcomes for your audience.

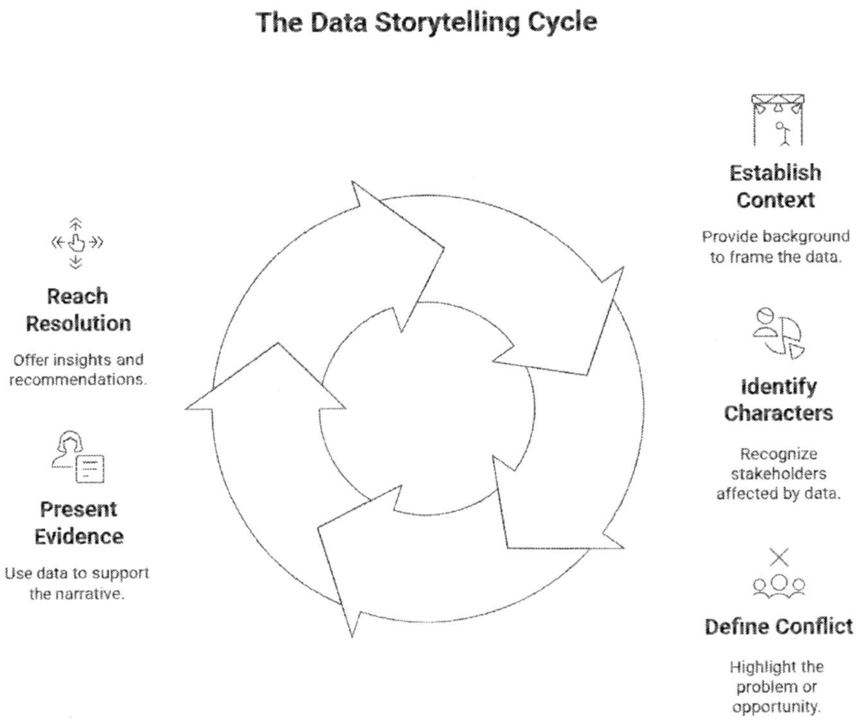


These elements mirror classic storytelling, ensuring your data narrative is engaging and memorable.

***Step-by-Step: Building Your Data Story***

To bring these elements to life, follow a logical sequence when crafting your story:

- **Set the Scene:** Start with context. Explain the business environment, market trends, or recent changes that make your analysis relevant.
- **Introduce the Stakeholders:** Identify who is involved or impacted. Are you analyzing customer behavior, internal processes, or market competition?

- **Highlight the Challenge:** Define the key business question or problem. Be specific—are sales declining in a region, or is customer churn increasing?
- **Present the Evidence:** Use data visualizations to illuminate the challenge. Select clear, relevant visuals such as line charts for trends, bar charts for comparisons, or maps for geographic patterns.
- **Reveal Insights:** Interpret the visuals, connect the dots, and extract actionable insights. What patterns or anomalies stand out?
- **Propose Solutions or Actions:** Based on your findings, recommend decisions or next steps.
- **Invite Engagement:** End with a call to action, encouraging stakeholders to act or discuss further.

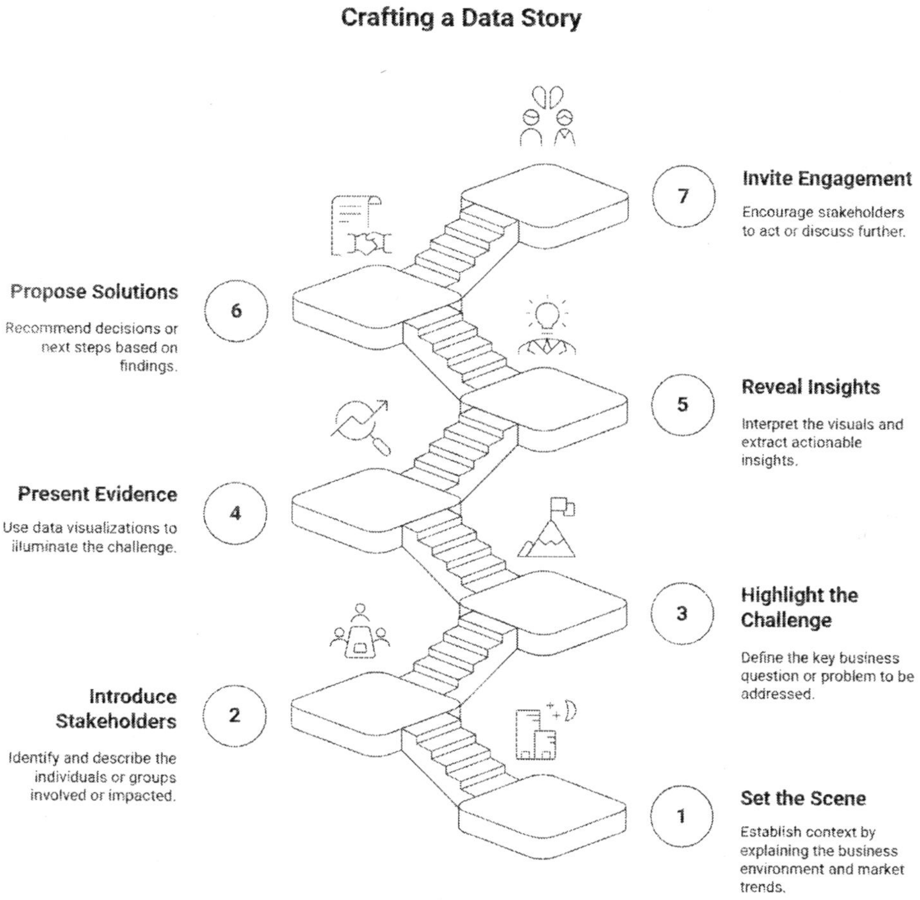


*Visualization Tools and Dashboards in Action*

Choosing the right tools and formats can make or break your data story. Business intelligence platforms like **Tableau** and **Power BI** offer powerful ways to visualize data and create interactive dashboards. For beginners, these tools provide drag-and-drop interfaces and templates for common business scenarios.

**Example: Sales Performance Dashboard**

A regional manager uses Power BI to build a dashboard tracking quarterly sales by product and territory. The dashboard includes:

- A map visualization highlighting underperforming regions.
- Bar charts comparing product lines.
- Trend lines showing sales growth over time.

By integrating context (quarterly goals), characters (regional sales teams), conflict (lagging territories), evidence (real-time sales data), and resolution (targeted coaching recommendations), the manager crafts a persuasive story that drives team action.

**Example: Customer Churn Analysis**

A SaaS company leverages Tableau to analyze customer churn. The analyst creates an interactive dashboard featuring:

- Cohort analysis to visualize retention rates by signup month.
- Heat maps showing usage patterns linked to churn.
- Annotations explaining spikes in cancellations after product updates.

Armed with these insights, the team identifies at-risk segments and tailors outreach, demonstrating how a clear data story can directly influence customer success strategies.

#### *Bringing Cultural and Global Perspectives*

Effective data stories transcend borders. For instance, a global retailer using Tableau may compare in-store versus online sales across continents, adapting visuals to suit local business contexts. In Japan, color palettes are chosen for cultural appropriateness, while in Germany, dashboard text is translated and localized. These adjustments ensure the story resonates with diverse audiences and avoids misinterpretation.

### 4.2. Finding the Story Within the Data

Just as a novelist uncovers themes and characters within the raw material of real life, data storytellers must reveal the hidden narrative within datasets. This process begins with curiosity and a clear understanding of your business objectives. Before building visuals or dashboards, it's essential to ask: What story does the data want to tell, and how does that story align with the decisions or actions I want my audience to take?

### *Understanding Your Business Context*

Every dataset exists within a broader business context. For example, sales figures aren't just numbers—they reflect customer behavior, market trends, and operational efficiency. Start by grounding your analysis in the business question at hand. Are you trying to identify growth opportunities, improve efficiency, or mitigate risks?

Visualization tools like **Tableau** and **Power BI** can help you quickly explore data, but the direction you take depends on understanding the "why" behind your analysis. For instance, a marketing analyst might use Tableau to explore campaign data, searching for patterns that explain a sudden spike in engagement. Meanwhile, an operations manager might focus on Power BI dashboards to spot bottlenecks in supply chain data.

### *Unearthing Patterns and Insights*

Finding the story within data is about more than highlighting the obvious. It involves looking for patterns, outliers, and trends that answer business-critical questions or challenge assumptions. Here's how you can approach this exploration:

**Explore Broadly:** Begin with an open mind. Use summary statistics and basic visualizations (like bar charts or scatterplots) to get a sense of the data's shape.

**Drill Down:** Once you spot an interesting trend or anomaly, dig deeper. Tableau's drill-down features or Power BI's interactive filters allow you to segment data by region, product, or demographic.

**Ask "Why" and "What If":** Don't settle for the first answer. Ask why a trend exists, and consider what might change if certain variables shifted.

For example, a global consumer goods company used Power BI to analyze declining sales in one region. By drilling into product categories and customer demographics, they uncovered that the drop was linked to a competitor's new launch, not a failure in their own marketing. This shifted their strategy from internal optimization to competitive response.

### *Connecting Data Points to Business Narratives*

Data storytelling bridges the gap between raw numbers and actionable insight. To craft a narrative, you need to connect the dots for your audience, guiding them from data discovery to business implications.

- **Chronological narratives** can show how performance evolves over time, such as tracking monthly revenue growth.
- **Comparative stories** highlight differences or similarities, like benchmarking sales against industry averages.
- **Cause-and-effect stories** reveal how one action leads to another, ideal for operational analysis or process improvement.

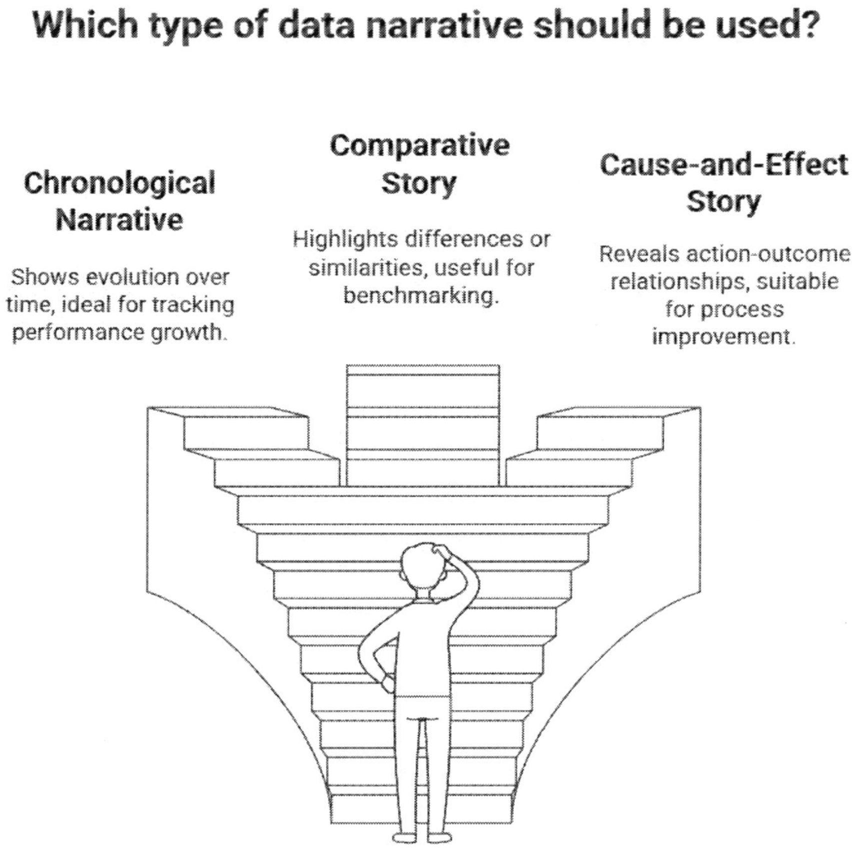


Consider the case of a Southeast Asian fintech startup. Using Tableau dashboards, the team visualized customer onboarding data and noticed that users were dropping off during the identity verification step. Digging deeper, they found this stage took significantly longer due to manual reviews. By sharing this story with cross-functional stakeholders through a clear visual narrative, they secured buy-in for process automation, resulting in a 30% increase in successful onboardings.

***Tools and Dashboards: Bringing Stories to Life***

Choosing the right tool and dashboard elements is crucial in illuminating your story. Platforms like Tableau and Power BI offer features that allow you to:

- Highlight key metrics with color or annotations.
- Use filters and interactivity to let users explore different facets of the story.
- Sequence visuals to mimic the structure of a narrative, moving from context to insight to action.

Interactive elements, such as dropdown menus or clickable region maps, help audiences explore the story at their own pace.

Finding the story within the data is a blend of detective work and creative thinking. By grounding your exploration in business context, actively seeking patterns, and using the right tools to visualize and communicate, you transform data from static tables into dynamic, persuasive narratives.

## 4.3. Developing a Central Message

Every compelling data story begins with a clear, focused central message. This message acts as the guiding star for your narrative, shaping the way information is selected, organized, and presented. Without a central message, even the most dazzling visuals risk becoming noise in a crowded information landscape. Developing this core idea is especially important when your audience—whether stakeholders, executives, or clients—may have limited time or attention.

***Defining Your Core Message***

Before opening Tableau, Power BI, or any visualization tool, step back and ask: What is the single most important insight I want my audience to remember? The answer to this question will clarify your central message and ensure your data story serves a specific business purpose.

Consider these guiding questions:

- What action do I want my audience to take after seeing this information?
- Which business goals or objectives does this data support?
- What is the most surprising, urgent, or valuable insight in my analysis?

By answering these, you shape not only your message but also the emotional resonance and business relevance of your story.

### *Aligning Data with Business Objectives*

Effective data storytelling connects analysis directly to organizational priorities. For example, a marketing analyst at a retail company analyzing campaign performance might identify that "Email campaigns drive 60% more repeat purchases than social media ads." The central message here highlights the impact of a specific channel and suggests where to focus future investments.

In contrast, an executive dashboard in Power BI for a logistics company might reveal, "Optimizing delivery routes could reduce fuel costs by 15% this quarter." This message ties analytics directly to cost-saving goals, making it actionable for decision-makers.

### *From Data Exploration to Message Refinement*

Data exploration often uncovers multiple interesting patterns, but not all findings are equally relevant. Refining your central message involves prioritizing insights based on business impact and audience needs.

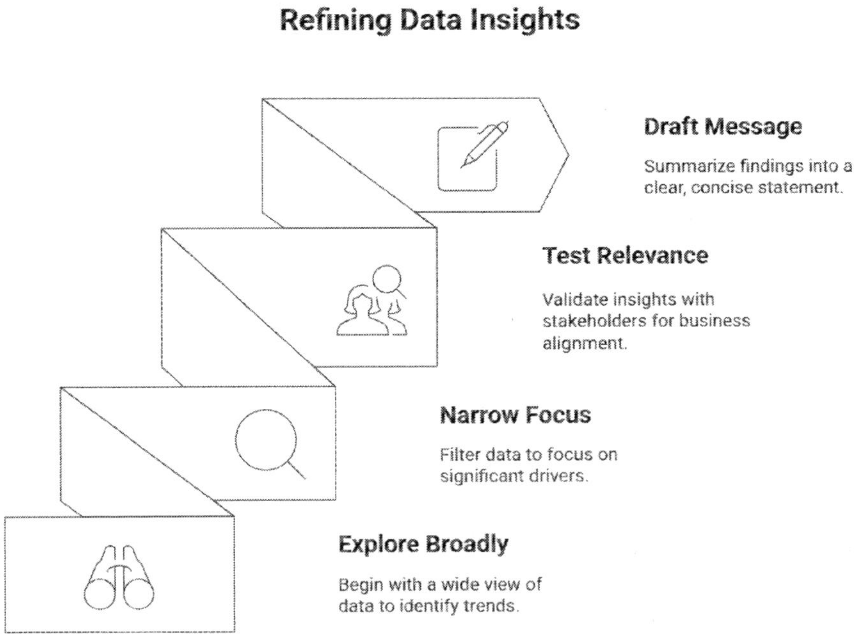


- **Explore Broadly:** Start with a wide view of your data, using basic charts or tables in Tableau or Power BI to identify standout trends or anomalies.
- **Narrow Focus:** Filter and segment the data to hone in on the most significant drivers behind your observations.

- **Test Relevance:** Ask colleagues or stakeholders if the insight aligns with current business challenges or opportunities.
- **Draft Your Message:** Create a one-sentence summary that captures the essence of your finding, using plain language.

For example, in Tableau:

```
# Simple calculation to identify top-performing regions

IF [Sales] > WINDOW_AVG([Sales]) THEN "Above Average"ELSE "Below
Average"END
```

This quick calculation can help you zero in on regions that outperform expectations, allowing you to focus your story on "Why the Northeast region is leading sales growth this year."

#### *Visualizing for Clarity and Impact*

Once your central message is clear, choose visuals that reinforce it rather than distract. In Power BI, you might use a simple bar chart to compare repeat purchase rates by campaign channel, highlighting the one that stands out. In Tableau, a heat map might reveal cost savings across delivery routes, visually supporting your main point.

Dashboards should avoid clutter and maintain a direct line of sight to the central message. For instance, a business dashboard designed to communicate cost reduction might feature:

- A headline metric: "Q2 Fuel Costs Down 15%"
- Supporting visuals: Line chart of monthly costs, map of optimized routes
- Call-to-action: "Expand optimization to additional regions"

This structure ensures the audience grasps the core message at a glance and understands the next steps.

#### *Global Perspective: Adapting the Message*

Different cultures and markets may respond to varying emphases in data storytelling. In a Japanese electronics firm, the central message might underscore process improvement and collective benefit, such as "Team-driven workflow changes have improved production efficiency by 10%." Meanwhile, a US-based tech startup could focus on innovation and market opportunity: "Our new feature adoption rate exceeds industry benchmarks by 25%."

Being mindful of these nuances helps tailor your message for maximum relevance and engagement across diverse audiences.

## 4.4. Storyboarding and Outlining Techniques

Transforming analytical insights into compelling business stories requires more than just effective visuals. The bridge between raw data and persuasive presentations is built through careful planning—specifically, through **storyboarding** and **outlining**. These techniques help you structure your narrative, ensuring each visualization supports a clear, logical flow that resonates with your audience.

Storyboarding, borrowed from film and design, involves sketching out the sequence of your narrative visually. Outlining, on the other hand, provides a textual roadmap, defining the key message, supporting points, and transitions. Both are crucial in avoiding information overload, highlighting the most impactful insights, and guiding your audience through a seamless data journey.

### *Why Storyboarding Matters in Data Storytelling*

A well-crafted storyboard lays out the journey your audience will take, panel by panel or slide by slide. This approach:

- Clarifies the logical progression of your story.
- Identifies gaps or redundancies in data or narrative.
- Ensures that each visualization has a specific purpose.
- Anticipates questions or objections, allowing you to address them proactively.

For beginners, storyboarding demystifies the often-intimidating process of turning data into a narrative. Instead of focusing on complex visualizations first, you start by mapping the story you want to tell.

### *Outlining Your Data Story*

An outline complements your storyboard by defining the narrative structure in words. A typical outline includes:

- **Opening (Hook):** The business context or problem statement that grabs attention.
- **Body (Development):** Key findings, evidence, and data visualizations supporting your message.
- **Climax (Insight):** The “aha” moment where data reveals a critical insight.
- **Resolution (Action):** Clear recommendations or next steps.

Outlining ensures your story isn't just a collection of charts, but a cohesive narrative that drives action.

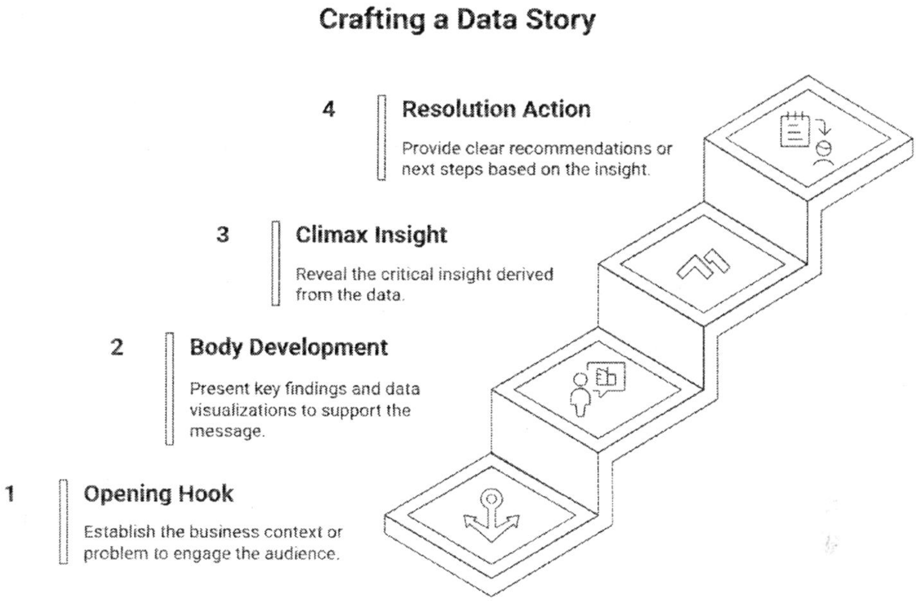


***Step-by-Step Storyboarding Process***

Let's break down a simple workflow for creating a data storyboard:

- **Clarify Your Objective**
    - Define what you want your audience to understand, decide, or do after your presentation.
- **Sketch a Sequence**
    - Use sticky notes, whiteboards, or digital tools (like PowerPoint or Miro) to arrange the major points you need to cover. Each "frame" represents a key message or visualization.
- **Map Visualizations to Each Frame**
    - Decide which type of chart, graph, or dashboard best supports each point. For instance, a trend over time might be best shown with a line chart.
- **Review for Flow and Gaps**

- Walk through your sequence. Does each step logically follow the previous one? Are transitions clear? Does every visualization earn its place?

- **Refine Based on Feedback**
  - Share your storyboard with colleagues or stakeholders. Gather feedback and adjust for clarity, emphasis, or missing elements.

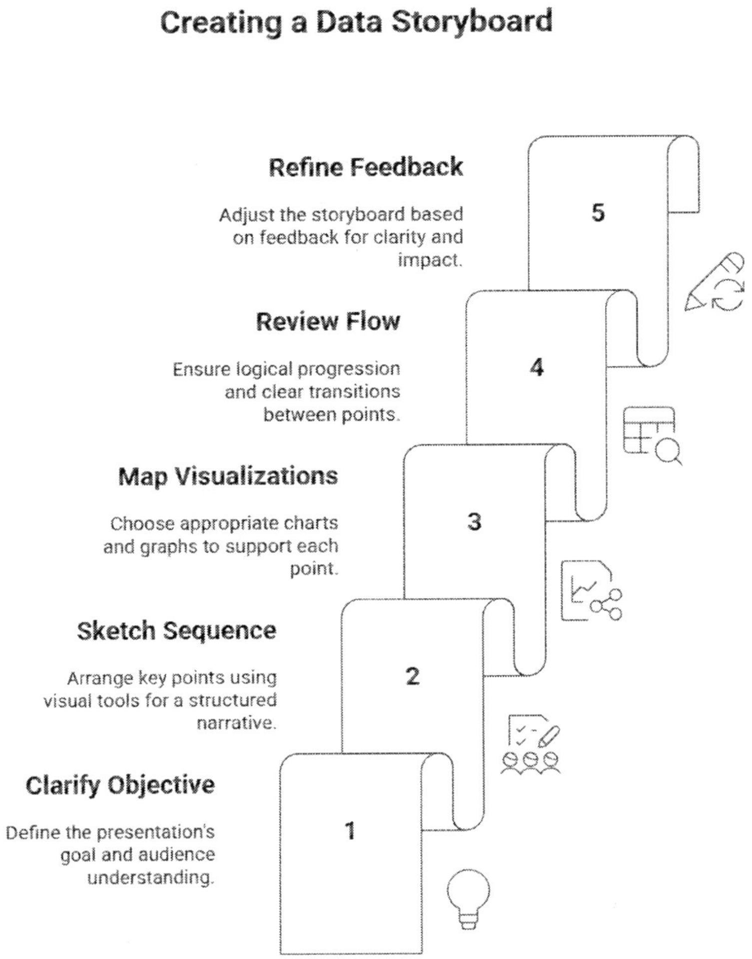


*Visualization Tool Applications*

Modern visualization tools streamline the storyboarding and outlining processes. For example:

**Tableau's Story Points:**

Tableau allows you to create "story points"—a sequence of visualizations with captions. This feature lets you build interactive data stories where users can follow a guided narrative or explore details at their own pace.

**Power BI's Report Pages:**

Power BI enables you to design multi-page dashboards, each acting as a chapter in your story. You can outline the flow using bookmarks and navigation buttons, making the journey intuitive for business users.

**Dashboard Illustrations:**

Imagine a sales performance dashboard. The storyboard might begin with a high-level overview (total sales per region), dive into problematic segments (regions with declining sales), and conclude with actionable insights (recommended focus areas). Sketching this sequence ensures each chart advances the plot, rather than overwhelming the audience with disconnected data.

### *Real-World Use Cases*

**Global Retail Expansion:**

A European retailer planning entry into Southeast Asia used storyboarding to present market analysis to its executive board. The team outlined the presentation: starting with macroeconomic trends, drilling into competitive landscapes, and finally projecting revenue opportunities by country. Visualizations in Power BI were mapped to each section, ensuring the narrative was clear and persuasive.

## 4.5. Integrating Data, Visuals, and Text

Successful data storytelling hinges on the seamless integration of data, visuals, and narrative text. Alone, numbers may appear abstract, and visuals can lack context, while text without supporting evidence risks sounding subjective. When combined thoughtfully, however, these elements reinforce each other, transforming dry analysis into a persuasive, memorable story that drives business outcomes.

### *The Power of Integration*

Effective data storytelling isn't simply about presenting charts or reporting results. It's about guiding your audience through a journey: introducing them to the data, helping them visualize key patterns, and framing those insights in a narrative that resonates. To do this, you must balance three core elements:

**Data:** The factual backbone, providing credibility and substance.
**Visuals:** The translation layer, making complex information accessible and engaging.

**Text:** The narrative glue, offering interpretation, context, and emotional connection.

Integrating these elements ensures that your audience not only understands your message but feels compelled to act on it.

### *Practical Approaches to Integration*

Bringing data, visuals, and text together requires deliberate structure and attention to detail. Consider the following strategies:

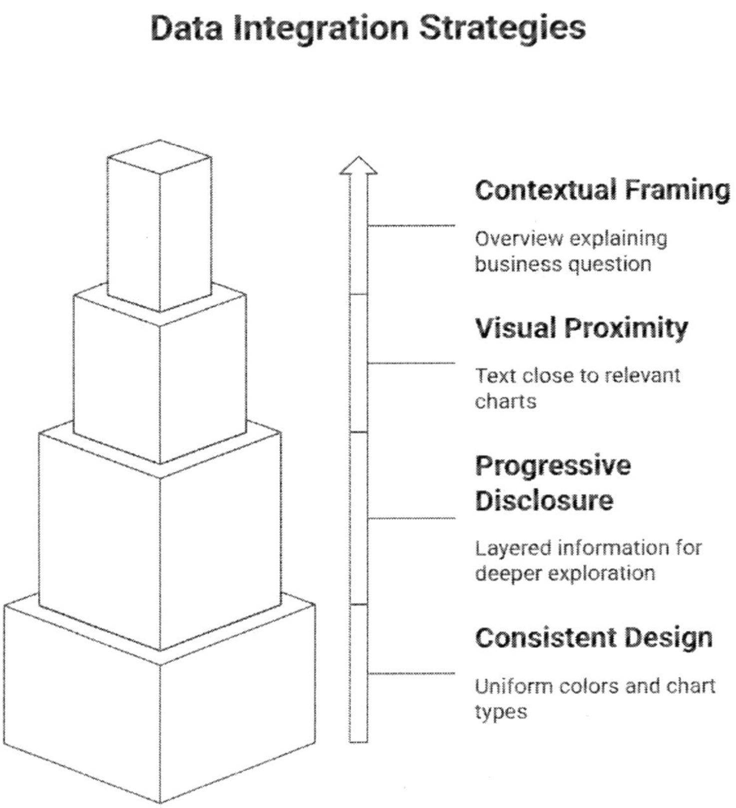


- **Contextual Framing:** Begin each dashboard or report with a brief overview explaining the business question being addressed. This primes your audience for what to look for in the data and visuals.
- **Visual Proximity:** Position explanatory text close to the relevant chart or graph. This reduces cognitive effort and helps viewers immediately connect narrative to evidence.
- **Progressive Disclosure:** Layer information, starting with high-level insights and enabling deeper exploration for interested stakeholders. Tools like Tableau

and Power BI support interactive drill-downs, making it easy for users to uncover more detail as needed.

- **Consistent Design Language:** Use uniform colors, fonts, and chart types to create a cohesive experience. Consistency enhances readability and aids in narrative flow.

### *Global Business Use-Case: Retail Sales Performance Dashboard*

Imagine a multinational retailer launching a new dashboard to monitor quarterly sales performance across regions. The team uses Power BI to integrate sales data from North America, Europe, and Asia, presenting it through a combination of maps, bar charts, and annotated text.

**Data:** Regional sales figures, historical trends, and product category breakdowns.
**Visuals:** A heat map highlights regions exceeding targets, while bar charts compare performance across quarters.
**Text:** Key insights are summarized above each visualization: "Asia-Pacific region outperformed forecasts, driven by strong electronics sales. See detailed figures below."

This integration allows executives in different countries to quickly grasp both the big picture and local specifics, fostering faster, more informed decision-making.

### *Scenario: Healthcare Claims Analysis in Tableau*

A health insurance analyst uses Tableau to investigate rising claim volumes. The dashboard integrates:

**Data:** Daily claim counts, categorized by type and region.
**Visuals:** Line charts show trends over time, while pie charts depict claim type distribution.
**Text:** Next to the charts, concise narrative explains anomalies: "Notice the sharp increase in outpatient claims in March, likely linked to the new telemedicine policy."

By layering these elements, the analyst helps both clinical and business teams understand the underlying drivers and align on operational responses.

### *Visualization Tools for Integration*

Modern business intelligence tools make it easier than ever to blend data, visuals, and narrative. Here are two prominent examples:

**Power BI:** Allows users to add text boxes, shape annotations, and narrative dashboards alongside interactive visuals. For instance, a KPI dashboard can feature callout boxes with business implications, supporting data-driven decision-making.

**Tableau:** Supports dashboard "story points," enabling a guided, step-by-step narrative with integrated commentary and visualization. This structure is ideal for walkthrough presentations or sharing findings with non-technical stakeholders.

```
# Example: Adding a text annotation in Power BI

from powerbi import Dashboard

dashboard = Dashboard()
dashboard.add_chart( 'sales_by_region')
dashboard.add_textbox( "Key Insight: Q2 sales in Europe rose by 15%,
driven by new product launches.")
dashboard.display()
```

***Dashboard Illustration: Bringing It All Together***

Consider a business operations dashboard designed for a logistics firm. The top section features a headline KPI and succinct commentary ("On-time deliveries improved by 8% this quarter"), followed by bar charts and maps with adjacent bullet-point summaries. Interactive filters allow users to dig deeper, with each visual supported by context-aware narrative, ensuring clarity and actionable insight.

## 4.6. Common Pitfalls in Narrative Crafting

As you strive to transform raw data into engaging stories, even the most well-intentioned narratives can falter if common pitfalls go unrecognized. Whether you're using Tableau, Power BI, or custom dashboards, understanding these missteps is essential for building narratives that truly resonate.

***Losing Sight of the Central Message***

A clear, focused narrative is the backbone of any effective data story. Many professionals fall into the trap of presenting too much information, overwhelming audiences with data points and visual clutter. This often happens when the storyteller is deeply familiar with the dataset and feels compelled to share every insight.

For example, a retail marketing manager using Tableau to analyze quarterly sales performance might include a dashboard with 15 different metrics. While comprehensive, this approach risks obscuring the key message—perhaps that a new promotional campaign drove a significant uptick in online sales. By failing to spotlight this central narrative, the audience may miss the actionable insight entirely.

To avoid this, always define your core message before you build your visualization. Ask yourself, "What is the one thing I want my audience to remember?" Then, design visuals and supporting narrative to reinforce that message, trimming away extraneous details.

#### *Overcomplicating Visuals*

Another frequent misstep is the use of complex or inappropriate visualizations. Selecting the wrong chart type or overloading a dashboard with unnecessary elements can confuse rather than clarify. Beginners sometimes opt for sophisticated visuals—such as intricate Sankey diagrams or dense scatterplots—when a simple bar or line chart would suffice.

Consider a global supply chain executive using Power BI to communicate quarterly shipping delays. If the dashboard includes a mix of heatmaps, animated flows, and granular tables, the narrative may become muddled, making it difficult for international partners to grasp the root causes of delays. In this scenario, a straightforward line chart comparing delivery times across regions would offer immediate clarity.

To prevent this pitfall, match your visualization type to the message and audience. Simpler visuals often have greater impact, especially for non-technical stakeholders.

#### *Ignoring Audience Context*

A successful data narrative accounts for the audience's knowledge, interests, and cultural context. Failing to tailor your story risks disconnecting with your listeners. This is particularly important when presenting to diverse, global teams.

For instance, consider a multinational financial services firm using Tableau dashboards to compare investment performance across Asia, Europe, and North America. Presenting data solely in USD without considering local currencies or reference points can alienate regional managers, who may find the information less relatable or actionable.

To avoid this, customize your narrative and visuals for your audience. Use relevant examples, localized data, and familiar terms. When possible, include region-specific context, such as using local currency symbols or benchmarks, to enhance engagement and understanding.

#### *Misleading With Data or Design*

Even unintentional misrepresentation can severely undermine trust and credibility. Common issues include truncated axes, cherry-picked data ranges, or color schemes that exaggerate differences. These mistakes may inadvertently lead audiences to draw incorrect conclusions.

In a dashboard illustrating employee turnover, for example, if the y-axis does not start at zero, minor changes may appear dramatic—potentially causing unwarranted concern among HR or leadership teams. Similarly, using aggressive color gradients in Power BI to represent minor fluctuations can overstate the significance of those changes.

To build trust, always strive for transparency in your data presentation. Clearly label axes, explain your data sources, and use color and scale judiciously.

#### *Neglecting the Story Arc*

A compelling narrative has a clear beginning, middle, and end. Some data storytellers present facts and figures without setting the scene or providing a resolution. This leaves audiences with information but no sense of direction or action.

Consider a project manager reporting on software development progress. If their Power BI dashboard only lists completed and pending tasks without context or next steps, stakeholders may struggle to see the broader impact or required actions.

Instead, frame your narrative as a journey: introduce the problem or opportunity, guide the audience through the analysis, and conclude with actionable recommendations.

In summary, crafting an effective data narrative means more than just assembling charts and numbers. Avoiding these common pitfalls—losing focus, overcomplicating visuals, ignoring your audience, misrepresenting data, and neglecting storytelling structure—will help ensure your insights are understood and impactful. As we move forward, we'll explore how to tailor your narrative for different audiences, further enhancing your ability to drive engagement and business results.

### 4.7. Reflection and Next Steps

Having explored the foundations of transforming data into a compelling narrative, it's important to pause and consider how these techniques can be put into action within real business environments. The journey from raw numbers to powerful stories is not just a creative exercise—it is a strategic skill that directly influences decision-making, stakeholder engagement, and business growth.

### *Visualization Tools: Bridging Data and Story*

Selecting the right tool is crucial for effective data storytelling. Tableau and Power BI are two widely used platforms that offer robust capabilities for crafting visual narratives:

**Tableau** excels at intuitive drag-and-drop dashboard creation, supporting dynamic maps, charts, and storytelling features like "story points," which guide viewers through data step by step.

**Power BI** is tightly integrated with Microsoft's ecosystem, making it ideal for organizations already using Excel and other Office tools. Its interactive dashboards, strong data modeling, and annotation tools make it a favorite for finance and operations teams.

Both tools allow for the integration of textual elements, callouts, and interactivity—essential ingredients for transforming dashboards from static reports into engaging stories.

### *Building on Your Learning: Next Steps*

As you reflect on the principles and examples from this chapter, consider the following actions to further develop your skills:

**Review your own data presentations:** Identify where a narrative or more intuitive visual could enhance understanding.

**Experiment with visualization tools:** Try building a simple dashboard in Tableau or Power BI, focusing on clarity and story flow.

**Seek feedback:** Share your narratives with colleagues from different departments or cultural backgrounds to ensure your story resonates broadly.

**Stay curious:** Explore data storytelling examples in your industry, noting how others use visuals and narrative to influence outcomes.

By continually refining your approach, you'll gain confidence and agility in using data storytelling to drive business success.

# 5. SELECTING THE RIGHT VISUALIZATION TOOLS

In today's fast-paced business world, the tools you choose to visualize data can make all the difference between a story that inspires action and one that falls flat. With an ever-expanding array of visualization platforms and technologies, selecting the right tool is no longer a technical decision alone; it's a strategic one that shapes how your insights are received, understood, and acted upon. The right visualization tool empowers you to communicate complex findings with clarity, foster collaboration across teams, and uphold data security in a global landscape.

This chapter serves as your essential guide through the landscape of modern data visualization tools. You'll begin with an overview of the most popular platforms, gaining clarity on their strengths and best-fit scenarios. We'll shine a spotlight on business mainstays like Excel and Power BI, as well as advanced platforms such as Tableau and Looker, highlighting how each can elevate your data storytelling in unique ways. For those seeking tailored, high-impact visuals, we'll explore the power of coding with Python and R, demystifying custom solutions for business professionals.

Beyond features and functionality, you'll learn how to evaluate tools through the lenses of collaboration, security, and scalability—critical factors in today's interconnected and compliance-driven business environment. Real-world insights come alive through a global bank's journey in selecting visualization tools across diverse regions, offering practical perspectives you can apply in your own organization.

By the end of this chapter, you'll be equipped to make informed choices about visualization tools, ensuring your data stories are not only clear and compelling but also secure and scalable. Let's embark on this exploration to ensure every business insight you share achieves maximum impact.

## 5.1. Overview of Visualization Tools

Selecting the right visualization tool is a crucial step in transforming raw data into compelling business stories. With the rapidly evolving landscape of analytics platforms, understanding your toolset not only shapes your ability to communicate insights but also maximizes your business impact. This section presents an overview of the most widely adopted data visualization tools, their core strengths, typical business applications, and hands-on scenarios where the right platform can make a measurable difference.

***Understanding the Visualization Tool Landscape***

Visualization tools range from intuitive drag-and-drop interfaces to highly customizable coding libraries. The choice depends on the complexity of your data, desired output formats, audience, and the technical resources available. For intermediate business professionals, the focus often lies in tools that balance ease of use, flexibility, and integration with existing business systems.

Some of the most popular tools in the business world include:

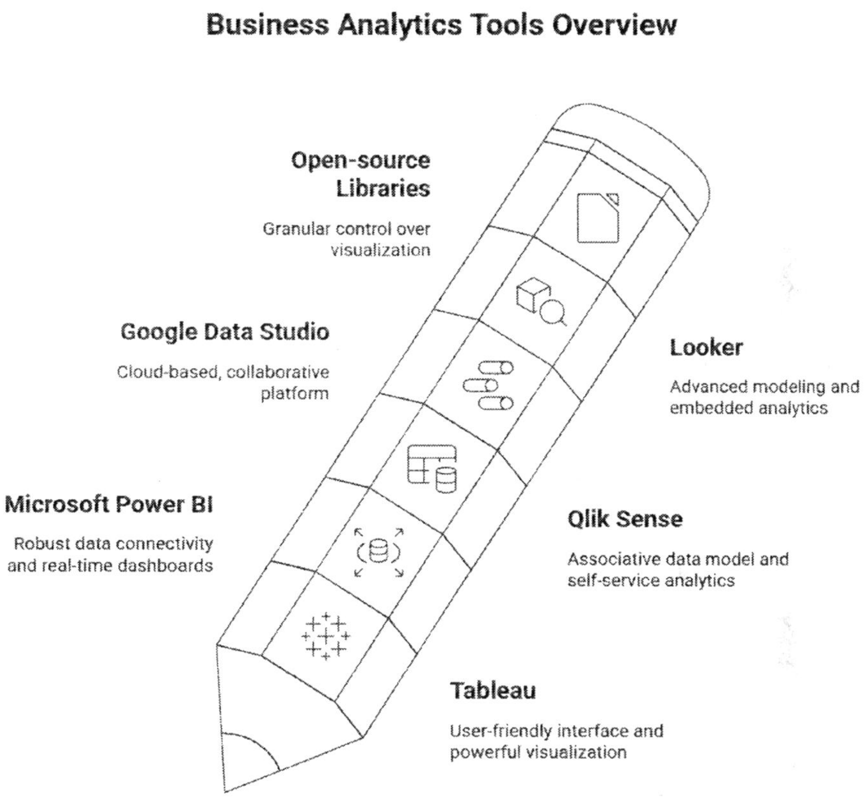


- **Tableau**: Known for its user-friendly interface and powerful visualization capabilities, Tableau is well-suited for interactive dashboards and deep data exploration.
- **Microsoft Power BI**: A favorite for organizations leveraging Microsoft ecosystems, Power BI offers robust data connectivity, real-time dashboards, and seamless integration with Office tools.
- **Qlik Sense**: Notable for its associative data model and self-service analytics, Qlik Sense excels in uncovering hidden relationships within complex datasets.

- **Google Data Studio**: A cloud-based, collaborative platform, Google Data Studio is ideal for sharing live, interactive reports across distributed teams.
- **Looker (now part of Google Cloud)**: Designed with advanced modeling and embedded analytics in mind, Looker bridges technical and business users through customizable, scalable dashboards.
- **Open-source libraries**: For those with coding expertise, libraries like D3.js, Plotly, and Matplotlib offer granular control over every aspect of the visualization process.

### *Core Features and Business Dashboard Examples*

Each tool comes with its own set of features tailored to different business needs. To illustrate, let's look at a few typical dashboard examples and how visualization tools bring them to life:

**Executive Sales Performance Dashboard (Tableau Example):**

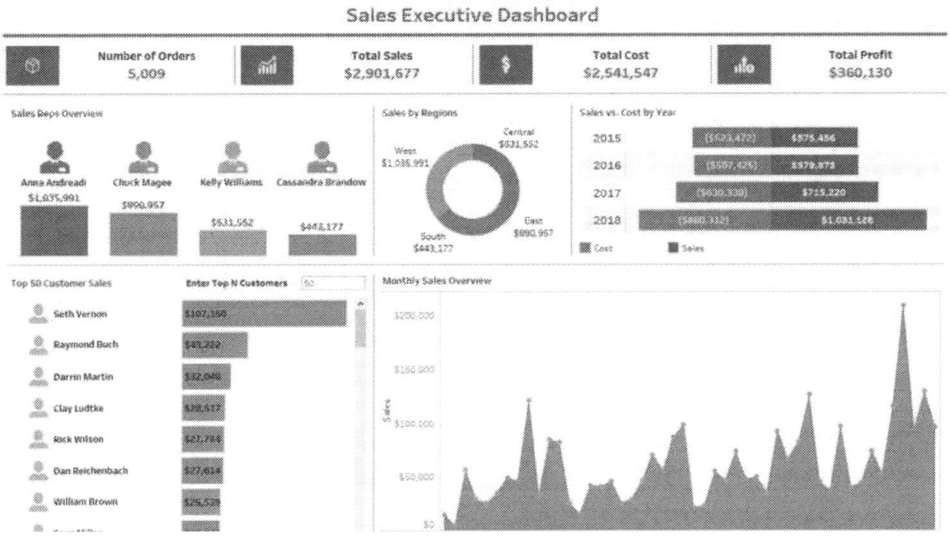


This dashboard provides C-suite leaders with a high-level overview of global sales, key regions, and top-performing products. Tableau's drag-and-drop interface allows users to blend multiple data sources and create interactive heat maps, allowing executives to drill down from global trends to individual product lines with a few clicks.

**Real-Time Marketing Campaign Monitoring (Power BI Example):**

A marketing team runs simultaneous campaigns across digital platforms. Power BI connects directly to sources like Google Analytics and social media APIs, presenting real-time visuals on impressions, conversions, and ROI. Custom alerts notify managers instantly when metrics deviate from targets, enabling agile decision-making.

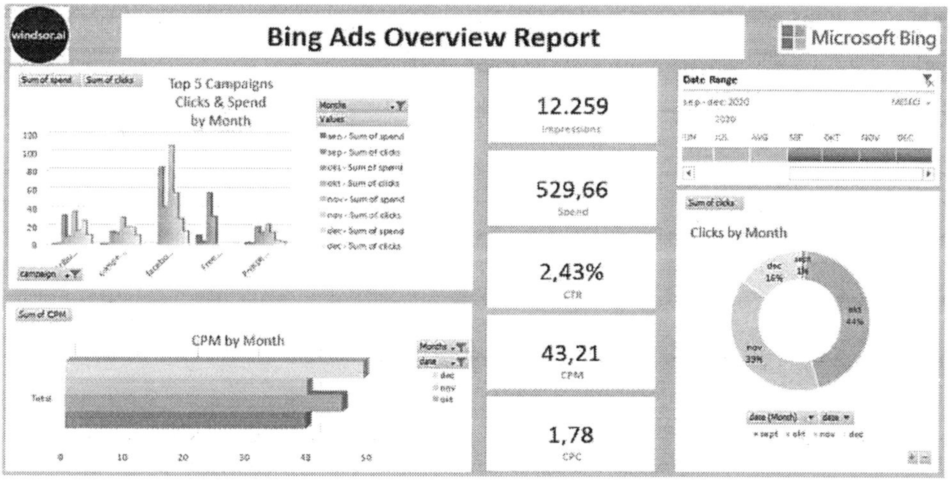


## Operational Efficiency Tracker (Qlik Sense Example):

A manufacturing company uses Qlik Sense to visualize end-to-end supply chain data. The associative model helps reveal unexpected relationships between production delays and supplier performance, supporting targeted process improvements.

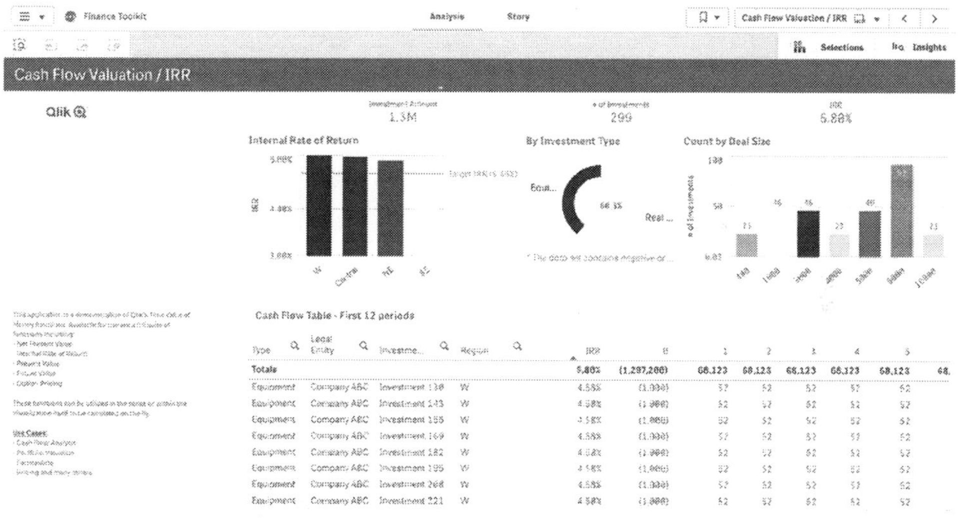


These examples highlight how the choice of tool can influence not just the appearance of dashboards but the speed, accuracy, and depth of business insights.

### *Practical Considerations for Tool Selection*

Choosing the best visualization tool involves more than comparing features. Business professionals should ask:

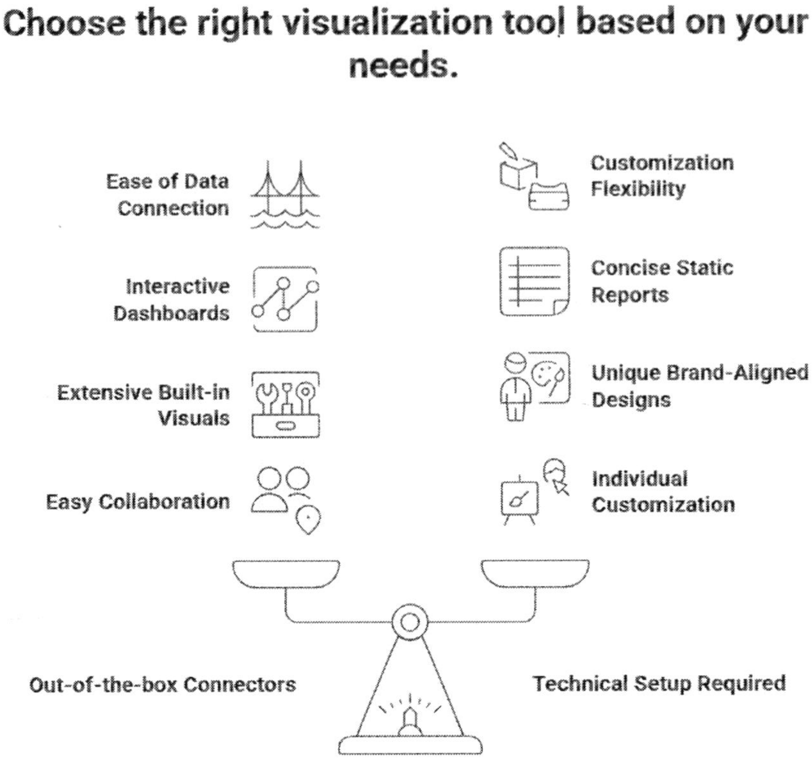


- **What types of data sources do I need to connect to?** Some platforms offer out-of-the-box connectors for databases, cloud services, and spreadsheets, while others require more technical setup.
- **Who is my audience?** Interactive dashboards may be perfect for analysts, while executives may prefer concise, static reports.
- **What level of customization is needed?** While Tableau and Power BI offer extensive built-in visuals, open-source tools like D3.js allow for unique, brand-aligned designs.
- **How important is collaboration?** Cloud-based tools like Google Data Studio make it easy to share live dashboards with global teams.
- **What are my resource constraints?** Consider licensing costs, user training, and IT support.

***Real-World Scenario: Global Retail Expansion***

Consider a global retailer planning to enter new markets in Southeast Asia. The analytics team uses Tableau to merge sales, demographic, and logistics data from multiple countries. By building a dynamic dashboard that visualizes regional demand trends, supply chain bottlenecks, and competitor presence, the team empowers leadership to make informed expansion decisions. The same project could leverage Power BI for real-time inventory monitoring, ensuring stock levels are optimized as new stores open.

Selecting the right visualization tool is foundational to effective data storytelling. The right platform transforms numbers into narratives, surfaces actionable insights, and ensures your message resonates with diverse business audiences.

## 5.2. Tool Spotlight: Excel and Power BI

When considering essential tools for data storytelling, Excel and Power BI consistently emerge as leading choices for business professionals. Each offers distinct strengths for transforming data into compelling narratives, and understanding their capabilities can help intermediate users elevate their storytelling impact. Let's delve into how these tools align with business objectives, illustrate their core features with practical applications, and compare them to other popular platforms such as Tableau.

Excel's enduring presence in the business world is rooted in its versatility, accessibility, and deep integration into daily workflows. Advanced features, including PivotTables, Power Query, and integrated charting options, make Excel a powerhouse for quick analysis and rapid prototyping of visualizations. Professionals across marketing, finance, and operations often use Excel as a starting point for exploring patterns, forecasting trends, and preparing datasets for broader distribution.

### *Core Visualization Features in Excel*

Excel offers a range of built-in chart types—bar, line, pie, scatter, and more—enabling users to visualize data with minimal setup. Its conditional formatting and sparklines add visual cues directly within data tables, highlighting anomalies or trends at a glance. For more complex storytelling, advanced users leverage features like:

- **PivotCharts and Slicers**: Dynamic filtering and drill-down capabilities to tell deeper stories.
- **Power Query**: Automated data cleaning and transformation, ensuring the foundation for any narrative is robust.
- **Custom Visuals**: Through VBA or add-ins, Excel allows the creation of tailored visuals specific to business needs.

Consider a retail manager tracking monthly sales performance. By integrating conditional formatting with sparklines, the manager quickly highlights top-performing regions in red or green, allowing executives to spot strengths and weaknesses in seconds.

### *Power BI: From Static Analysis to Interactive Storytelling*

While Excel excels at static reporting and quick analyses, Power BI takes data storytelling to the next level with interactive dashboards and rich, real-time visualizations. Designed for scalability, Power BI connects to diverse data sources—databases, online services, and even live streams—enabling comprehensive business intelligence.

Key features include:

- **Drag-and-Drop Visualization**: Build dashboards with a wide variety of charts, maps, and custom visuals without coding.
- **Cross-Filtering and Drill-Down**: Empower viewers to explore data stories at their own pace, uncovering insights through interactive exploration.
- **Data Modeling**: Integrate multiple data sources and relationships, supporting complex narratives that span departments or regions.
- **Sharing and Collaboration**: Publish dashboards securely, ensuring stakeholders always have access to the latest insights.

A global marketing team, for example, might use Power BI to visualize campaign performance across regions. By integrating data from Google Analytics, CRM systems, and social platforms, the team builds a unified dashboard. Executives can drill into specific countries to see which campaigns drive engagement, filter by product line, or even view real-time updates during a product launch.

### *Comparing Excel and Power BI to Tableau and Other Tools*

Though Tableau shares similarities with Power BI—offering interactive dashboards, sophisticated visualizations, and a focus on user-friendly data exploration—Power BI's tight integration with the Microsoft ecosystem provides a unique advantage for organizations already invested in Office 365. Excel's ubiquity also means that transitioning between Excel and Power BI is seamless, supporting iterative analysis and rapid scaling.

The illustration below demonstrates a typical business dashboard workflow using Excel and Power BI:

```
1. Data Preparation in Excel:
   - Cleanse and format sales data using Power Query.
   - Build summary PivotTables and static charts.

2. Seamless Export to Power BI:
   - Import refined datasets from Excel into Power BI.
   - Design an interactive dashboard with drill-down filters for
product, region, and time period.
```

```
3. Business Impact:
   - Share the Power BI dashboard with stakeholders.
   - Enable managers to interact with live data, driving informed
decision-making.
```

***Real-World Scenario: Supply Chain Optimization***

A manufacturing firm in Southeast Asia faced bottlenecks due to fluctuating supplier lead times. Analysts consolidated operational data in Excel, using PivotCharts to identify patterns across months. Transitioning to Power BI, they built interactive dashboards mapping delays by supplier, shipment route, and material type. This visualization enabled procurement managers to quickly isolate chronic issues and collaborate with suppliers on targeted improvements. The result was a 15 percent reduction in average lead time within one quarter.

## 5.3. Tool Spotlight: Tableau and Looker

Choosing the right visualization tool can be the difference between a data story that captures attention and one that falls flat. Among the diverse options available, **Tableau** and **Looker** stand out for their robust features and adaptability across industries. Both platforms empower professionals to build impactful visual narratives, yet they approach data visualization from distinct angles. Understanding their strengths and ideal use cases will help you elevate your data storytelling, regardless of your organization's size or sector.

***Tableau: Interactive Visual Analytics for Business Impact***

Tableau has built a reputation as a leader in intuitive, interactive dashboards. Its drag-and-drop interface allows users to swiftly create compelling visualizations, even with limited technical backgrounds. Tableau's strength lies in its ability to connect to numerous data sources, from simple spreadsheets to complex cloud databases, making it a go-to solution for analysts and business teams worldwide.

Consider a multinational retail corporation that wants to analyze sales performance across different regions and product categories. Using Tableau, the marketing team can quickly build a dashboard displaying:

- Dynamic heat maps of sales by region
- Year-over-year growth line charts
- Product-wise sales breakdowns with filter options

By enabling users to filter data interactively—such as selecting a specific country or product line—Tableau helps decision-makers drill down into granular details. This interactivity transforms static data into an evolving story, allowing executives to identify trends, spot anomalies, and act quickly.

A Tableau dashboard example for this scenario might include:

```
[Sales Performance Dashboard]
- Filters: Country, Product Category, Time Period
- Main View: Map of Sales by Region (color-coded)
- Secondary View: Line Chart of Sales Over Time
- Drill-down Section: Top 10 Products Table
```

This structure not only communicates complex information clearly but also invites exploration, making the data story both accessible and actionable.

***Looker: Data Modeling and Consistent Metrics for Scalable Insights***

While Tableau excels at quick, visual exploration, Looker distinguishes itself with its powerful data modeling capabilities. Looker uses a modeling language called LookML, which allows data teams to define business metrics and data relationships centrally. This ensures that every dashboard and report reflects consistent, organization-wide definitions—an essential feature for larger businesses or those with strict governance needs.

Imagine a global fintech company that needs to standardize financial metrics across regional offices. With Looker, data analysts can define key measures such as "Monthly Recurring Revenue" or "Customer Churn Rate" in LookML. Marketing and finance teams then build their dashboards using these centrally governed metrics, ensuring consistency across all reports.

A typical Looker dashboard for this use case could include:

```
[Financial Health Dashboard]
- Consistent Metrics: MRR, Churn Rate, Customer Lifetime Value
- Visuals: Bar Charts for Monthly Revenue Growth, Pie Chart for Revenue
by Segment, Trend Lines for Churn Rate
- Filters: Region, Customer Type, Time Frame
```

This approach reduces the risk of conflicting numbers in board meetings and enables scalable storytelling as the company grows. Furthermore, Looker's integration with Google Cloud Platform makes it a strong choice for organizations with complex, cloud-based data environments.

***Practical Dashboard Illustration: A Comparative View***

To further clarify, suppose a European telecommunications provider wants to monitor its customer satisfaction and service performance:

**Tableau**: The operations team quickly assembles a dashboard that visualizes customer satisfaction survey results alongside network outage data. Drag-and-drop filters allow managers in different countries to view their specific metrics.

**Looker**: The company's data team defines standardized metrics for customer sentiment and service uptime in LookML. All regional managers access dashboards with identical metric definitions, ensuring that comparisons across countries are accurate and meaningful.

Both tools support engaging, persuasive data stories; the choice depends on the organization's need for agility (Tableau) versus governance and consistency (Looker).

#### *Summary and Transition*

Selecting between Tableau and Looker is less about choosing the "best" tool and more about aligning with your organization's requirements and the nature of your data stories. Tableau offers unmatched flexibility and rapid visualization, ideal for dynamic exploration. Looker excels when standardized, reliable metrics are paramount, fostering trust in cross-functional storytelling.

### 5.4. Coding for Customization: Python and R

As we expand our exploration beyond GUI-based visualization platforms like Power BI and Qlik, it's essential to consider the flexibility that coding environments offer. For business professionals seeking bespoke visualizations or requiring advanced analytics, Python and R stand out as powerful tools for customization. Their open-source ecosystems enable you to design, automate, and scale visual storytelling in ways that static dashboards often cannot.

#### *Why Code for Customization?*

While platforms such as Tableau and Power BI are celebrated for their user-friendly interfaces and rapid dashboard deployment, they can sometimes limit your ability to tailor visuals to complex business needs. Coding provides the following advantages:

- **Unlimited Customization:** Build unique chart types or brand-specific designs beyond default templates.
- **Advanced Analytics Integration:** Seamlessly blend statistical analysis and machine learning with visualization.
- **Automation and Reproducibility:** Script repetitive reporting tasks or generate real-time, data-driven stories.
- **Integration with Business Systems:** Connect directly to APIs, databases, or cloud services for dynamic updates.

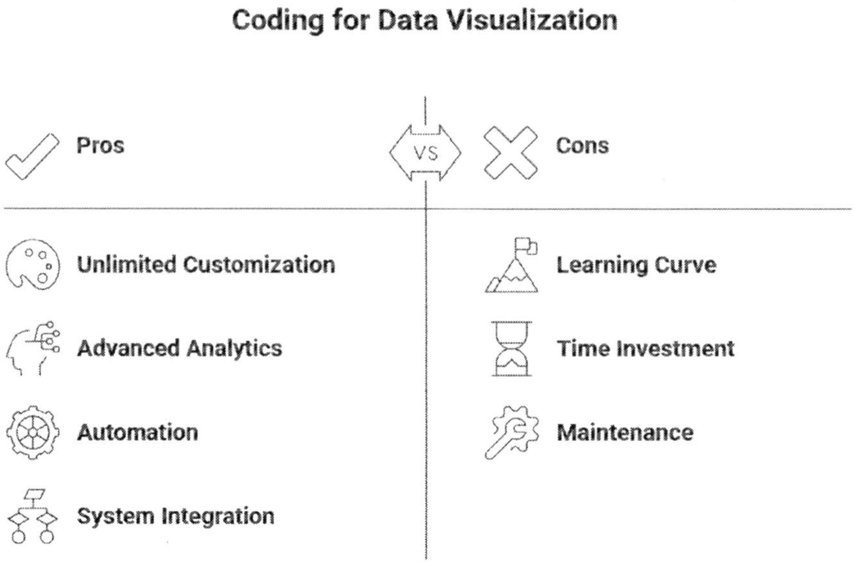


For organizations with evolving requirements or global teams, coding also ensures consistency and scalability, especially when distributing or automating business insights.

*Python for Business Data Visualization*

Python's popularity in data science circles is matched by its robust visualization libraries and ease of integration with enterprise analytics workflows. Libraries like **Matplotlib**, **Seaborn**, **Plotly**, and **Altair** empower users to craft everything from simple bar charts to intricate interactive dashboards.

Consider a multinational retailer aiming to monitor sales trends across regions. Using Python, the analytics team can:

- **Aggregate sales data** from multiple sources (databases, CSVs, APIs).
- **Visualize regional performance** with interactive maps using Plotly.
- **Embed statistical forecasts** directly within the visuals.
- **Automate dashboard updates** for weekly executive briefings.

A sample Python snippet using Plotly might look like this:

```
import plotly.express as px
import pandas as pd

# Sample sales data

df = pd.DataFrame({
    'Region': [ 'Americas', 'EMEA', 'APAC'],
```

```
    'Sales': [120000, 95000, 104000]
})

fig = px.bar(df, x= 'Region', y= 'Sales', title= 'Quarterly Sales by Region')
fig.show()
```

This approach not only provides interactivity but also allows analysts to customize every aspect of the visualization, from color schemes to tooltips, ensuring alignment with the company's branding and stakeholder preferences.

***R for Statistical Storytelling***

R shines in statistical analysis and is favored by many in finance, healthcare, and academia for its precision and rich visualization packages such as **ggplot2**, **plotly for R**, and **shiny** (for web apps).

A financial services firm, for instance, might use R to:

- **Analyze customer churn rates** across product segments.
- **Visualize survival curves** to inform retention strategies.
- **Develop interactive dashboards** using Shiny for real-time insight delivery to executives.

An example using ggplot2 in R:

```
library(ggplot2)

# Customer churn data

data <- data.frame(
    Segment = c( "Retail", "Corporate", "SME"),
    ChurnRate = c(0.12, 0.08, 0.15)
)

ggplot(data, aes(x=Segment, y=ChurnRate)) +
    geom_col(fill= "steelblue") +
    labs(title= "Churn Rate by Customer Segment", y= "Churn Rate", x= "Segment")
```

Such custom visuals can be tailored to highlight specific business questions, such as identifying at-risk customer segments or forecasting future performance under different scenarios.

### *Integrating Python and R with Business Dashboards*

Organizations often blend the strengths of coding environments with business intelligence platforms. For example, Power BI and Tableau both support integration with Python and R scripts, allowing you to:

- **Embed advanced analytics directly into dashboards.**
- **Deploy interactive widgets** (e.g., sliders, filters) that leverage custom code.
- **Scale insights** by linking scripts to live data sources for real-time updates.

A global pharmaceutical company, for instance, may use Tableau's Python integration to visualize real-time clinical trial results, overlaying predictive analytics for decision-makers.

Custom coding with Python and R unlocks a new realm of creativity and analytical depth in data storytelling. By bridging complex analytics with tailored visualizations, business professionals can deliver narratives that resonate with diverse audiences and drive impactful decisions.

## 5.5. Evaluating Tools for Collaboration and Security

As you move from selecting the technical fundamentals of visualization tools to evaluating their role within your organization, collaboration and security become essential criteria. Today's business landscape demands not just effective visuals but also seamless teamwork and robust data protection. Visualization tools are no longer isolated, stand-alone applications; they are integral to cross-functional workflows that span departments, locations, and sometimes even continents. Understanding how these tools enable secure collaboration will help you choose solutions that fit both your storytelling ambitions and your enterprise's data governance requirements.

### *Collaborative Features: Driving Team Success*

In many organizations, data storytelling is a team sport. Marketers, analysts, and executives need to contribute insights, review visualizations, and provide feedback—often in real time. Leading visualization platforms have responded by embedding collaboration features directly into their offerings.

For instance, **Tableau** allows multiple users to work on dashboards simultaneously, leave comments, and share workbooks securely within an organization. **Microsoft Power BI** integrates with Office 365 and Teams, enabling users to co-author reports, track version history, and embed dashboards in collaborative channels.

Business dashboards are often the focal point for collaborative decision-making. Consider a multinational retail company using Power BI to visualize sales trends across regions. Country managers can annotate dashboards with local market insights, while headquarters monitors global performance in real time. This level of interactivity ensures that data-driven stories are enriched with context and collective expertise.

Some collaboration features to consider when evaluating visualization tools include:

- **Version control** to track changes and revert to previous states if needed.
- **Commenting and annotation** capabilities for asynchronous feedback.
- **Role-based access** to define who can view, edit, or publish dashboards.
- **Integration with productivity suites** for streamlined workflows.

#### *Security: Safeguarding Data and Insights*

With shared access comes the critical responsibility of securing sensitive business data. Data visualizations often incorporate confidential sales figures, customer information, or proprietary algorithms, all of which require strong protection against unauthorized access and data breaches.

Leading tools like Tableau and Power BI have extensive security features, such as:

- **User authentication**: Single sign-on (SSO) and multi-factor authentication (MFA) help verify user identities before granting access.
- **Data encryption**: Both at rest and in transit, ensuring that sensitive data remains unreadable to unauthorized parties.
- **Granular permissions**: Allowing administrators to set dashboard- or report-level access, so users see only what is relevant to their role.
- **Audit trails**: Logging user activity for compliance and monitoring.

A practical example comes from a global financial services firm that needs to share performance dashboards with executives in different regions. Using Tableau Server, they set permissions so that only authorized leaders can view regional results, while analysts can access aggregated, anonymized data for broader analysis. This ensures both effective collaboration and rigorous compliance with data privacy laws.

#### *Balancing Collaboration with Security: A Strategic Approach*

While robust collaboration can drive innovation and faster decision-making, it must be balanced with the need for security. Overly restrictive permissions can stifle teamwork, whereas lax controls can expose your business to risk. The most effective organizations establish clear policies for dashboard sharing and data access, leveraging the flexibility of modern tools.

For instance, a healthcare provider implementing Power BI established a tiered access model: clinicians could view and annotate patient outcomes dashboards, while administrators had rights to edit and publish new reports. This approach fostered collaborative analysis while protecting patient confidentiality and adhering to regulatory standards.

#### *Key Considerations When Evaluating Tools*

When assessing visualization tools for your organization, ask:

- Does the tool support real-time and asynchronous collaboration?
- What authentication, encryption, and audit features does it offer?
- Can access be customized by user role, region, or department?
- How easily does the tool integrate with existing communication and productivity platforms?
- Are security features kept up-to-date with evolving compliance requirements?

By aligning your tool selection with your team's collaboration style and your organization's security posture, you empower business storytelling that is both impactful and protected.

### 5.6. Case Study: Global Bank's Tool Selection Across Regions

When Global Bank, a multinational financial institution with operations spanning North America, Europe, and Asia-Pacific, set out to modernize its data storytelling practices, it faced a unique challenge: selecting and implementing the right visualization tools for teams with diverse regional needs and technological maturity. The bank's goal was to create unified, actionable business dashboards that would empower both regional managers and global executives to make informed decisions quickly and confidently.

#### *Evaluating Visualization Tools*

Global Bank shortlisted several leading tools, including **Tableau**, **Power BI**, and **Qlik Sense**, each offering distinct advantages:

**Tableau**: Known for its powerful data visualization options, ease of use, and strong community support. Tableau's ability to connect with a wide variety of data sources made it a strong contender for the North American and European teams.

**Power BI**: Integrated seamlessly with Microsoft's suite of products, offered strong data governance features, and was cost-effective for large deployments. Its real-time dashboard capabilities appealed to executive stakeholders.

**Qlik Sense**: Provided a self-service approach, excellent associative data modeling, and offline capabilities, making it attractive for Asia-Pacific's mobile-focused teams.

#### *Lessons Learned and Key Takeaways*

Global Bank's experience demonstrates that tool selection is not just a technical decision but a business-critical process requiring sensitivity to regional needs and organizational culture. Early stakeholder engagement, careful evaluation of tool capabilities, and piloting solutions in real-world scenarios ensured that each region received a tailored, impactful data storytelling solution.

In summary, aligning visualization tool selection with both global strategy and local context enabled Global Bank to elevate its data storytelling effectiveness worldwide. As you move forward, consider how your organization's unique structure and needs can inform the best-fit tools for your own data storytelling journey.

## 5.7. Summary and Recommendations

Selecting the right visualization tools is more than a technical decision—it's a strategic choice that shapes how your organization interprets, shares, and acts on data insights. Throughout this chapter, we've examined how different platforms like Tableau, Power BI, and Google Data Studio can empower teams to transform raw data into actionable stories. The right tool supports not only the technical requirements of your data but also the communication needs of your stakeholders, ensuring clarity, engagement, and impact.

#### *Key Takeaways*

When choosing a visualization tool, it's crucial to align your selection with your business objectives, technical capabilities, and audience expectations. Consider the following:

**Purpose and Audience:** Match the tool with the complexity of your data and the sophistication of your audience. Executives may require high-level dashboards, while analysts might need granular, interactive reports.

**Integration and Scalability:** Evaluate how seamlessly the tool connects with existing data sources and whether it can scale as your business grows.

**Ease of Use and Adoption:** Tools with intuitive interfaces and robust support resources reduce training time and encourage widespread adoption.

**Customization and Interactivity:** The ability to tailor visuals and enable user-driven exploration enhances storytelling and makes insights more accessible.

#### *Real-world Business Use Cases*

To illustrate the impact of selecting the right visualization tool, let's explore two practical scenarios that highlight both global and industry-specific perspectives.

### Scenario 1: Retail Chain Expansion with Power BI

A multinational retail chain sought to optimize its supply chain operations across Asia and Europe. The data analysis team deployed Power BI to integrate sales, logistics, and inventory data from diverse sources. By creating interactive dashboards with geographic mapping and trend analysis, regional managers could identify bottlenecks and adjust inventory allocation in real time. The intuitive interface encouraged store managers, many of whom lacked advanced technical skills, to explore performance trends independently, fueling a culture of data-driven decision-making.

### Scenario 2: Marketing Campaign Optimization in Tableau

A digital marketing agency with clients spanning North America and Africa faced challenges in communicating campaign ROI to stakeholders with varying data literacy. Using Tableau, the agency built dynamic dashboards that visualized campaign reach, conversion rates, and customer engagement with rich, easy-to-understand visuals. Color-coded metrics and interactive filters allowed clients to drill down by region or demographic. This approach not only improved transparency but also fostered collaborative discussions, enabling clients to co-create future campaign strategies.

### *Business Dashboard Illustration*

A well-designed dashboard is the centerpiece of effective data storytelling. Consider the following Power BI dashboard layout for a global sales team:

This design ensures that executives see actionable metrics at a glance, while analysts can use filters and drill-down features for deeper insights.

### *Recommendations for Implementation*

To maximize your investment in visualization tools, follow these strategic recommendations:

- **Start with a Pilot Project:** Test your chosen tool on a high-impact, well-defined business question to build momentum and demonstrate value.
- **Involve Stakeholders Early:** Gather input from end users to ensure the tool addresses real business needs and encourages buy-in.
- **Invest in Training and Support:** Provide resources such as tutorials, workshops, or internal champions to accelerate adoption and proficiency.
- **Promote Iterative Improvement:** Regularly solicit feedback and update dashboards to keep visualizations relevant and aligned with evolving business priorities.
- **Foster a Data Storytelling Culture:** Recognize and celebrate data-driven wins, encouraging teams to share insights and best practices across the organization.

In summary, selecting the right visualization tool is essential for clear, persuasive data storytelling that resonates with your audience and drives business results. By aligning your choice with organizational goals, investing in user adoption, and continuously refining your approach, you'll empower your teams to unlock the full potential of your data.

# 6. VISUAL DESIGN PRINCIPLES FOR BUSINESS IMPACT

A memorable data story is more than just numbers and charts—it's a thoughtfully crafted visual experience that guides your audience from curiosity to clarity, and ultimately to action. The most brilliant insights can easily be lost if the accompanying visuals are cluttered, confusing, or inconsistent. This chapter unlocks the essential design principles that transform routine data displays into persuasive business communications, ensuring your message stands out and resonates.

Building on the storytelling foundations established earlier, here we delve into the practical art and science of visual design for business impact. You'll explore how **color theory** can influence perception and decision-making, and why your choice of palette should be strategic, not just aesthetic. We'll unravel the power of **typography and layout** in making complex information accessible and engaging, so your audience absorbs what matters most. Next, you'll discover how **Gestalt principles**, the psychological underpinnings of visual organization, can help you structure visuals that are both intuitive and memorable.

Consistency is critical for building trust and reinforcing your organization's identity, so we'll discuss ways to align your visualizations with broader **branding efforts**. In today's increasingly remote and mobile-first business landscape, designing visuals that are clear and compelling across devices and contexts is more important than ever.

By mastering these design principles, you'll be equipped to create business visualizations that do more than inform—they inspire, persuade, and drive results. As you move through this chapter, you'll find actionable guidance and real-world examples to help you apply these concepts immediately, elevating both your data storytelling and your professional impact.

## 6.1. Color Theory and Its Business Implications

Color is far more than a decorative element in data visualization; it is a powerful communicator that shapes how business audiences interpret and act on information. Understanding color theory enables professionals to craft visuals that are not only aesthetically pleasing but also purposeful, driving clarity, focus, and emotional engagement. In the context of business impact, mastering color choices can mean the difference between a presentation that inspires decisive action and one that confuses or alienates stakeholders.

### *The Fundamentals of Color Theory for Business Visuals*

To use color effectively, it's essential to grasp a few foundational principles from color theory. At its core, color theory explores how colors interact, the emotions they evoke, and how viewers perceive them. In business data storytelling, these principles translate into practical guidelines for highlighting trends, distinguishing categories, and guiding attention.

The three key attributes of color are:

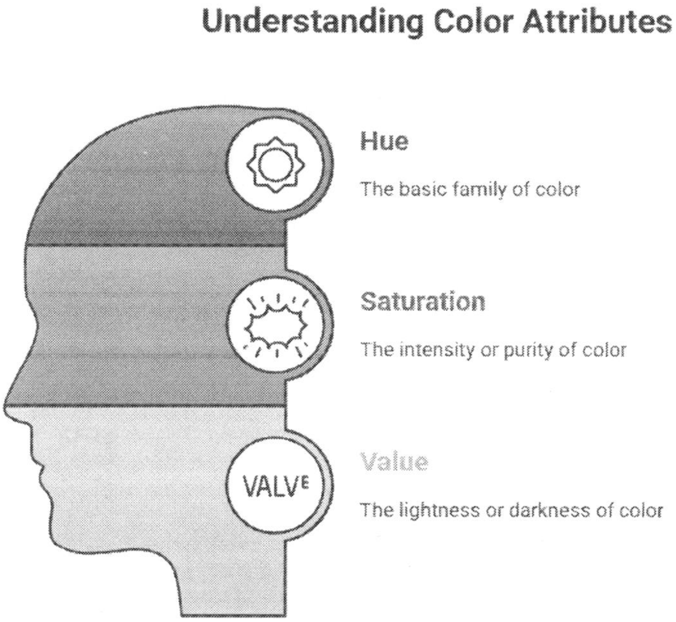


- **Hue:** The basic family of color, such as red, blue, or green.
- **Saturation:** The intensity or purity of the color.
- **Value:** The lightness or darkness of a color.

Beyond these basics, color combinations matter. Using a **color palette**—a carefully curated selection of hues—ensures consistency and supports corporate branding.

### *Business-Driven Color Choices: What Works and What to Avoid*

In business settings, color selections should serve the narrative and business objectives. Consider the following guidelines when designing dashboards and charts:

- **Limit the palette:** Too many colors can overwhelm or distract. Stick to a primary palette with clear distinctions.

- **Use color to encode meaning:** Assign consistent colors to categories (e.g., red for losses, green for gains) across reports and dashboards.
- **Ensure accessibility:** Choose color combinations that are distinguishable for people with color vision deficiencies. Tools like Tableau and Power BI offer color-blind-friendly palettes.
- **Prioritize contrast:** High contrast improves readability, especially on business dashboards viewed in varied lighting conditions.

A common pitfall is the misuse of corporate branding colors in ways that conflict with intuitive associations. For example, using a brand's primary red to represent positive growth can confuse stakeholders accustomed to red indicating loss.

***Real-World Use Case 1: Sales Dashboard in Tableau***

Imagine a multinational retail company aiming to optimize sales performance across regions. The data team uses Tableau to build a dashboard for executives. They select a palette where:

- **Green** indicates regions exceeding targets.
- **Yellow** signals regions meeting, but not surpassing, targets.
- **Red** highlights underperforming regions.

By adhering to these intuitive color codes, executives can immediately identify problem areas and direct resources appropriately. Tableau's built-in palette options and color legends make it simple to apply these standards consistently.

```
// Tableau Example: Setting Conditional Colors for Sales Performance
IF [Sales] >= [Target] THEN 'Green'
ELSEIF [Sales] >= [Minimum Acceptable] THEN 'Yellow'
ELSE 'Red'
END
```

This approach not only clarifies the data but also leverages universal color associations for faster decision-making.

***Real-World Use Case 2: Diversity Dashboard in Power BI***

A global technology firm wants to showcase progress in workforce diversity. The data analyst builds a Power BI dashboard with:

- **Blues and purples** to represent various departments, ensuring each is distinct but visually harmonious.
- **Neutral grays** for benchmarks and non-highlighted categories, keeping the focus on diversity metrics.

- **Accent colors** for key achievements, such as surpassing a gender parity milestone.

Power BI allows users to customize palettes and preview color accessibility, ensuring stakeholders across regions and backgrounds can interpret the visuals without ambiguity.

```
// Power BI: Applying Custom Color Themes
{
  "name": "DiversityDashboardTheme",
  "dataColors": ["#4F81BD", "#8064A2", "#C0504D", "#9BBB59",
"#F79646"],
  "background": "#FFFFFF",
  "foreground": "#000000",
  "tableAccent": "#4F81BD"
}
```

This thoughtful use of color supports the company's inclusivity mission and ensures the story resonates globally.

#### *Cultural Sensitivity in Color Application*

Colors carry different meanings across cultures. For instance, while red may signal danger or loss in Western contexts, it symbolizes prosperity in many Asian cultures. A global business must consider these differences when designing dashboards for international audiences. Many visualization tools, including Tableau and Power BI, let users customize palettes to accommodate regional preferences or provide alternative color-coded legends.

#### *Color Pitfalls and Best Practices*

Avoiding common color-related mistakes is crucial for effective storytelling:

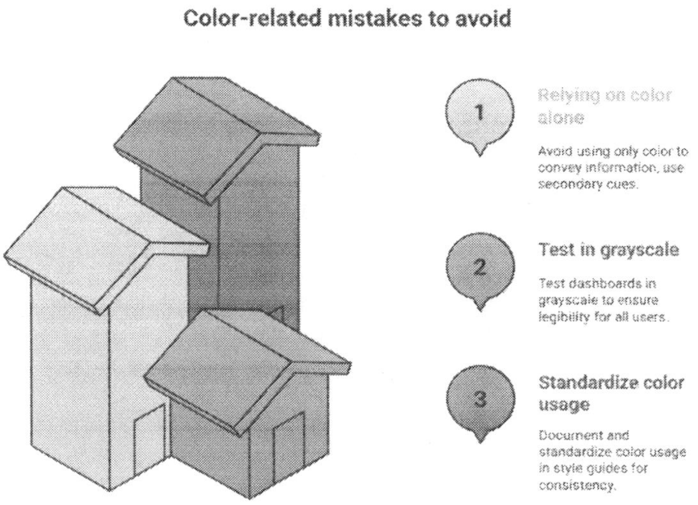

- Don't rely on color alone to convey critical information; use labels, icons, or patterns as secondary cues.
- Test dashboards in grayscale to ensure legibility for all users.
- Document and standardize color usage in style guides for consistency across business communications.

By applying color theory thoughtfully, business professionals can ensure their data visuals are not only attractive but also actionable and inclusive. Effective color choices support faster insight, stronger emotional resonance, and better alignment with business objectives.

In the next section, we'll explore typography and layout—two additional pillars of visual design that, when combined with strategic color use, elevate your data storytelling to new heights.

## 6.2. Typography and Layout for Readability

Typography and layout are often underestimated in data visualization, yet they serve as the backbone of clarity and engagement in business storytelling. Where color helps guide the eye and emphasize insights, typography and layout work together to structure information, enhance comprehension, and create a positive user experience. By mastering these elements, you ensure that your data stories are not only visually appealing but also intuitively easy to understand, a critical factor in driving impactful business decisions.

### *The Power of Typography in Data Visualizations*

Typography is more than just choosing a font; it defines how your audience reads and interprets information. The right typographic choices can mean the difference between a dashboard that feels overwhelming and one that feels inviting and accessible.

**Key Principles of Effective Typography:**

- **Legibility:** Always prioritize clear, readable typefaces for your data labels, headlines, and annotations. Sans-serif fonts such as Arial, Helvetica, or Segoe UI are popular choices in business dashboards because they maintain clarity at various screen sizes.
- **Hierarchy:** Establishing a typographic hierarchy—using different font sizes and weights—guides the viewer through your story. Headlines should be bold and prominent, subheadings slightly smaller, and body text or data labels clear but less dominant.

- **Consistency:** Using a consistent font family and sizing structure across your visualization builds trust and reduces cognitive load, making it easier for audiences to focus on the data rather than the design.

**Application Example:**

Imagine a sales performance dashboard in Tableau, shared across a multinational retail company. The dashboard uses Segoe UI in three distinct sizes: large for section titles, medium for key performance indicators (KPIs), and small for detailed data labels. This clear separation ensures that executives can quickly spot critical figures while analysts can dive deeper into supporting details.

### *Layout: Structuring Information for Maximum Impact*

Layout is the art of arranging elements to communicate your message with maximum efficiency and minimum friction. In the context of business data storytelling, a well-structured layout provides a logical flow and prevents users from feeling lost or distracted.

**Essential Layout Strategies:**

- **Alignment and Grids:** Aligning charts, tables, and text along invisible grids creates a sense of order. Both Power BI and Tableau offer grid and snap-to-grid features, allowing you to maintain even spacing and alignment among elements.
- **Grouping and Proximity:** Place related items close together and separate distinct sections with whitespace. This helps viewers intuitively connect related information and navigate between different story points.
- **Whitespace Utilization:** Whitespace, or negative space, is not wasted space. It gives breathing room to your visuals, preventing overwhelming clutter and allowing key insights to stand out.

**Sequential Layout for Storytelling:**

- **Start with Context:** Place the main headline and a brief narrative at the top, setting the stage for your audience.
- **Present Core Insights:** Position KPIs or summary charts in a prominent area, usually the upper left, as this is where most viewers naturally begin scanning.
- **Provide Supporting Details:** Arrange secondary charts or tables below or to the right, allowing users to drill down into specifics without crowding the main story.

- **Conclude with Action:** End with recommendations, next steps, or a call to action, guiding decision-makers towards meaningful outcomes.

### *Business Use-Cases: Typography and Layout in Action*

#### Scenario 1: Financial Dashboard for Global Stakeholders

A financial services firm in Singapore designs a quarterly performance dashboard using Power BI for its Asia-Pacific leadership team. Recognizing the cultural and linguistic diversity of its audience, the team selects fonts that support multiple languages, ensuring legibility in both English and Chinese characters. Headings are bold and consistent, while detailed notes are aligned in a clean, left-justified column. Strategic use of whitespace separates revenue data from expense breakdowns, reducing confusion and making cross-country comparisons effortless.

#### Scenario 2: Marketing Campaign Tracker in a US-Based SaaS Company

A marketing analyst creates a campaign tracker dashboard in Tableau. The dashboard uses a clear typographic hierarchy: campaign names in large, bold headers, conversion rates in medium-sized numerals, and footnotes in a subtle, smaller font. The layout places headline metrics at the top, visual trend lines in the center, and campaign-level details at the bottom. This structure enables marketing leaders to grasp high-level performance instantly and empowers team members to investigate specific campaigns as needed.

### *Visualization Tools: Implementing Typography and Layout*

Modern visualization platforms make it easy to apply strong typographic and layout principles:

**Tableau:** Offers customizable text boxes, font settings, and dashboard layout containers for precise alignment and grouping. The device preview feature ensures layouts adjust for different screens.

**Power BI:** Provides theme customization, grid alignment, and responsive layout controls. Users can standardize fonts and colors across reports for consistent branding and clarity.

**Qlik Sense:** Supports responsive design, allowing for automatic reformatting of typography and layout to suit desktop or mobile viewing.

Here's a sample Tableau dashboard layout code snippet for aligning key elements:

```
DashboardTitle: font-size: 24px; font-weight: bold;
KPISection: margin-top: 20px; display: flex; justify-content: space-between;
DetailTable: margin-top: 30px; font-size: 12px;
```

Typography and layout are more than aesthetic choices—they are critical tools for guiding your audience through data stories with clarity and impact. By applying these principles in your dashboards and reports, you transform complex information into actionable insights that resonate with stakeholders across cultures and business functions.

## 6.3. Gestalt Principles in Visualization

Gestalt principles, rooted in psychology, describe how humans naturally perceive visual elements as organized patterns and unified wholes rather than isolated components. Understanding and leveraging these principles is essential for designing business visualizations that are not only aesthetically pleasing but also intuitively understood. By aligning your dashboard layouts, charts, and infographics with Gestalt principles, you can guide viewers' attention, minimize misinterpretation, and deliver insights with greater clarity and impact.

### *The Core Gestalt Principles for Data Visualization*

Let's explore the main Gestalt principles most applicable to business data storytelling:

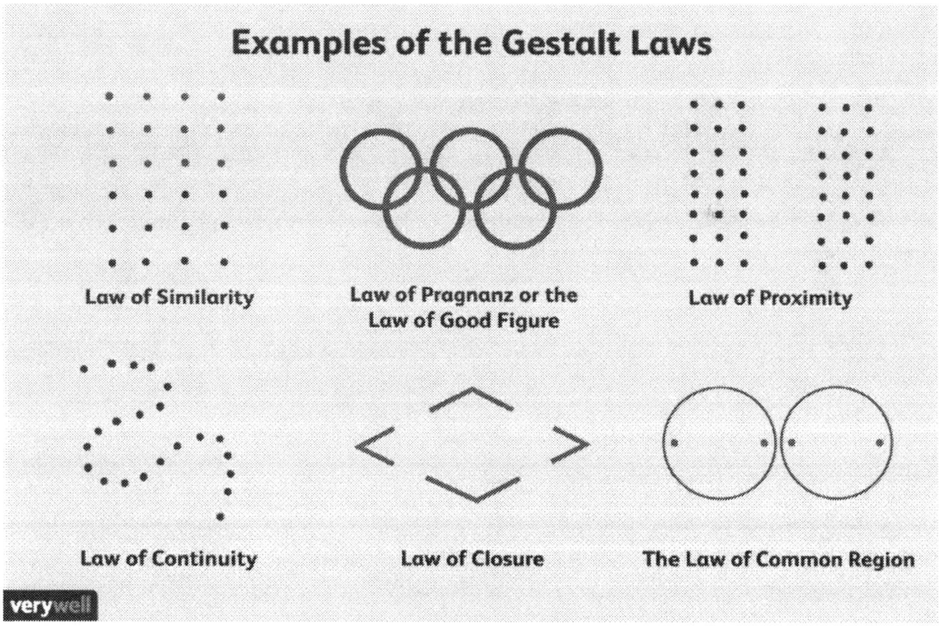


- **Proximity**: Elements that are close together are perceived as related.
- **Similarity**: Objects that look alike are grouped mentally.
- **Enclosure**: Elements enclosed by a boundary are seen as part of a group.
- **Closure**: The mind tends to fill in missing information to create whole shapes.

- **Continuity**: The eye follows lines, curves, or a sequence, perceiving them as related.
- **Figure/Ground**: The mind distinguishes between a main object (figure) and the background (ground).

Applying these principles can dramatically improve the readability and effectiveness of your business dashboards and reports.

#### *Proximity: Grouping by Spatial Arrangement*

When designing a dashboard in Tableau or Power BI, placing related metrics—such as sales figures, conversion rates, and customer feedback—close together signals their connection. For example, on a retail performance dashboard, grouping store revenue, foot traffic, and average transaction value in a single card or section ensures users interpret these KPIs as part of the same performance narrative.

**Practical Application**:

Suppose you're building a sales performance dashboard for a multinational company using Power BI. By aligning regional sales charts side by side and separating them from unrelated operational metrics with white space, you leverage proximity to help viewers quickly compare performance across markets.

#### *Similarity: Using Consistent Visual Cues*

Similarity helps users connect data points that share visual characteristics, such as color, shape, or size. In a Tableau dashboard tracking customer acquisition channels, using the same color for all referral sources (e.g., blue for social media channels, green for email, orange for search) enables viewers to instantly recognize patterns or discrepancies.

**Dashboard Illustration**:

Imagine a financial health dashboard for a bank. You use blue circles for deposits, red triangles for withdrawals, and green squares for investments. Even as the data grows more complex, the repeated use of color and shape makes it easy for stakeholders across regions to identify trends and anomalies at a glance.

#### *Enclosure: Framing Related Information*

By enclosing related elements with borders, shading, or subtle backgrounds, you create a visual boundary that signals cohesion. In a business intelligence tool like Tableau, you can use containers or background colors to frame a set of KPIs or charts.

**Use-Case Example**:

A marketing manager in a global e-commerce firm creates a quarterly campaign dashboard. She uses shaded panels to enclose campaign performance metrics—such as impressions, click-through rate, and conversion—separating them from long-term brand health indicators. This enclosure helps executives focus on campaign-specific results, reducing cognitive load.

***Closure: Encouraging the Mind to Complete Patterns***

Closure leverages our tendency to fill in missing information. In data storytelling, sparing use of partial shapes or implied lines can simplify visuals without sacrificing clarity. For example, a progress gauge showing only three-quarters of a circle for 75% completion allows viewers to intuitively recognize the whole.

### **Visualization Tool Example**:

In Power BI, you can use donut charts with a segment missing, prompting the viewer to mentally complete the circle and grasp the proportion represented, which is particularly effective for illustrating market share or project milestones.

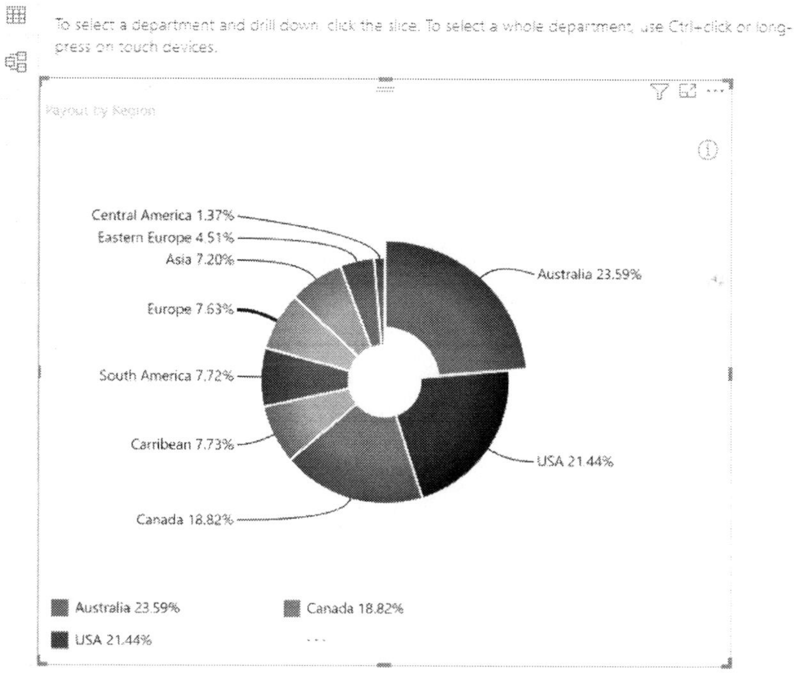


***Continuity: Leading the Eye Along a Path***

Continuity guides viewers through a sequential flow, such as a customer journey or sales funnel. In Tableau, you might use connected scatterplots or line graphs with smooth curves to show how sales progress across months, encouraging the eye to follow the trend without interruption.

**Business Scenario**:

A telecom analyst visualizes churn over time, using a line graph that subtly curves through data points. The viewer's eye follows the decline or spikes smoothly, revealing seasonal patterns and making it easier to identify when interventions succeeded.

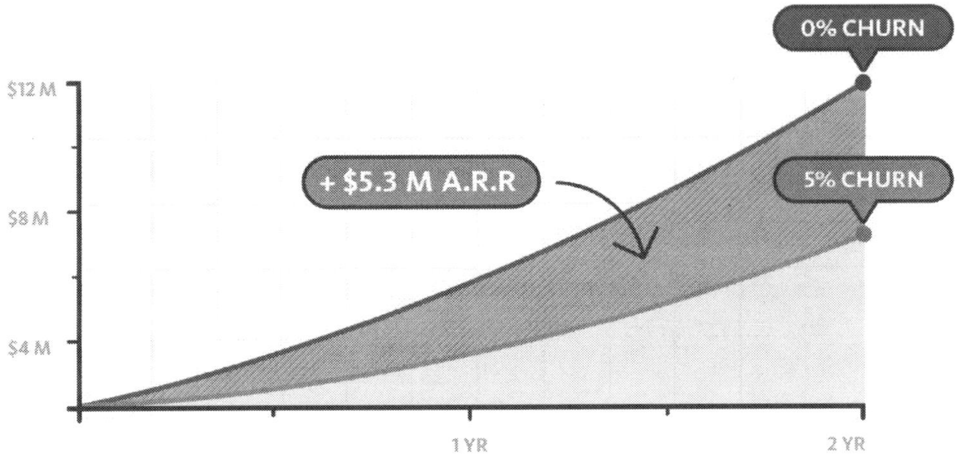


### *Figure/Ground: Highlighting What Matters*

Distinguishing the main message (figure) from the background (ground) is crucial. This can be achieved with contrast, color, or depth effects. For instance, highlighting a key KPI in a bold color against a muted background ensures that stakeholders focus on the most important insight.

**Dashboard Example**:

A CEO's snapshot dashboard in Tableau uses vibrant color only for the quarterly net profit figure, leaving supporting data in grayscale. This instantly draws attention to business-critical performance, allowing for swift executive decision-making.

### *Bringing it All Together: Gestalt in Action*

Consider a global logistics company presenting its delivery efficiency metrics. By:

- Grouping on-time delivery rates and average delivery times spatially (proximity)
- Using consistent icons for domestic and international shipments (similarity)
- Framing urgent orders in a colored box (enclosure)

- Displaying an incomplete route map that visually suggests the completed journey (closure)
- Using directional arrows to guide viewers from order receipt to delivery (continuity)
- Highlighting exceptions in red against a soft gray background (figure/ground)

The company transforms a complex dataset into a dashboard that tells a clear, actionable story to regional managers worldwide.

Gestalt principles offer a powerful toolkit for transforming raw business data into intuitive, impactful visuals. By thoughtfully applying proximity, similarity, enclosure, closure, continuity, and figure/ground, you ensure your dashboards and reports resonate with diverse audiences and drive strategic decision.

## 6.4. Ensuring Consistency and Branding

Consistency and branding are essential pillars in maximizing the business impact of your data visualizations. After exploring the power of icons and imagery to enrich your visual narratives, it's time to focus on how standardized design elements and brand alignment can elevate your dashboards and reports from merely informative to truly influential.

A consistent visual language not only enhances clarity but also builds trust and recognition with your audience. When every chart, dashboard, and report echoes your organization's brand identity, you reinforce a sense of professionalism and reliability—key factors in persuasive business storytelling.

### *The Foundations of Consistency in Data Visualization*

Consistency in data visualization extends beyond using the same chart types or color palettes. It encompasses the alignment of fonts, spacing, iconography, and even the interaction patterns in digital dashboards. These elements work together to create a seamless experience that reduces cognitive load, enabling stakeholders to focus on insights rather than deciphering new layouts with each report.

Consider these core areas where consistency matters:

- **Color Schemes:** Select a unified palette that reflects your brand's colors. This not only makes visuals more aesthetically pleasing but also anchors your audience in your company's identity.
- **Typography:** Use a limited set of typefaces, ideally those specified in your brand guidelines. Consistent font usage enhances readability and visual harmony.

- **Layout and Spacing:** Standardized placement of titles, legends, and filters allows users to intuitively navigate dashboards and reports.
- **Data Formatting:** Uniform date, number, and currency formats prevent misinterpretation and streamline cross-report analysis.

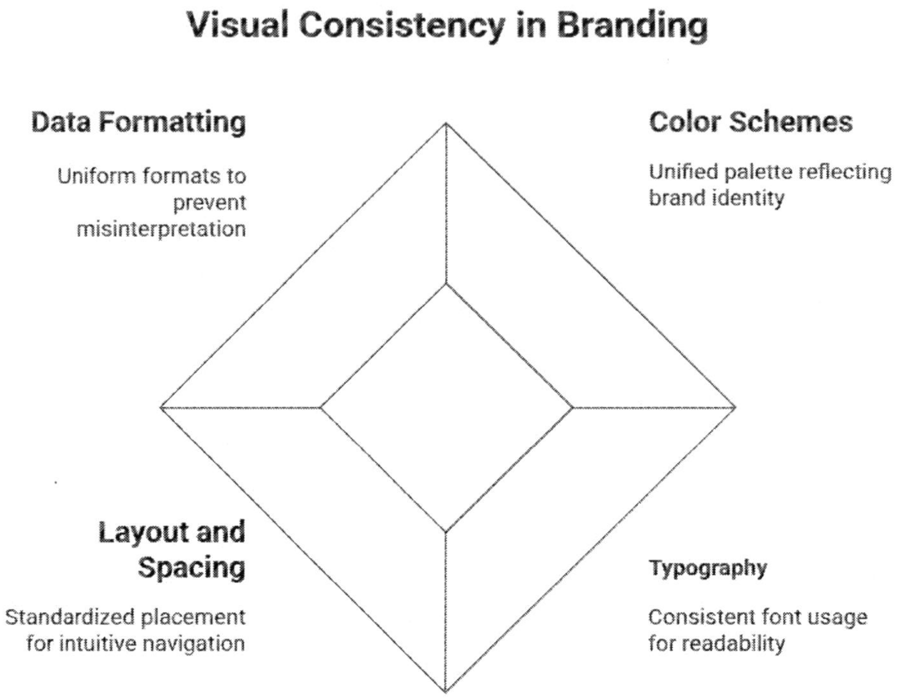


*Bridging Branding and Business Storytelling*

Branding in data visualization isn't simply about adding your company's logo to a dashboard, it's about weaving your brand's essence into every visual element. This approach ensures your data stories not only inform but also reinforce your organizational culture and values.

For example, a global consumer goods company might use its signature blue and silver in all executive reports, while a fintech startup could leverage bold, modern fonts and dynamic color gradients to reflect innovation and agility. When stakeholders see these familiar elements, they instantly recognize the source and credibility of the insights.

*Practical Application: From Guidelines to Execution*

Creating and enforcing consistency and branding in data visualizations requires both strategic planning and practical execution. Here's a streamlined process that teams can follow:

- **Establish Design Guidelines:** Collaborate with marketing and design teams to adapt corporate brand guidelines for data visualization. This includes specifying colors, fonts, logos, and acceptable chart types.
- **Create Templates and Style Guides:** Develop reusable templates in your primary visualization tool—such as Tableau, Power BI, or Google Data Studio. These templates should include branded color palettes, standard font settings, and pre-formatted layouts.
- **Educate and Onboard Teams:** Conduct training sessions or provide documentation to ensure all analysts and report creators understand and apply the standards.
- **Audit and Refine:** Periodically review dashboards and reports to ensure adherence and gather feedback for refinement.

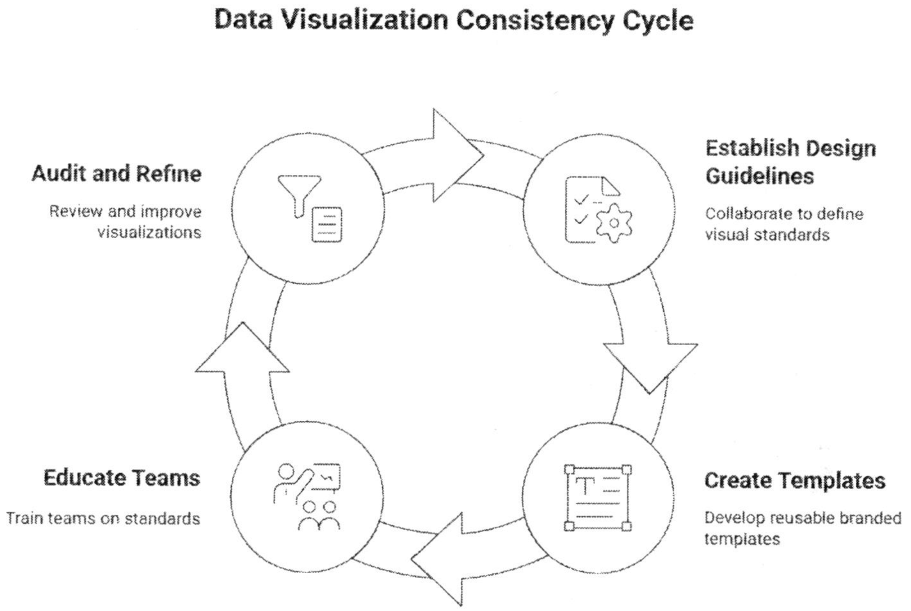


Here is an example of setting a custom color palette in Tableau to align with a brand's guidelines:

```
# In Tableau Desktop, define your custom palette in the Preferences.tps
file

<preferences>
  <color-palette name="Brand Colors" type="regular">
    <color>#003366</color> <!-- Corporate Blue -->
    <color>#00AEEF</color> <!-- Accent Blue -->
    <color>#F2F2F2</color> <!-- Light Gray -->
    <color>#C0C0C0</color> <!-- Silver -->
```

```
  </color-palette>
</preferences>
```

Similarly, in Power BI, you can import a theme JSON file that specifies your brand's colors, fonts, and visual settings for use across all reports.

***Business Use-Cases: Consistency and Branding in Action***

Let's look at two organizations that leveraged consistency and branding to enhance their data storytelling:

### 1. International Retailer: Standardized Executive Dashboards

A multinational retailer with operations across Asia, Europe, and North America faced challenges due to disparate reporting standards in each region. By rolling out a centralized Power BI template aligned with their global brand (including color schemes, typography, and logo placement), they ensured that every executive dashboard looked and felt the same worldwide. This consistency built trust among senior leaders and made it easier to compare performance metrics across markets, accelerating decision-making and fostering a unified corporate culture.

### 2. African Fintech Startup: Building Trust Through Visual Identity

A rapidly growing fintech company in Kenya wanted to stand out in a crowded market. By embedding their vibrant brand colors and modern iconography into every Tableau dashboard shared with investors and partners, they projected a cohesive, forward-thinking image. This visual consistency not only improved the user experience but also reinforced the startup's brand promise of transparency and innovation, helping to attract new funding and partnerships.

***Dashboard Illustration: Bringing Consistency to Life***

Imagine opening your sales dashboard and instantly recognizing your organization's brand—deep greens reflecting your eco-driven mission, a clean sans-serif font for approachable professionalism, and consistent iconography guiding you to key metrics. Filters and legends are always in the same location, and every chart follows the same visual conventions. This predictability not only saves time but also instills confidence in the data and the decisions it supports.

Ensuring consistency and integrating branding into your data visualizations transforms raw information into trusted, persuasive business tools. By applying standardized design principles and aligning with your organization's visual identity, you elevate both the clarity and impact of your data stories.

## 6.5. Designing for Mobile and Remote Audiences

As digital transformation accelerates, business professionals are increasingly expected to communicate insights across a spectrum of devices and locations. With mobile technology now integral to the way executives, analysts, and teams access business intelligence, designing data visualizations for mobile and remote audiences is essential for maximizing engagement and business impact. This section explores best practices, practical considerations, and real-world scenarios for optimizing data storytelling in a mobile-first, globally connected environment.

### *Understanding the Mobile and Remote Context*

Designing for mobile and remote audiences means adapting your visualizations for smaller screens, variable connectivity, and the unique demands of a workforce that may be distributed across geographies and time zones. Unlike traditional desktop dashboards, mobile data stories must prioritize clarity, speed, and relevance.

Remote professionals often access dashboards on the go, during travel, or in locations with limited bandwidth. They require immediate, actionable insights without the cognitive overload of dense or overly complex visuals. This shift demands a fundamental rethink in both design strategy and tool selection.

### *Key Principles for Mobile-Optimized Data Visualizations*

To ensure your data stories remain effective in mobile and remote contexts, consider the following design principles:

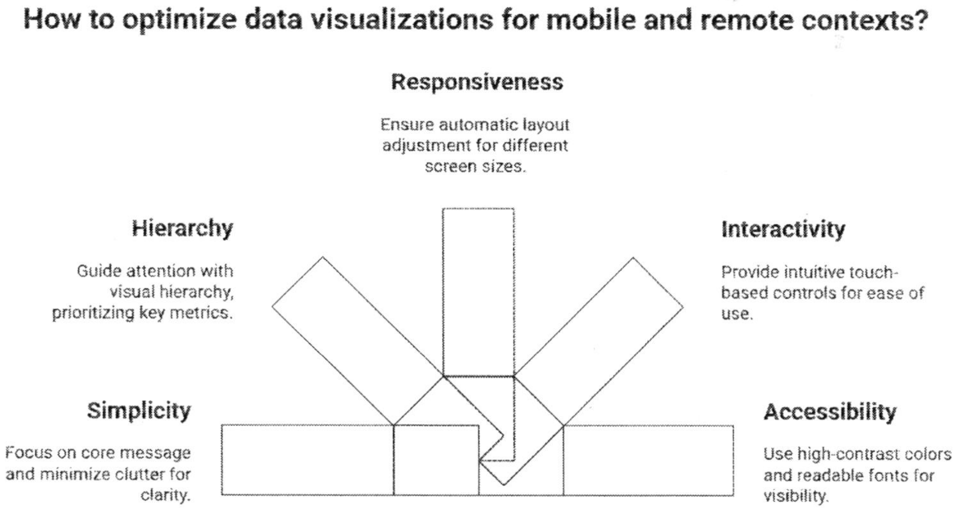

- **Simplicity:** Strip away non-essential elements. Focus on the core message and minimize clutter.
- **Hierarchy:** Use visual hierarchy to guide attention, starting with the most important metrics at the top.
- **Responsiveness:** Ensure your dashboards automatically adjust layout and content to fit different screen sizes.
- **Interactivity:** Provide intuitive touch-based controls, such as tap-to-filter or swipe-to-scroll, instead of mouse-dependent features.
- **Accessibility:** Use high-contrast color schemes and readable fonts for visibility in various lighting conditions.

By prioritizing these principles, you not only enhance usability but also foster faster, more confident decision-making among remote and mobile users.

### *Visualization Tool Examples: Tableau and Power BI*

Modern business intelligence platforms like Tableau and Power BI have recognized the importance of mobile and remote accessibility. Both tools offer dedicated mobile apps and responsive dashboard design capabilities.

In Tableau, you can create **device-specific dashboards**, allowing you to design different layouts for desktops, tablets, and phones. The platform's "Device Preview" feature enables you to see how your visualizations will appear on various devices before publishing.

```
# Example: Auto-sizing dashboard in Tableau

# Select "Dashboard" > "Device Preview" > Choose device type
(Phone/Tablet)

# Drag and drop visual components, resize for optimal mobile viewing
```

Power BI also provides **responsive visuals**, which automatically adjust to different screen sizes. Its mobile app supports push notifications and touch-friendly navigation, making it easier for remote teams to stay informed on critical metrics.

```
Power BI Responsive Visuals:
- Enable "Responsive" option in visual format settings
- Visual adjusts layout based on device screen size
```

These features ensure that your data stories maintain their impact, regardless of where or how they are accessed.

### *Practical Business Scenarios*

To illustrate the importance of designing for mobile and remote audiences, let's consider two real-world examples:

### 1. Retail Operations Dashboard for Field Managers

A global retail chain uses Tableau to provide field managers with a mobile dashboard tracking daily sales, inventory, and staffing levels. The dashboard features a clean, card-based layout, with large touch targets and high-contrast color to ensure readability in sunlight. Managers can filter by store location with a tap, allowing them to quickly identify underperforming outlets during store visits, even with spotty Wi-Fi connectivity.

### 2. Executive KPI Monitoring at a Multinational Financial Firm

A financial services executive travels frequently between Tokyo, London, and New York. Using Power BI's mobile app, she receives real-time alerts on key performance indicators (KPIs) such as revenue growth, client onboarding rates, and regulatory compliance status. The dashboard is designed with minimalist gauges and sparklines, enabling her to absorb critical insights at a glance between meetings or while commuting.

Both scenarios demonstrate the competitive advantage gained by tailoring data visualizations for mobile and remote consumption: faster responses, more informed decisions, and increased productivity.

#### *Dashboard Design Strategies for Distributed Teams*

When designing dashboards for distributed or multicultural teams, consider these additional strategies:

- **Localization:** If your audience is global, ensure that date formats, currencies, and units are localized for each region.
- **Bandwidth Optimization:** Compress graphics and limit the use of heavy images or animations for users with limited connectivity.
- **Offline Access:** Where possible, leverage BI tools' offline capabilities, allowing users to download and view key dashboards when internet access is intermittent.

Designing for mobile and remote audiences is not just a technical necessity but a strategic imperative in today's business landscape. By embracing simplicity, responsiveness, and contextual relevance, you empower every stakeholder—regardless of location or device—to act on your insights with confidence.

## 6.6. Reflection and Application

As we reflect on the visual design principles discussed in this chapter, it's essential to translate theory into practice—bridging the gap between conceptual knowledge and tangible business outcomes. By applying these principles deliberately, you can elevate the effectiveness of your data visualizations, ensuring they not only inform but also inspire action. Let's explore how these principles come alive in real-world business scenarios, examine the use of leading visualization tools, and consider practical steps for embedding these techniques into your own work.

***Bringing Design Principles to Life: Business Scenarios***

Consider two diverse business settings where visual design principles make a measurable impact: a global retail company's executive dashboard and a regional healthcare organization's operational report.

**Scenario 1: Executive Dashboard for Retail Growth**

A multinational retailer sought to empower its leadership team with actionable insights across global markets. Using Power BI, the data analytics team created an executive dashboard that distilled complex sales, inventory, and customer behavior data into a cohesive, visually intuitive story.

Key design decisions included:

**Prioritizing Visual Hierarchy:** High-level KPIs such as total sales, market growth, and customer satisfaction were placed prominently at the top, using bold, consistent colors and larger fonts.

**Strategic Use of Color:** Color was employed not for decoration, but to signify performance thresholds (e.g., green for on-target, red for underperformance), reducing cognitive load and enabling quick scanning.

**Consistent Iconography and Layout:** Icons representing product categories and regions were standardized, making the dashboard universally understandable regardless of the user's native language or location.

**Interactive Filters:** Users could drill down from global to regional data, with visual cues guiding them through each layer without overwhelming detail.

By applying these design principles, the retailer's dashboard became a central tool for strategic discussions, fostering alignment across international teams and driving agile, data-informed decisions.

**Scenario 2: Healthcare Operational Report**

In a Southeast Asian healthcare network, operational managers were tasked with improving patient flow efficiency. Leveraging Tableau, analysts designed a report to visualize bottlenecks and highlight opportunities for process improvement.

Key approaches included:

**Use of Gestalt Principles:** The design grouped related metrics (e.g., average wait times, bed occupancy rates) using proximity and similarity, making patterns and anomalies easy to spot.

**Accessibility and Inclusivity:** Colors and contrasts adhered to accessibility standards, ensuring all users—including those with color vision deficiencies—could interpret the data accurately.

**Annotation and Contextual Aids:** Strategic annotations explained spikes in wait times, while embedded tooltips provided additional context without cluttering the main view.

This visualization empowered non-technical stakeholders, from nurses to administrators, to quickly grasp operational challenges and collaborate on targeted interventions—demonstrating how thoughtful design can bridge expertise gaps and catalyze positive change.

### *Visualization Tools: From Principle to Practice*

To implement these principles effectively, modern business professionals have access to a range of visualization tools that support best-in-class design practices:

**Tableau**: Renowned for its intuitive drag-and-drop interface and flexible dashboard capabilities, Tableau enables users to apply visual hierarchies, color schemes, and interactive filtering with ease. Its "Show Me" feature suggests optimal chart types based on your data, encouraging thoughtful design decisions.

**Power BI**: Microsoft's Power BI excels in seamless integration with business data sources and offers rich customization options. Users can apply conditional formatting, create responsive layouts, and leverage built-in templates to ensure consistency and professionalism.

**Looker, Qlik, and Google Data Studio**: These platforms further empower business users with collaborative features, customizable themes, and the ability to embed visualizations into broader business workflows.

### *Applying Principles to Your Own Work*

To put these concepts into action in your business context, consider the following steps:

**Audit Existing Visualizations**: Review your current dashboards and reports, assessing them against the principles of clarity, hierarchy, color use, and accessibility.

**Engage Stakeholders**: Involve end-users early in the design process to understand their needs, ensuring that visualizations are both relevant and actionable.

**Prototype and Iterate**: Use the prototyping capabilities of tools like Tableau or Power BI to test different layouts, color schemes, and annotation strategies. Gather feedback and refine iteratively.

**Document and Standardize**: Develop a style guide or set of templates that institutionalize your best practices, supporting consistency as your organization's data culture matures.

Applying visual design principles is not merely an aesthetic exercise—it is a business imperative that shapes how information is received, understood, and acted upon. By grounding your data storytelling in clarity, intentionality, and inclusivity, you transform numbers into narratives that resonate across cultures, roles, and industries.

As you move forward, remember that mastery in data storytelling is a journey. The principles explored here set a strong foundation, but the most impactful stories arise from continuous learning, adaptation, and real-world experimentation.

# 7. TELLING THE RIGHT STORY WITH THE RIGHT CHART

This chapter invites you to master the art and science of chart selection, a critical skill for anyone seeking to turn data into compelling business narratives. You'll discover practical frameworks for selecting visuals that fit your data and your audience, ensuring clarity and resonance in every presentation. We'll explore the most common business charts—bar graphs, line charts, pie charts, and more—and unpack when each shines or falls flat. For those grappling with more intricate datasets, advanced visualizations will be demystified, empowering you to communicate complexity without confusion.

Equally important, we'll spotlight common pitfalls—those subtle missteps that can distort meaning or erode trust—and how to avoid them. Through a real-world case study on presenting revenue trends to the C-suite, you'll see these principles in action, gaining insight into what works when the stakes are highest. By the chapter's end, you'll be equipped with a checklist for smart chart selection, ready to craft stories that not only inform, but inspire action. Let's unlock the techniques that transform your data into the right story, told with the right chart.

## 7.1. Chart Selection Frameworks

Choosing the right chart is not just a technical decision, it is a strategic act of storytelling that determines how effectively your audience will understand, engage with, and act on your data. As organizations become more data-driven, business professionals must be adept at matching data with visuals that clarify, not confuse, their core message. This section introduces practical frameworks for chart selection, ensuring your data stories are not only visually compelling but also aligned with business goals and audience needs.

### *Understanding the Purpose Behind Your Data*

Before selecting a chart, it's vital to clarify the specific question your data should answer. Are you comparing performance, showing trends over time, illustrating part-to-whole relationships, or communicating correlations? Each purpose aligns with particular chart types. Frameworks help you systematically evaluate your options and make choices that enhance—not obscure—your message.

### *The Four Pillars of Chart Selection*

Chart selection can be guided by four foundational pillars:

- **Data Structure:** Is your data categorical, numerical, time-based, or hierarchical?

- **Analytical Task:** What action or insight do you want to prompt—comparison, distribution, composition, or relationship?
- **Audience Needs:** Are viewers data-savvy executives, marketing teams, or external clients? Tailor complexity and design accordingly.
- **Context of Use:** Will your chart be static in a report, interactive in a dashboard, or presented live?

These pillars serve as a checklist to ensure the chart you select not only fits the data but also the business narrative and audience expectations.

***Chart Selection Matrix: A Practical Framework***

One widely adopted approach is the **Chart Selection Matrix**. This matrix maps data types and business tasks to recommended chart types, streamlining the selection process for tools like Tableau and Power BI.

| Analytical Task | Data Example | Suggested Charts | Visualization Tools Example |
|---|---|---|---|
| **Comparison** | Sales by region | Bar, Column, Bullet | Tableau, Power BI |
| **Trend Over Time** | Monthly revenue | Line, Area, Sparkline | Tableau, Power BI |
| **Distribution** | Customer ages | Histogram, Box Plot | Tableau, Power BI |
| **Composition** | Market share | Pie, Stacked Bar, Tree Map | Tableau, Power BI |
| **Relationship** | Sales vs. ad spend | Scatter, Bubble | Tableau, Power BI |

For instance, if your goal is to compare quarterly sales across regions, a bar chart in Power BI provides clear, quick insights, while a line chart would serve better for visualizing revenue trends over several months.

***Real-World Use Case: Dashboard Design in a Global Retail Company***

Consider a global retail company launching a new executive dashboard using Tableau. The leadership team needs to monitor sales performance, identify best-selling products, and track regional market share. Using a chart selection framework, the design team matches each business question to an optimal visual:

- **Sales Performance Over Time:** Line charts summarize monthly sales trends, making seasonality and growth patterns instantly visible.
- **Best-Selling Products:** Horizontal bar charts compare product categories side-by-side for easy ranking.
- **Regional Market Share:** A treemap or stacked bar chart illustrates how each region contributes to total global sales.

By structuring the dashboard around these frameworks, the retailer ensures that every chart supports a business decision and communicates insights succinctly, regardless of the viewer's location or cultural background.

***Scenario: Marketing Campaign Analysis in a Multinational Corporation***

A marketing analyst at a multinational corporation is tasked with evaluating the effectiveness of recent campaigns across different countries. Using Power BI, the analyst applies a chart selection framework:

- **Campaign Reach by Country:** A map visualization highlights geographic differences, making regional trends immediately apparent.
- **Response Rates Over Time:** Line charts reveal spikes or drops in engagement following campaign launches.
- **Conversion Rate Comparison by Channel:** Grouped bar charts allow quick comparison between digital, print, and social media channels.

Such strategic chart selection ensures the analysis caters to both data-literate managers and non-technical stakeholders, fostering clear, actionable discussions across cultures.

#### *Integrating Chart Selection in Visualization Tools*

Modern business intelligence platforms such as Tableau and Power BI offer built-in recommendations and templates based on data structure and analytical goals. For example, Tableau's "Show Me" panel suggests chart types based on selected data fields, while Power BI's quick insights feature guides users toward effective visuals.

```
# Example: Automated Chart Recommendation in Power BI# After selecting
fields, Power BI suggests visuals:# Sales (Numeric) + Region (Category)
=> Bar Chart# Revenue (Numeric) + Time (Date) => Line Chart
```

However, human judgment remains critical. Automated suggestions are helpful, but the nuanced understanding of business context and audience needs ensures that the chosen chart truly tells the intended story.

Selecting the right chart is the cornerstone of effective data storytelling. By leveraging structured frameworks and aligning visuals with business objectives, you transform raw data into narratives that inspire action. Whether using Tableau, Power BI, or another tool, a thoughtful approach to chart selection bridges the gap between technical data and compelling business stories.

### 7.2. Common Business Charts and When to Use Them

Selecting the right chart is a vital decision in the process of data storytelling. The chart you choose not only shapes how information is perceived, but also directs your audience's attention to the insights that matter most. While there are countless ways to visualize data, certain chart types have become foundational in business communication due to their clarity and effectiveness. Let's explore these common business charts, understand when to use them, and see how they come to life in real-world scenarios and visualization tools.

***Bar and Column Charts: Comparing Categories***

Bar and column charts are among the most recognizable and versatile visualizations. By displaying rectangular bars whose lengths are proportional to the data values, these charts are perfect for comparing discrete categories or tracking changes over time when categories are limited.

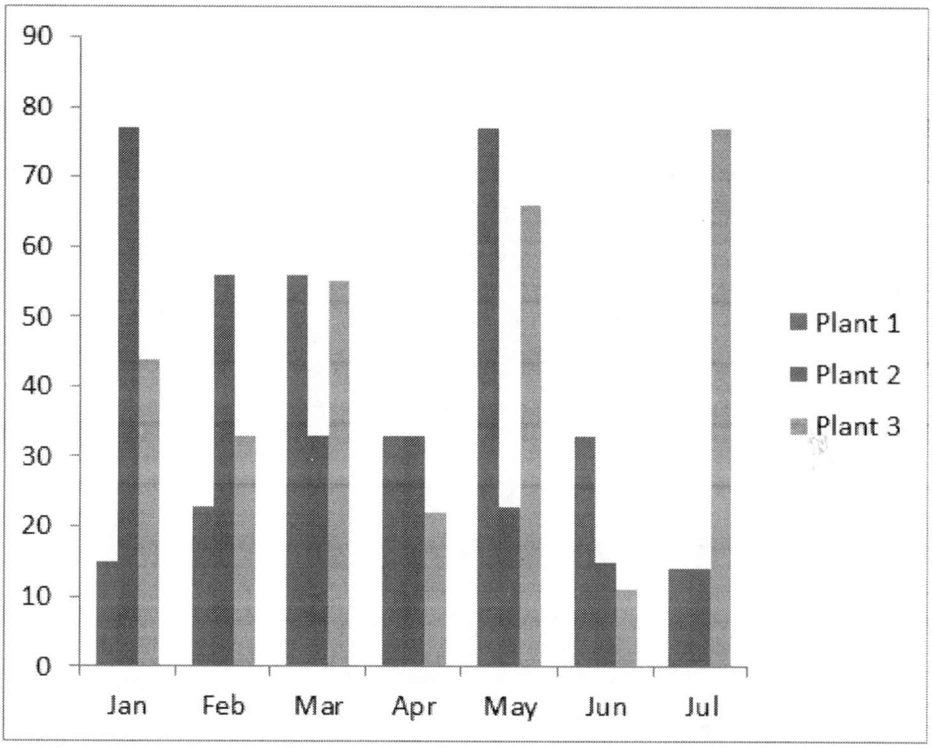


For example, a marketing manager may use a column chart in Power BI to compare quarterly sales across different regions. The chart quickly reveals which regions are outperforming others, guiding resource allocation decisions.

**When to use:**

- Comparing values across categories (e.g., product lines, departments)
- Highlighting differences or trends over discrete intervals
- Displaying rankings or standings

**Tool tip:** Both Tableau and Power BI offer drag-and-drop interfaces for creating bar and column charts, allowing you to filter, group, and drill down into categories interactively.

### *Line Charts: Showing Trends Over Time*

Line charts excel at illustrating how values change over continuous intervals, such as time. They are ideal for highlighting trends, patterns, and fluctuations.

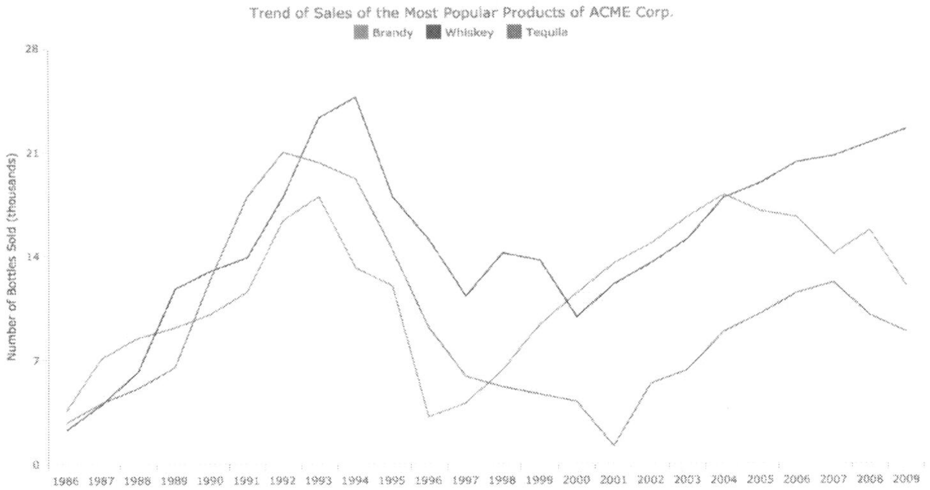


A finance team might rely on a line chart in Tableau to track monthly revenue growth for a SaaS product. The visual trend line instantly communicates the business's trajectory, helping executives determine if corrective action is needed.

**When to use:**

- Visualizing trends over time (days, months, years)
- Comparing multiple time series (e.g., product sales over different years)
- Revealing seasonality or cyclical behavior

**Business dashboard illustration:** Consider a dashboard that displays line charts for both sales and customer support tickets. This allows a business leader to correlate spikes in support demand with product launches, providing a narrative that goes beyond raw numbers.

### *Pie and Donut Charts: Showing Parts of a Whole*

Pie and donut charts represent data as slices of a circle, each slice showing a proportion of the whole. Although often misused, they can be effective for illustrating simple composition with a handful of categories.

Imagine an HR executive using a donut chart in Power BI to show workforce composition by department. If there are only four or five departments, the distribution is immediately clear, supporting discussions about diversity or resource planning.

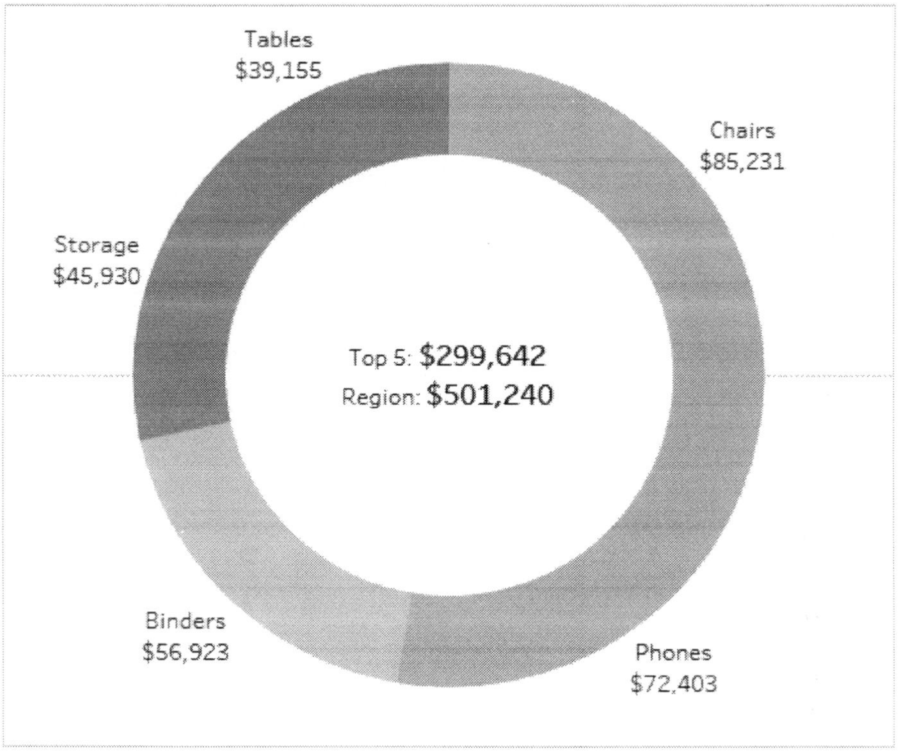


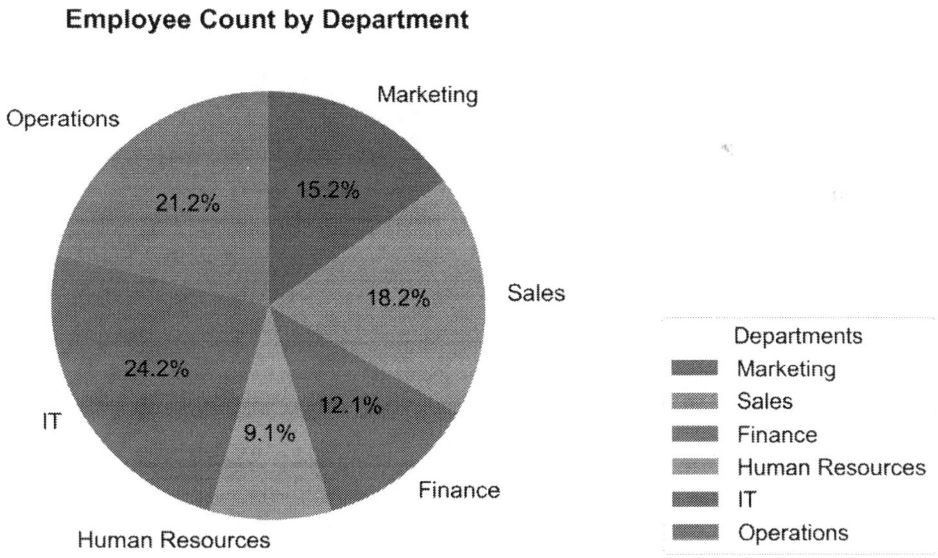


**When to use:**

- Displaying proportions or percentages of a total
- Comparing a small number of categories (ideally fewer than six)

- Emphasizing a dominant segment

**Caution:** Avoid using pie charts for detailed comparisons or when categories are numerous or values are similar, as this can hinder clarity.

***Scatter Plots: Revealing Relationships and Correlations***

Scatter plots display two variables on Cartesian axes, using points to show how the variables relate. These are powerful tools for uncovering correlations, clusters, or outliers in data.

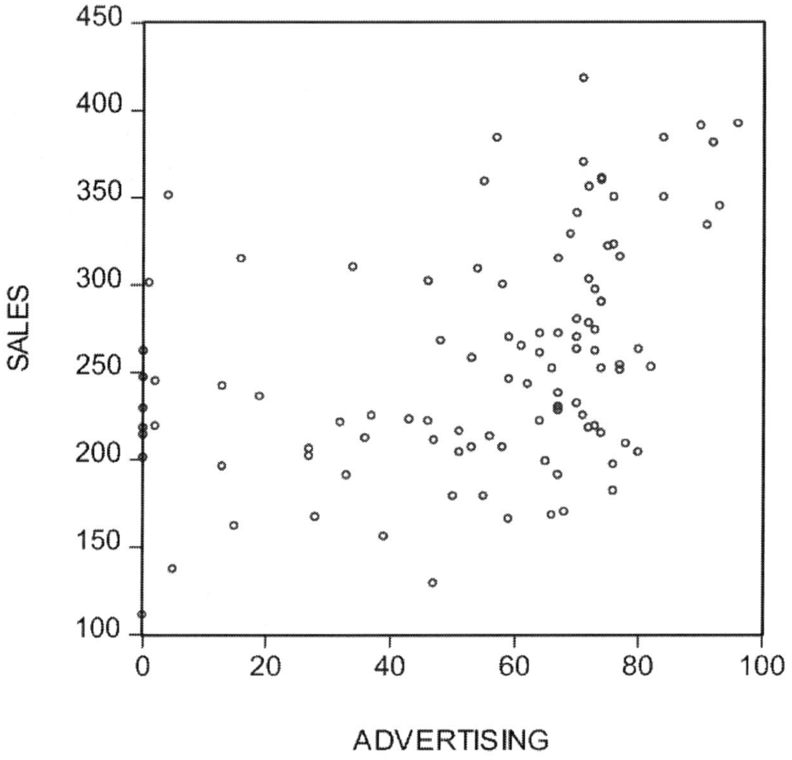


A global retail chain might use a scatter plot in Tableau to examine the relationship between advertising spend and monthly sales across different countries. The visualization can reveal whether increased spending translates into higher sales equally in diverse markets.

**When to use:**

- Investigating correlations or relationships between two numeric variables
- Spotting clusters, trends, or outliers
- Supporting regression analysis or predictive modeling

**Tool tip:** Scatter plots in Power BI can be enhanced with interactive filtering, allowing users to zoom into specific segments or anomalies.

***Stacked Bar and Area Charts: Understanding Composition Over Time***

Stacked bar and area charts build on their traditional counterparts by showing how sub-categories contribute to a total. They are especially useful for tracking how different segments evolve or compare within a whole.

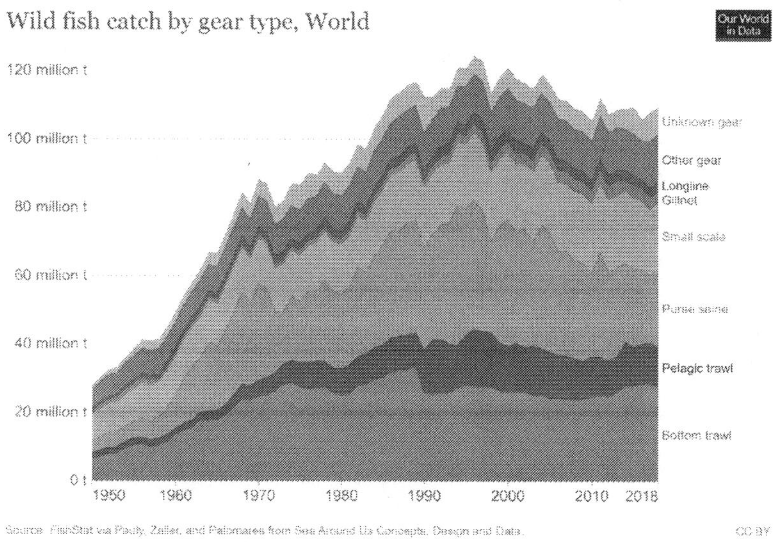


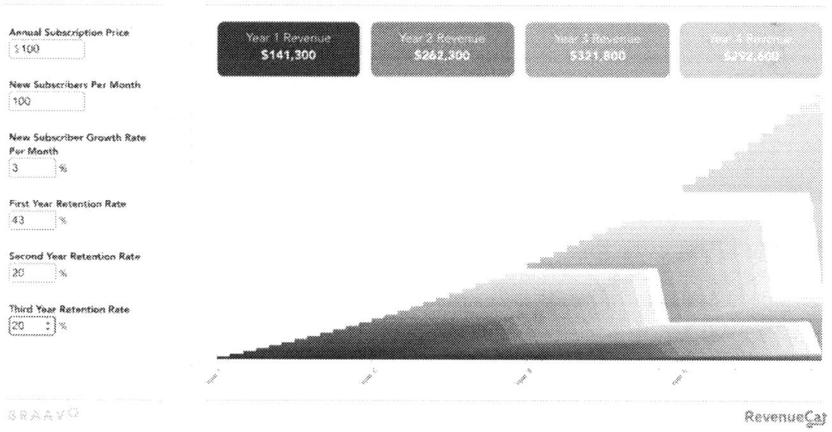


A SaaS business may use a stacked area chart in Tableau to visualize monthly revenue streams from new subscriptions, renewals, and upsells. This helps the executive team quickly see which revenue stream is growing or shrinking, informing product and sales strategies.

**When to use:**

- Comparing overall trends and segment contributions
- Displaying part-to-whole relationships over time
- Visualizing cumulative data

***Heatmaps: Highlighting Patterns and Concentrations***

Heatmaps use color intensity to show data density or values across two dimensions, making them ideal for spotting patterns or concentrations.

An operations manager at a logistics company might use a heatmap dashboard in Power BI to monitor delivery delays by region and time of day. This highlights bottlenecks, enabling targeted process improvements.

**When to use:**

- Visualizing frequency, volume, or intensity across categories
- Identifying hotspots or anomalies
- Comparing many categories or time periods simultaneously

***Real-World Business Scenarios***

To bring these charts to life, consider this scenario: An international bank uses a combination of bar, line, and heatmap visualizations in Tableau to tell a cohesive story to stakeholders about customer acquisition, transaction volume, and service bottlenecks across different regions. By selecting the right chart for each insight, the data narrative becomes intuitive and actionable.

In another case, a fast-growing e-commerce startup leverages Power BI dashboards featuring stacked area and scatter plots. These charts help leadership understand how marketing campaigns drive multi-channel sales and identify which customer segments are most engaged, providing a roadmap for scaling growth.

Choosing the right chart is a foundational skill in data storytelling, ensuring that your visuals communicate insights clearly and drive business impact. By aligning your chart choice with your message and data type, you set the stage for more advanced techniques that further enhance your narrative.

## 7.3. Advanced Visuals for Complex Data

As your data narratives mature, so too must your approach to visualizing complexity. While basic charts like bar graphs and line plots offer clarity for straightforward stories, business realities often demand more sophisticated visuals to capture intricate relationships, reveal multi-dimensional trends, and engage a diverse audience. In this section, you'll learn how advanced visuals such as heatmaps, network diagrams, and small multiples can illuminate deeper insights without overwhelming your viewers. We'll also discuss how to leverage modern tools like Tableau and Power BI to implement these visuals in practical business contexts.

***Understanding When to Use Advanced Visuals***

Complex data sets often feature multiple variables, time periods, or categories that interact in non-linear ways. In such cases, advanced visuals are not just helpful—they are essential. The right choice of visualization can:

- Uncover hidden patterns across large or dense datasets.
- Simplify multi-layered relationships for business stakeholders.
- Provide interactive exploration, empowering users to find their own insights.

Before diving into specific chart types, it's important to clarify your objective: Are you comparing segments, showing distribution, tracking change over time, or mapping relationships? The answer will guide your selection of advanced visuals.

### *Key Advanced Visual Techniques*

Let's explore some of the most powerful chart types for complex business data, along with practical examples and tool-based implementations.

#### Heatmaps: Illuminating Patterns in Large Datasets

**Heatmaps** use color intensity to display the concentration, frequency, or value of data points across two dimensions. This makes them ideal for identifying patterns or anomalies in large tables—common in sales, operations, and customer behavior data.

**Business Scenario:**

A global retailer wants to analyze sales performance across regions and product categories over the past year. A heatmap quickly highlights underperforming combinations or unexpected hotspots.

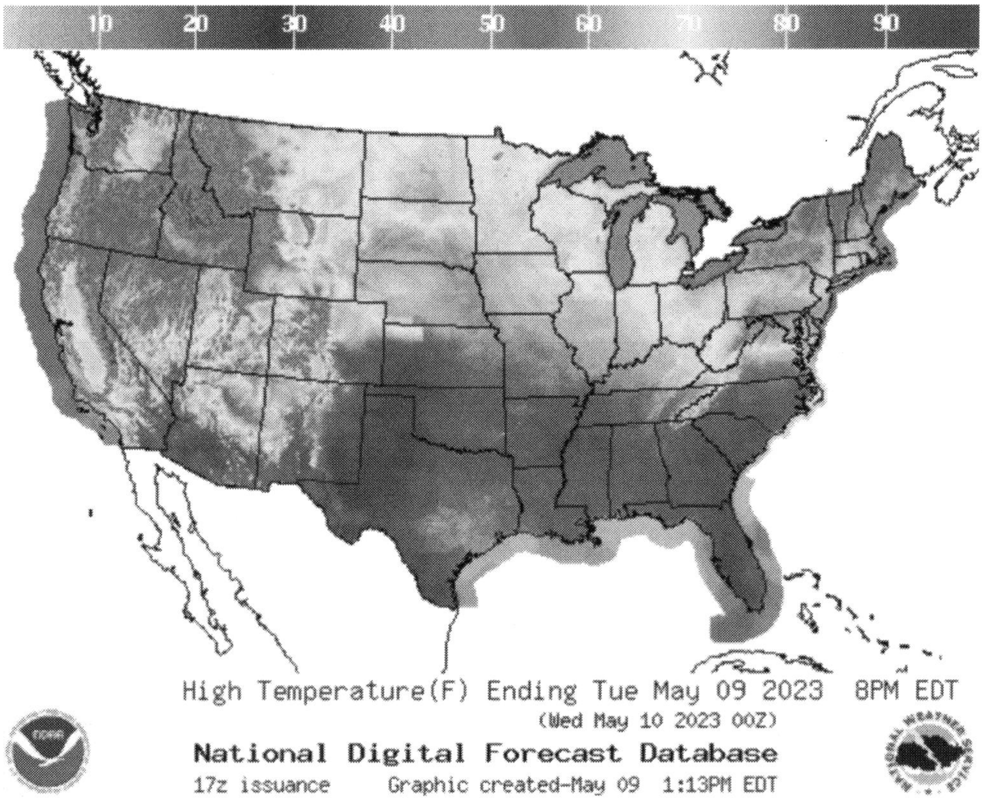


**Tool Example (Tableau):**

In Tableau, you can create a heatmap by placing 'Region' on the rows, 'Product Category' on the columns, and 'Sales' as the color-encoded value. The color gradient instantly surfaces outliers for further investigation.

### Network Diagrams: Mapping Relationships

**Network diagrams** (also called node-link diagrams) visualize relationships between entities, such as supply chain partners, social networks, or financial transactions. They are invaluable for revealing clusters, bottlenecks, or influential nodes within a system.

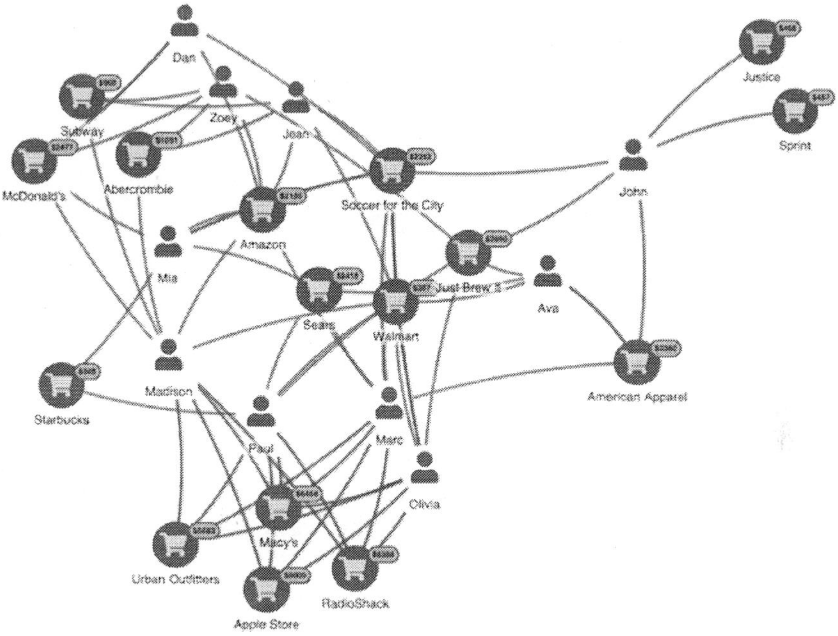


**Business Scenario:**

A fintech company analyzes fraudulent transaction patterns. By mapping transactions as edges between customer accounts (nodes), network diagrams expose suspicious clusters and high-risk connections.

**Tool Example (Power BI):**

Power BI offers custom visuals like the 'Network Navigator' chart. By importing this visual, you can drag fields representing source and target entities, instantly mapping complex relationships and enabling interactive exploration.

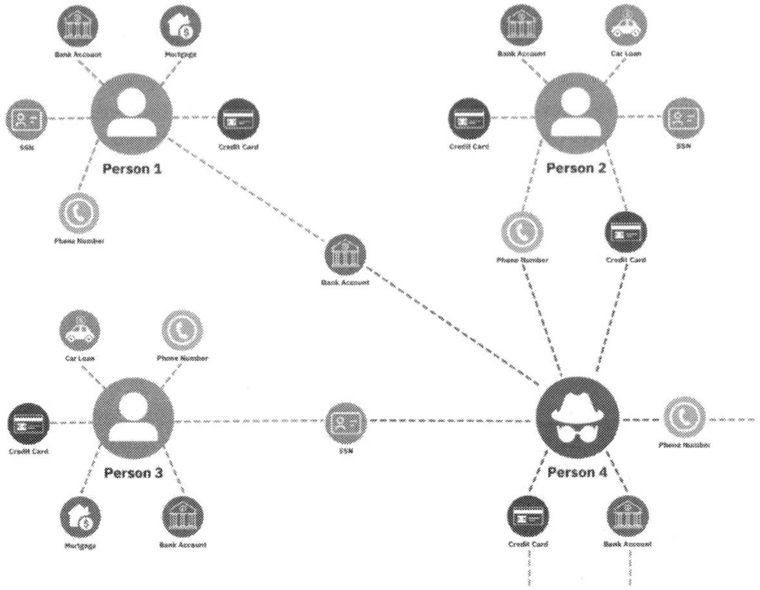


### Small Multiples: Comparing Many Related Charts

**Small multiples**—a series of similar charts sharing the same axes and scale—allow for side-by-side comparison of multiple categories, time periods, or segments. This technique is especially effective for highlighting variations or trends without clutter.

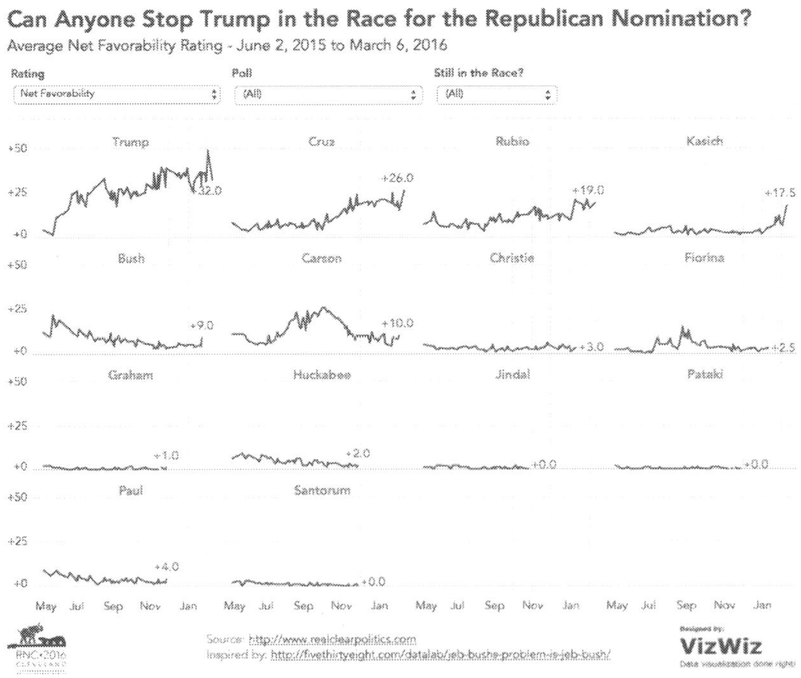

**Business Scenario:**

A pharmaceutical company tracks drug adoption rates across 15 countries. Instead of a single cluttered line chart, small multiples present each country's data in its own panel, making country-level trends and outliers easy to spot.

**Tool Example (Tableau):**

Tableau's 'Show Me' panel enables quick creation of small multiples by dragging multiple dimensions onto the grid. Users can scan across panels for holistic or granular insights.

### Sankey Diagrams: Visualizing Flow and Proportion

**Sankey diagrams** illustrate the flow of resources, money, or information between stages or categories, with the width of the lines representing quantity. They provide a compelling narrative for processes like customer journeys or supply chains.

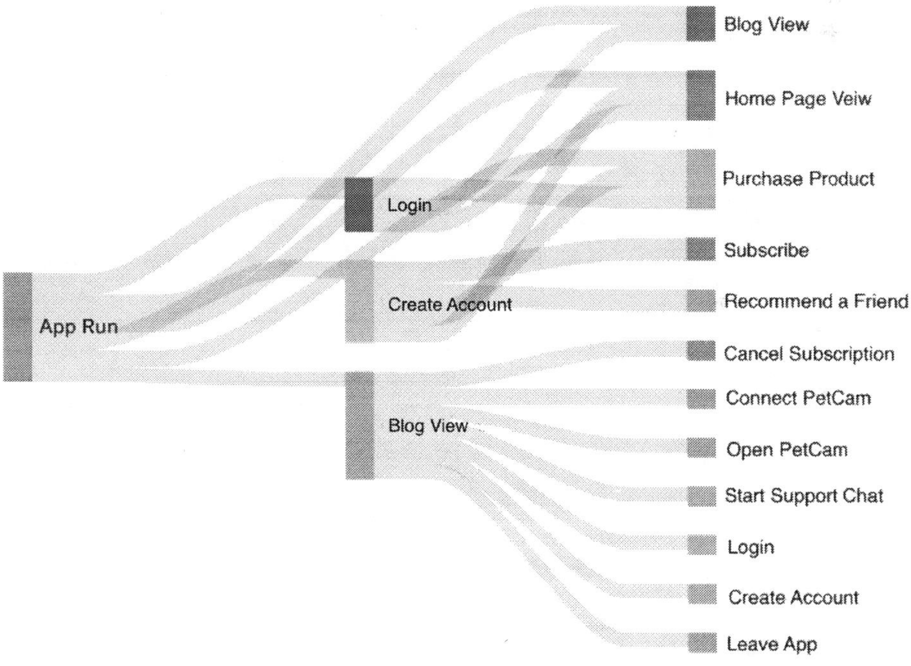


**Business Scenario:**

A telecommunications company visualizes customer movement through its service funnel—from awareness to retention. A Sankey diagram reveals where users drop off, helping marketers target interventions.

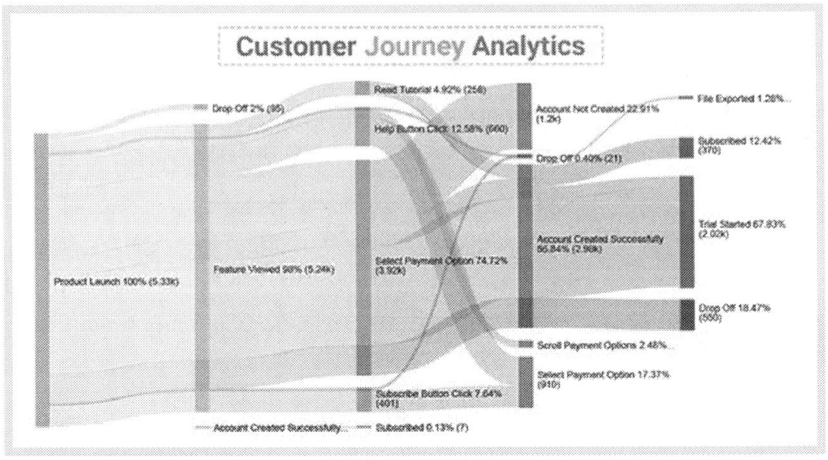


Customer Journey Analytics: Are You Using It Effectively?

### Tool Example (Power BI):

The 'Sankey Chart' custom visual in Power BI allows you to map sources and targets, customizing node colors and widths to match business logic and branding.

#### *Best Practices for Advanced Visuals*

When working with advanced visuals, clarity and accessibility are paramount. Follow these guidelines to ensure your charts enhance rather than hinder your story:

- **Simplify where possible:** Use filtering, aggregation, or interactive controls to prevent information overload.
- **Label effectively:** Advanced visuals can be complex; clear labels, legends, and tooltips are vital for interpretation.
- **Provide context:** Frame your visual with a concise title and annotations that guide viewers toward key findings.
- **Test with stakeholders:** Gather feedback to ensure your visual meets the audience's needs and background.

#### *Business Dashboard Integration*

Advanced visuals reach their full potential within business dashboards, where they are combined with summary metrics, filters, and explanatory text. For example, a sales dashboard in Tableau might feature:

- A heatmap for regional sales performance.
- A line chart for historical trends.

- Interactive filters allowing users to drill down by product, region, or time period.

Similarly, a Power BI executive dashboard could include:

- A Sankey diagram illustrating customer flow.
- Small multiples comparing regional KPIs.
- Drill-through actions for in-depth analysis.

***Global Perspective: Cultural Sensitivity in Visuals***

In multinational contexts, it's crucial to ensure that advanced visuals are culturally sensitive and accessible. For example, certain color schemes may have different meanings in Asia versus Europe. Localizing dashboards and using universally understood symbols can increase engagement and accuracy across regions.

Advanced visuals enable you to tackle complex data challenges head-on, surfacing insights that might otherwise remain hidden. By mastering tools like Tableau and Power BI, and applying techniques such as heatmaps, network diagrams, and small multiples, you can elevate your data storytelling and facilitate smarter business decisions.

## 7.4. Avoiding Common Chart Missteps

As we delve deeper into the art of selecting the right chart to tell your story, it's crucial to recognize that even well-intentioned visualizations can fall short if common chart missteps are not carefully avoided. Misapplied charts can obscure insights, mislead stakeholders, or even erode trust in your data-driven narratives. By being mindful of these pitfalls—and knowing how to sidestep them—you can ensure your visualizations remain clear, credible, and compelling across business contexts.

***The Dangers of Misleading Visuals***

When charts are designed without careful attention to accuracy and clarity, they can unintentionally (or sometimes deliberately) distort the underlying data. These issues are not just technical missteps; they carry significant business consequences, from flawed decision-making to reputational risk.

Consider a scenario where a multinational retailer uses a sales dashboard built in Power BI to compare quarterly revenues across regions. If the designer uses a truncated y-axis to exaggerate small differences, executive management might overreact to insignificant fluctuations, diverting resources based on perceived trends that are not truly impactful.

### *Common Chart Pitfalls and How to Avoid Them*

The following are some of the most frequent charting errors encountered in business environments, along with practical guidance on circumventing them:

#### 1. Truncated or Inconsistent Axes

Charts that do not start their axes at zero (particularly bar or column charts) can exaggerate differences between categories, misleading the viewer.

**How to avoid:**

Always start axes at zero for bar and column charts. For line charts tracking change over time, truncation may sometimes be justified but must be clearly labeled and used with caution.

**Tool Example:**

In Tableau, you can set axis starting points manually. Always review the default settings to ensure they align with your intent.

#### 2. Overcomplicated Visuals (Chartjunk)

Adding unnecessary elements—such as heavy gridlines, 3D effects, or excessive color—can distract from the data's message.

**How to avoid:**

Simplify your visuals. Remove extraneous decorations and focus on clean, direct representation. Use color purposefully, reserving it for highlighting key data points.

**Tool Example:**

Power BI offers minimalist themes and formatting panes that help strip away non-essential elements. Use these features to reinforce clarity.

#### 3. Inappropriate Chart Types

Selecting the wrong chart type for your data can obscure trends or relationships. For example, using a pie chart to compare more than four or five categories often results in a confusing visual.

**How to avoid:**

Match your chart to the data and the story you need to tell. Use bar charts for categorical comparisons, line charts for trends over time, and scatterplots for correlations.

**Business Scenario:**

A marketing manager in Singapore attempted to use a stacked area chart in Tableau to show website traffic sources over time. However, the overlapping colors made it difficult for stakeholders to discern changes in individual channels. Switching to a grouped bar chart clarified the relative performance of each channel, leading to more targeted campaign adjustments.

### 4. Cherry-Picking or Omitting Data

Excluding relevant data, or only displaying data that supports a particular conclusion, undermines the integrity of your story.

**How to avoid:**

Present a balanced view. If data is omitted, be transparent about the reasons. Always include context so the audience can properly interpret the findings.

### 5. Inconsistent Scales or Units

Combining different scales or units within a single chart can confuse your audience and make comparisons invalid.

**How to avoid:**

Standardize units and scales wherever possible. If combining metrics is necessary, clearly label each axis and consider using dual-axis charts carefully, ensuring viewers are not misled.

**Tool Example:**

In Power BI dashboards comparing revenue (in USD) and units sold, use clear axis titles and tooltips to help users understand the distinctions.

***Real-World Use Case: Financial Reporting Dashboard***

A global financial services firm implemented a dashboard in Tableau to track expense ratios across international offices. Initially, the designer used multiple pie charts, one per region, to illustrate departmental spending. However, stakeholders struggled to compare slices across pies, and subtle changes in proportions were nearly impossible to discern.

After consulting data storytelling best practices, the team replaced the pie charts with a single stacked bar chart, enabling straightforward side-by-side comparisons. The revised visualization quickly revealed regions where administrative costs were disproportionately high, prompting a targeted review and subsequent cost savings.

#### *Recognizing and Correcting Chart Missteps*

To ensure your charts consistently support accurate, impactful storytelling, consider these steps:

- Review your charts for clarity and accuracy before sharing.
- Solicit feedback from colleagues with varied backgrounds to catch potential misinterpretations.
- Continuously update your visualization skills by exploring best practices in your preferred tools.

By adopting a critical eye and a user-focused mindset, you can avoid the most common pitfalls and deliver visualizations that drive informed business action.

Avoiding common chart missteps is essential for ensuring your visualizations maintain credibility and influence within your organization. By remaining vigilant about potential pitfalls, leveraging the capabilities of visualization tools, and drawing on real-world business lessons, you can keep your data stories clear, honest, and actionable.

### 7.5. Case Study: Revenue Trends Presentation for C-Suite

Presenting revenue trends to the C-suite is a high-stakes opportunity to shape strategic direction and influence key business decisions. This case study unpacks a real-world scenario where choosing the right charts and storytelling techniques not only clarified complex financial data but also inspired decisive executive action. By grounding our approach in thoughtful chart selection and design best practices, we'll see how visualization tools like Tableau and Power BI can transform raw numbers into a compelling narrative tailored for executive audiences.

Revenue trends often span multiple regions, product lines, or customer segments, making the data inherently multi-dimensional. The goal is not just to display these trends, but to surface insights—such as growth drivers, seasonality, or emerging risks—in a format that supports rapid C-suite comprehension and action. Let's walk through the process, from stakeholder needs to final presentation.

### *Understanding the Audience and Context*

Before building the presentation, it's vital to clarify what matters most to the executive team. Typically, C-suite leaders want answers to questions like:

- Are we meeting or exceeding revenue targets?
- What are the key drivers of growth or decline?
- How do current trends compare to past performance?
- Where are the opportunities and risks?

In this case, our global manufacturing client needs to present quarterly revenue trends broken down by region (North America, EMEA, APAC), product segment, and sales channel. The dashboard must be concise, visually striking, and allow for quick comparisons.

### *Selecting the Right Charts: Clarity Over Complexity*

With multi-faceted data, it's tempting to overload the dashboard with detail. However, effective data storytelling requires discernment. Let's explore how to select the right chart for each insight.

- **Line Charts for Trends**: To show revenue over time, a line chart offers clear visibility into fluctuations, seasonality, and long-term growth.
- **Stacked Column Charts for Contribution**: These are excellent for comparing revenue contributions by region or product within each period.
- **Bar Charts for Ranking**: When highlighting top-performing regions or products, horizontal bar charts quickly communicate rankings.
- **Heatmaps for Patterns**: If seasonality or anomalies are important, a heatmap using color gradients can immediately draw attention to outliers.

#### Visualization Example: Tableau Dashboard

Using Tableau, the analyst constructs a dashboard with three main elements:

**Global Revenue Trend Line**: A line chart shows total global revenue by quarter for the past three years, color-coded by region. This immediately reveals periods of strong or weak growth and allows C-suite members to spot regional divergences at a glance.

**Regional Contribution Stacked Columns**: Stacked column charts break down each quarter's revenue by region, highlighting shifts in regional performance over time. Interactive filters allow executives to drill down into specific product lines within any region.

**Product Segment Bar Chart**: A bar chart ranks product segments by year-to-date revenue, making it easy to identify growth leaders and laggards.

#### Visualization Example: Power BI Interactive Dashboard

In Power BI, the analyst takes advantage of interactivity by enabling executives to:

Click on a region in the trend line to see a detailed breakdown by product and sales channel.
Use a date slider to focus on specific quarters or years.
Hover over any segment to reveal precise values and percentage changes.

These interactive features empower the C-suite to explore "what-if" scenarios, such as projecting revenue if certain regions maintain current momentum.

### *Crafting the Narrative: From Data to Executive Action*

A successful revenue trends presentation isn't just a collection of charts—it's a carefully crafted story. The analyst structures the presentation as follows:

- **Executive Summary**: Begin with a high-level narrative, summarizing key trends and headline performance metrics. This primes executives to interpret the visuals in context.
- **Visual Walkthrough**: Guide the audience through each dashboard element, using annotations and callouts to highlight inflection points, such as a surge in APAC revenue or a dip in EMEA.
- **Insight Synthesis**: Conclude with a synthesis of findings and recommendations, linking the data to strategic priorities. For example, "Investment in APAC digital channels has driven a 15 percent revenue increase, suggesting further expansion could yield significant returns."

### *Global Perspectives: Adapting the Story*

Consider a multinational retailer preparing a similar revenue trends presentation. In Japan, business culture values harmony and consensus, so the analyst uses color schemes that are culturally appropriate (avoiding red for declines, which may signal alarm) and provides context around fluctuations to avoid singling out underperforming teams. Meanwhile, a North American tech company facing rapid market shifts emphasizes the ability to interact with the dashboard in real-time, supporting agile decision-making.

This case study demonstrates that aligning chart selection and narrative flow with executive needs is essential for impactful data storytelling. Tools like Tableau and Power BI offer flexibility to tailor visuals for clarity, interactivity, and cultural context. By focusing on insights, not just information, you empower leaders to act swiftly and confidently.

### 7.6. Summary and Chart Selection Checklist

As you strive to transform data into actionable business insights, selecting the right chart is both an art and a science. The visual representation you choose can make the difference between a message that resonates and one that falls flat. This section consolidates core principles from the chapter and provides a practical checklist for chart selection. Alongside, you'll find real-world business scenarios and examples of visualization tools to illustrate how the right choice elevates your data storytelling.

#### *Recap: Aligning Chart Types with Your Narrative*

Each data story has a purpose, whether it's to compare performance, show trends, highlight relationships, or illustrate parts of a whole. Choosing the appropriate chart ensures your message is clear and compelling. Let's revisit the main chart types and their strengths:

- **Bar and Column Charts:** Ideal for comparing categories or discrete items. Use in sales performance dashboards to compare quarterly revenue across regions.
- **Line Charts:** Best for illustrating trends over time, such as tracking monthly website visits or stock prices.
- **Pie and Donut Charts:** Useful for showing proportions or percentage breakdowns, but should be used sparingly and only when categories are few.
- **Scatter Plots:** Reveal correlations and relationships between two numeric variables, often used in customer segmentation or market analysis.
- **Heat Maps:** Visualize data density or intensity, ideal in operational dashboards for identifying high-activity zones.
- **Maps (Geospatial Visualizations):** Show geographical distribution, such as customer locations or supply chain routes.

Selecting the right chart is not just about data type, but also about the business question you seek to answer and the audience you aim to engage.

#### *Chart Selection Checklist*

A structured approach helps ensure your chart choice aligns with your data, narrative, and stakeholder needs. Use the following checklist as a guide whenever you prepare a visualization:

- **Define the Objective**

- What is the central message or decision you want to support?
- Are you comparing, trending, categorizing, or revealing relationships?

- **Understand the Data**
  - What types of variables are involved (categorical, numerical, time-based, geographic)?
  - Are there outliers or exceptions that require special attention?

- **Know Your Audience**
  - Are they executives looking for high-level trends or analysts seeking detailed breakdowns?
  - What is their level of data literacy?

- **Select the Most Effective Chart Type**
  - Does the chart type highlight the story you want to tell?
  - Is the visualization intuitive and easy to interpret?

- **Refine for Clarity and Impact**
  - Is the chart free from unnecessary clutter?
  - Are labels, legends, and colors used purposefully?
  - Have you tested alternative visualizations?

- **Test and Iterate**
  - Solicit feedback from a colleague or sample user.
  - Adjust based on comprehension and engagement.

***Real-World Use Cases***

To bring these principles to life, consider two business scenarios where chart selection is pivotal to storytelling:

**Scenario 1: Retail Sales Performance Dashboard in Tableau**

A multinational retailer wants to understand quarterly sales performance across regions. In Tableau, the analyst creates a dashboard with:

A **column chart** comparing sales by region for each quarter, making it easy to spot top and underperforming areas.

A **line chart** showing sales trends over the year, highlighting seasonality.

A **heat map** layered on a geographical map to quickly identify sales hotspots.

By choosing distinct chart types for comparison, trend analysis, and geographic insight, the dashboard tells a multi-dimensional story. Executives can immediately see not only where sales are strong, but also how performance fluctuates over time and location.

**Scenario 2: Customer Segmentation Insights in Power BI**

A marketing team at a European telecom provider is tasked with understanding customer segments based on usage and satisfaction scores. Using Power BI, the analyst:

Deploys a **scatter plot** to map customer satisfaction (Y-axis) against monthly data usage (X-axis), with point size representing account tenure.
Adds a **bar chart** breaking down average revenue per segment.
Incorporates a **pie chart** for a high-level view of segment size distribution.

This combination helps the team identify high-value, satisfied customers (top-right quadrant), and segments needing engagement. The right charts make the insights actionable, informing targeted campaigns.

***Visualization Tools: Practical Considerations***

Modern business intelligence platforms like Tableau and Power BI offer built-in chart selection recommendations based on your dataset. These features can guide you, but always apply human judgment to ensure your visualization aligns with your storytelling objectives.

For example, Tableau's "Show Me" panel suggests chart types based on selected fields, while Power BI's AI visualizations can auto-generate insights. However, automated suggestions are only starting points; your expertise in audience context and narrative focus remains crucial.

***Dashboard Illustration: Chart Selection in Action***

Imagine a business dashboard for a global logistics company tracking delivery performance:

- **Map visualization** shows delivery routes and delays by region.
- **Bar chart** compares on-time deliveries by distribution center.
- **Line chart** tracks average delivery times week-over-week.

This multi-chart dashboard leverages the strengths of each visualization type, ensuring stakeholders see both the big picture and actionable details.

Selecting the right chart is foundational to compelling data storytelling. By following a structured checklist and considering real-world use cases, you can transform raw data into stories that drive business action. The tools you use, while powerful, are only as effective as the choices you make in design and narrative alignment.

# 8. FROM DASHBOARDS TO DATA STORIES: EVOLVING YOUR PRESENTATIONS

Imagine walking into a meeting where your data isn't just displayed, it's alive, interactive, and tells a story that inspires action. In today's fast-paced business landscape, merely presenting numbers on a dashboard is no longer enough. Audiences expect more: clarity, engagement, and insights that drive results. This chapter guides you beyond static dashboards and into the dynamic world of data storytelling, where every visualization becomes a powerful narrative tool.

Here, we unravel the crucial distinctions between dashboards and data stories, helping you understand when to monitor key metrics and when to weave information into a compelling narrative. You'll learn how to design interactive dashboards that do more than report—they invite exploration, encourage questions, and empower stakeholders to discover insights on their own terms. As businesses become increasingly global, the chapter also addresses the nuances of presenting data across different cultures and regions, ensuring your visuals resonate universally and avoid misinterpretation.

Transitioning from static to dynamic visuals can transform your presentations, making them more persuasive and memorable. We'll walk you through this evolution, offering practical strategies and real-world examples from diverse business environments. To measure your progress, you'll discover methods for evaluating the effectiveness of your dashboards and stories, ensuring your efforts translate to business impact. Along the way, we'll reflect on the best practices and common pitfalls, equipping you with the confidence to deliver data-driven presentations that stand out in any boardroom.

As you dive in, expect to gain the skills to move from simply sharing data to truly connecting with your audience, empowering you to turn insights into action and elevate your influence as a master data storyteller.

## 8.1. The Difference Between Dashboards and Stories

As organizations increasingly rely on data-driven strategies, the way insights are presented can dramatically enhance—or diminish—their impact. Two primary approaches dominate business data communication: dashboards and data stories. While both aim to translate complex data into actionable knowledge, they serve distinct purposes and require different design philosophies. Understanding the difference between dashboards and stories is crucial for evolving your presentations from static displays of information to dynamic narratives that influence decisions.

### *Understanding Dashboards: Purpose and Practice*

Dashboards are ubiquitous in modern business environments. Designed as interactive tools, they provide real-time access to a range of metrics, enabling users to monitor performance, identify trends, and respond swiftly to changes. Dashboards typically aggregate key performance indicators (KPIs) and other relevant data into a single, easily accessible interface.

For example, in **Tableau** or **Power BI**, a sales dashboard might display:

- Monthly sales figures by region
- Year-over-year growth trends
- Top-performing products or services
- Customer acquisition rates

These visualizations allow managers to explore data on demand, filter by parameters, and drill down into specifics. The core strength of a dashboard lies in its ability to empower users to investigate data independently, supporting ongoing monitoring and operational decision-making.

However, this strength can also be a limitation. Dashboards are excellent for "what" questions but often fall short in answering "why" or "what next." In other words, dashboards are repositories of facts, not interpreters of meaning.

### *The Essence of Data Stories: Crafting Narrative and Meaning*

Data stories, on the other hand, are purposeful narratives built around data. Rather than presenting all available information, a data story curates specific insights and weaves them into a compelling sequence that guides the audience toward a conclusion or recommended action.

A well-crafted data story:

- Selects the most relevant data points for the intended audience
- Provides context, interpretation, and implications
- Uses visualizations not just for information, but for emphasis and persuasion
- Follows a narrative arc: introduction, rising action, climax, and resolution

In practical terms, a data story in **Power BI** might use a sequence of visuals to explain why regional sales have declined, identify contributing factors, and conclude with targeted recommendations for improvement. The story is not an open-ended exploration; it is a guided journey with a clear message and a call to action.

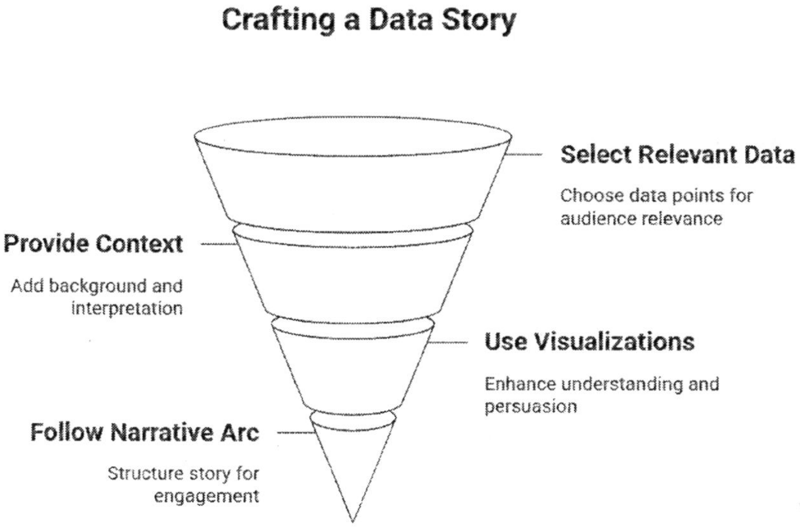


*Comparing Dashboards and Stories: Key Distinctions*

To further clarify the distinction, consider the following comparison:

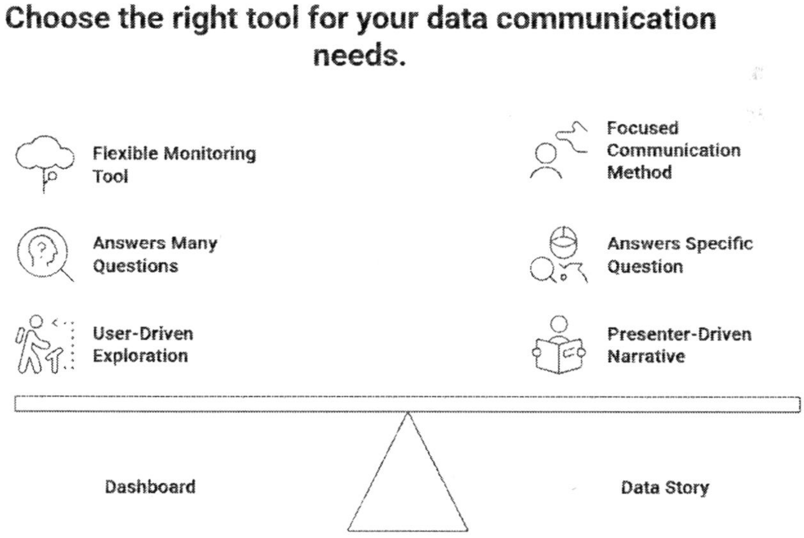


**Dashboard**: A flexible tool for ongoing monitoring; answers many questions; user-driven exploration.

**Data Story**: A focused, guided communication; answers a specific question; presenter-driven narrative.

Dashboards are like the cockpit of an airplane, providing constant streams of data to help pilots adjust in real time. Data stories, by contrast, are like a flight report, explaining how the journey unfolded and what should be done differently next time.

#### *Real-World Use Cases*

Let's look at two scenarios that highlight these differences:

### Global Retail Operations Dashboard (Tableau Example)

A multinational retailer uses a Tableau dashboard to track daily inventory levels, sales performance, and supply chain bottlenecks across various regions. Regional managers log in to the dashboard every morning to monitor KPIs and respond to emerging issues—stockouts, surges in demand, or delivery delays. The dashboard supports operational decisions but does not, by itself, explain why a particular region is underperforming or what actions should be taken beyond adjusting inventory orders.

#### *When to Use Dashboards vs. Data Stories*

Choosing between a dashboard and a data story depends on your audience and objectives:

Use **dashboards** when your audience needs to explore data independently, monitor performance, or answer a broad array of operational questions.

Use **data stories** when you need to persuade, explain, or recommend a specific course of action based on data.

Visualization tools such as Tableau, Power BI, and Qlik Sense offer features for both approaches. Dashboards excel with interactive filters, drill-downs, and real-time data feeds. For storytelling, these tools support features like guided navigation, annotated visuals, and narrative sequencing to shape the audience's journey.

In summary, dashboards and data stories are both vital in the business data toolkit, but they serve distinct roles. Dashboards empower ongoing exploration and monitoring, while data stories guide audiences to insights and action. Recognizing when and how to shift from dashboard to story elevates your data presentations from informative to transformative.

## 8.2. Building Interactive Dashboards

An effective dashboard does more than simply display data—it empowers users to explore, discover, and act. Building interactive dashboards is a transformative step in the data storytelling journey, allowing your audience to engage directly with information, uncover insights relevant to their context, and make data-driven decisions with confidence. This interactivity is the bridge between passive consumption and active exploration, turning your presentations into collaborative experiences.

### *Understanding the Power of Interactivity*

Traditional dashboards often present a static snapshot: charts, tables, and KPIs arranged for quick reference. While useful, these static views can be limiting when stakeholders need to answer follow-up questions or dig deeper into trends. Interactive dashboards, by contrast, invite users to filter, drill down, and pivot the data themselves, supporting a more nuanced understanding.

Interactivity transforms a dashboard from a mere reporting tool into a dynamic decision support system. For business professionals, this means:

- Gaining real-time answers to "what if" scenarios
- Tailoring insights to specific business units, clients, or regions
- Uncovering hidden patterns by slicing and dicing data on demand

This level of engagement is crucial for effective data storytelling, where the story adapts to the audience's curiosity and business needs.

### *Key Elements of Interactive Dashboards*

Designing an effective interactive dashboard involves more than adding buttons or drop-down menus. Each interactive element should serve a clear purpose, guiding the user through the data story without overwhelming or distracting them.

Consider these core features:

- **Filters and Slicers:** Allow users to view data for specific timeframes, geographies, product lines, or customer segments, encouraging personalized exploration.
- **Drill-downs and Drill-throughs:** Enable deeper dives from summary to detail, supporting root-cause analysis and nuanced storytelling.
- **Dynamic Highlights and Tooltips:** Provide additional context or explanations when users hover or click, making complex data approachable.
- **Responsive Visuals:** Automatically update charts and indicators based on user selections, maintaining narrative coherence.

For example, a sales performance dashboard in Power BI might include slicers for region, product category, and sales period, with bar charts and maps updating accordingly. A Tableau dashboard could feature a clickable map, letting users explore sales by country, and then by city, with tooltips displaying key metrics.

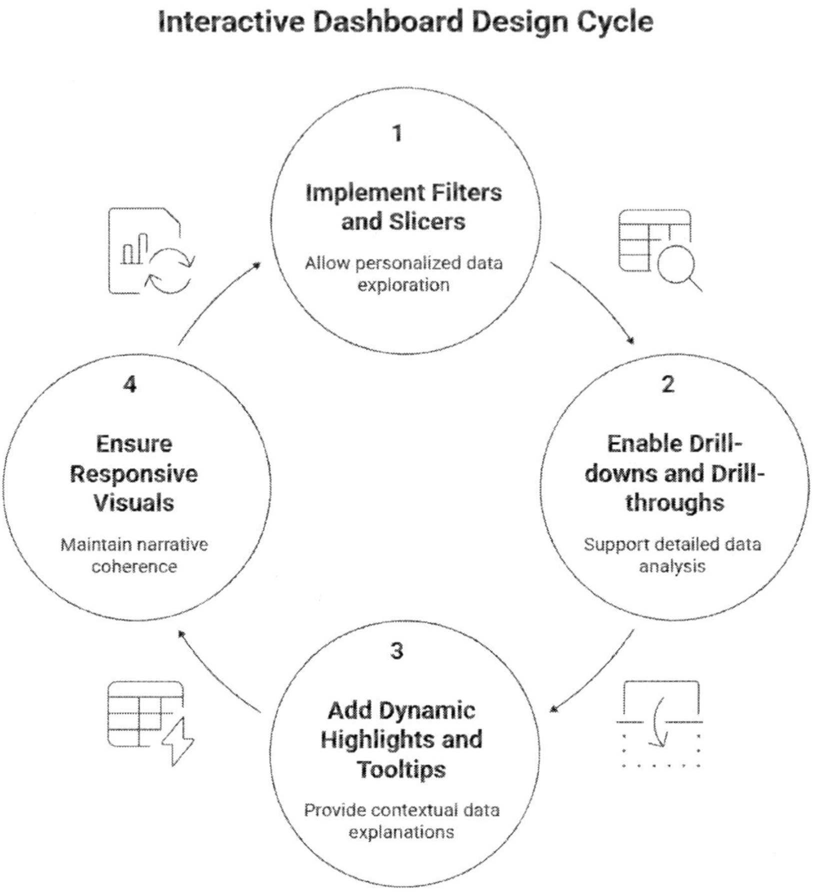


***Steps for Building Interactive Dashboards***

Creating an interactive dashboard requires both technical proficiency and a storyteller's mindset. Follow these sequential steps to ensure your dashboard not only works smoothly but also communicates effectively:

- **Define the Business Question:** Start by identifying the main question or challenge your dashboard will address. This keeps the design focused and the interactions purposeful.
- **Map the User Journey:** Anticipate the paths users might take as they explore the data. Consider what questions they are likely to ask and in what sequence.

- **Select the Right Tool:** Choose a dashboard tool that aligns with your audience's needs and your organization's infrastructure. Tableau and Power BI are industry leaders, offering robust interactivity and sharing options.
- **Design with Clarity:** Lay out visuals to guide the user's eye, grouping related information and minimizing clutter. Use color, size, and hierarchy to emphasize key points.
- **Implement Interactive Features:** Add filters, drill-downs, and dynamic visual elements. Test each for usability, ensuring they enhance rather than hinder the narrative.
- **Iterate with Stakeholders:** Share prototypes with end-users, gather feedback, and refine the dashboard based on real-world usage.

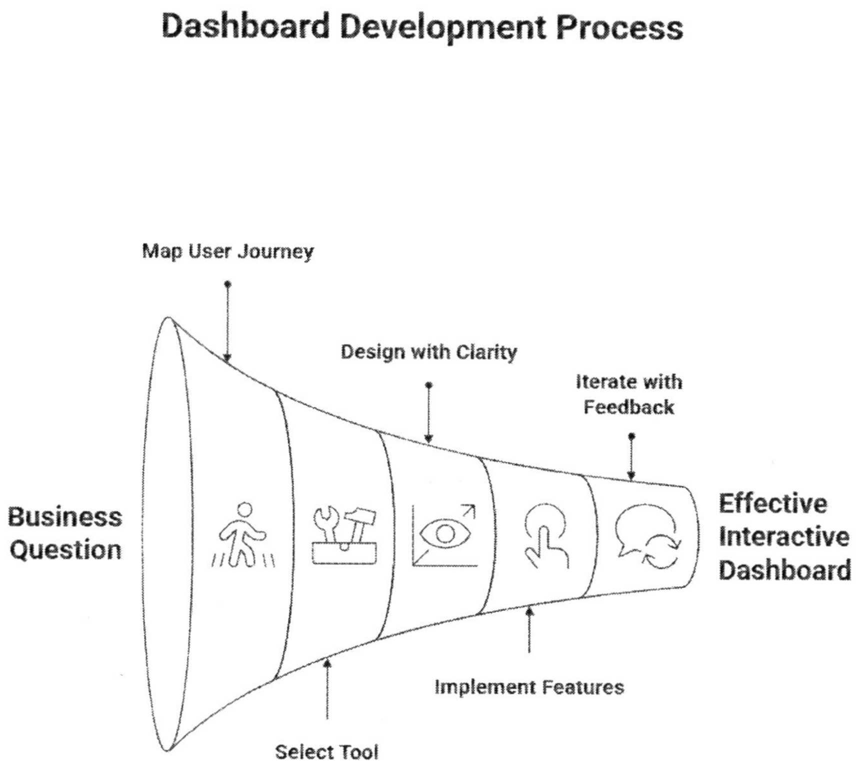


*Real-World Scenarios*

To illustrate the impact of interactive dashboards, consider the following business scenarios:

### Global Retail Chain: Sales Optimization

A multinational retail chain sought to optimize its inventory and sales strategies across diverse markets. Using Tableau, the analytics team built an interactive dashboard where regional managers could filter sales data by country, product category, and promotion period. Drill-down capabilities allowed managers to identify underperforming stores and adjust inventory in near real-time. The result was a more agile response to market changes and a measurable increase in sales performance.

**Marketing Agency: Campaign Performance**

A digital marketing agency used Power BI to track campaign effectiveness for multiple clients. Through interactive dashboards, clients could view metrics such as click-through rates, conversions, and ROI by campaign, channel, and audience segment. Dynamic filters enabled granular analysis, helping clients quickly identify which messages resonated with specific demographics. This transparency fostered trust and empowered clients to make informed marketing investments.

Both examples underscore how interactivity turns dashboards into strategic assets, enabling diverse users—from frontline managers to executives—to engage with data in ways that drive business value.

***Choosing the Right Visualization Tools***

Selecting the appropriate technology is essential for successful interactive dashboards. Popular options include:

**Tableau:** Renowned for its intuitive interface and powerful visualization capabilities, Tableau excels at creating visually striking, interactive dashboards suitable for global enterprises and small businesses alike.

**Power BI:** Integrates seamlessly with Microsoft's ecosystem, offering robust self-service analytics and extensive sharing features, making it a favorite for organizations standardizing on Microsoft products.

**Qlik Sense and Google Data Studio:** Also provide interactive dashboarding capabilities, with strengths in rapid prototyping and cloud-based collaboration.

Regardless of the tool, prioritize ease of use, scalability, and security. Ensure your dashboards are accessible on multiple devices, including mobile, to maximize reach and impact.

Building interactive dashboards is a pivotal skill for modern business professionals, enabling both compelling data stories and actionable insights. By carefully considering user needs, purposefully designing interactions, and leveraging the right tools, you transform static data into dynamic narratives that drive results.

## 8.3. Transitioning from Static to Dynamic Visuals

As organizations strive to make their data presentations more impactful, many are recognizing the limitations of static dashboards and reports. While static visuals—like traditional bar charts, tables, and printed dashboards—provide a snapshot of information at a specific point in time, they often fall short in engaging audiences or supporting deeper exploration. Dynamic visuals, by contrast, empower users to interact with the data, uncover insights, and personalize their journey through the story. This transition marks a pivotal step in data storytelling: from presenting facts to enabling discovery and dialogue.

### *Understanding Static vs. Dynamic Visuals*

Static visuals are fixed images or reports. These may include PDF exports, slide decks, or printed charts, offering no interactivity. Dynamic visuals, on the other hand, are interactive and responsive. They allow the viewer to filter data, drill down into specific segments, animate changes over time, or even customize views according to their unique questions.

Consider a sales dashboard. A static version might show regional sales for the last quarter as a simple bar chart. A dynamic version lets users select different time frames, compare regions, or click on a region to see product-level details.

### *Why Transition to Dynamic Visuals?*

Making the shift to dynamic visuals delivers significant business advantages:

- **Enhanced Engagement**: Viewers become active participants, not passive recipients.
- **Deeper Insight**: Interactivity enables users to explore root causes, trends, and outliers.
- **Personalization**: Stakeholders can tailor the story to their specific needs or interests.
- **Real-Time Decision Making**: Live dashboards update automatically, facilitating agile responses.

These benefits are particularly valuable in fast-paced business environments, where timely, data-driven decisions can mean the difference between seizing an opportunity and missing it.

### *Making the Transition: Tools and Techniques*

Transitioning from static to dynamic visuals is both a technical and a cultural shift. It requires the adoption of modern tools and a mindset that values exploration as much as explanation.

#### Popular Tools for Dynamic Visualization:

**Tableau**: Renowned for its user-friendly drag-and-drop interface and powerful interactive dashboards, Tableau allows users to filter data, create calculated fields, and design compelling, story-driven presentations.

**Power BI**: Microsoft's Power BI integrates seamlessly with existing business systems, offering interactive reports, drill-through capabilities, and real-time data streaming.

**Qlik Sense**: Known for its associative data model, Qlik Sense empowers users to explore data freely, uncovering hidden relationships and trends.

#### Illustrative Example: Interactive Sales Dashboard in Tableau

Suppose a regional sales manager wants to understand quarterly performance. A static dashboard might simply show total sales by region. A dynamic Tableau dashboard, however, allows the manager to:

- Select a specific quarter using a slider.
- Filter results by product category or sales channel.
- Click on a region to see city-level breakdowns.
- Animate revenue growth over time.

This interactivity turns a one-size-fits-all report into a personalized exploration tool, fostering richer conversations and more nuanced decision-making.

### *Business Use Cases: Real-World Scenarios*

Let’s examine how organizations across diverse sectors have benefited from transitioning to dynamic visuals:

#### 1. Global Retail Chain: Enhancing Executive Decision-Making

A European-based retail group operated in over 20 countries, relying on static spreadsheets for monthly performance reviews. Executives found it difficult to spot emerging trends or drill into underperforming regions. By adopting Power BI, the company transformed its performance dashboards into interactive, real-time tools. Executives could now:

- Instantly filter sales by country, store, or product.

- Visualize inventory levels and promotions' impact.
- Share customized dashboards across teams.

This led to faster interventions, more targeted marketing strategies, and increased sales in lagging markets.

**2. Financial Services Firm: Improving Client Engagement**

An asset management firm in Singapore provided clients with quarterly investment summaries as static PDF reports. Clients wanted more transparency and flexibility. By shifting to a dynamic dashboard using Tableau, clients could:

Adjust timeframes and compare portfolio performance across sectors.
Simulate different investment scenarios.
Access real-time updates rather than waiting for the next report cycle.

Client satisfaction improved, and the firm differentiated itself in a competitive market by offering a superior data experience.

These scenarios illustrate how dynamic visuals not only improve internal decision-making but also enhance external relationships and brand value.

### *Practical Steps for Your Organization*

If you're ready to move beyond static dashboards, follow these foundational steps:

- **Assess Needs and Stakeholders**: Identify who will use the dashboards and what decisions they need to make.
- **Choose the Right Platform**: Evaluate tools like Tableau, Power BI, or Qlik Sense based on your organization's data infrastructure and user requirements.
- **Design for Interactivity**: Plan dashboards with filters, drill-downs, and other interactive elements that align with your stakeholders' workflows.
- **Pilot and Iterate**: Roll out dynamic dashboards to a pilot group, gather feedback, and refine the experience.
- **Foster a Culture of Exploration**: Encourage users to ask questions, explore scenarios, and share insights.

### *Summary and Next Steps*

Transitioning from static to dynamic visuals transforms data presentations from passive reports to engaging experiences that drive action. By leveraging interactive tools and thoughtful design, businesses can unlock deeper insights and foster a data-driven culture. In the next section, we'll explore how to weave these dynamic elements into cohesive data stories—ensuring that your presentations not only inform but also inspire and persuade your audience.

## 8.4. Presenting Data Across Cultures and Regions

Effective data storytelling requires more than just technical expertise or creative visualization. When presenting to audiences across different cultures and regions, it's essential to consider how diverse backgrounds, values, and expectations shape the interpretation of data. This sensitivity not only prevents miscommunication but also deepens engagement, ensuring your message resonates globally.

### *Understanding Cultural Context in Data Presentation*

Culture profoundly influences how people perceive colors, symbols, numbers, and even storytelling styles. For instance, a color that signals prosperity in one region may represent caution or negativity in another. Similarly, the preference for directness or subtlety in communication varies widely across cultures.

Let's explore key factors to consider when tailoring data presentations for international audiences:

- **Color Associations:** Colors evoke different emotions globally. Red, for example, often represents good fortune in China but can signify warning or loss in Western contexts.
- **Numerical Formats:** Date formats (MM/DD/YYYY vs. DD/MM/YYYY), decimal separators (comma vs. period), and currency symbols differ by country.
- **Reading Direction:** While most Western cultures read left-to-right, others, such as Arabic-speaking regions, read right-to-left, influencing dashboard layout and data flow.
- **Symbolism and Icons:** Common icons or metaphors may not have universal meaning. A mailbox icon may be unfamiliar or carry a different connotation in some regions.
- **Storytelling Preferences:** Some cultures value concise, data-driven arguments, while others expect context, narrative, and relationship-building.

By accounting for these factors, you can design data stories that are both accurate and culturally attuned.

### *Adapting Dashboards for Global Stakeholders*

Business dashboards are a staple for organizations to monitor key metrics and make informed decisions. However, a dashboard that performs well in one region may be confusing or ineffective elsewhere if cultural nuances are overlooked.

### Example: Multinational Sales Performance Dashboard

A global retail company uses Tableau to present sales data to regional managers in Asia, Europe, and North America. To ensure clarity and impact:

- **Localization:** The dashboard automatically adapts date formats and currency based on the viewer's location. For example, European managers see sales in euros with dates formatted DD/MM/YYYY, while American managers see dollars and MM/DD/YYYY.
- **Color Customization:** The design team avoids using red to highlight positive performance in Asia, opting for green or gold instead, recognizing regional associations with prosperity.
- **Language Options:** Tooltips and axis labels are translated for each audience, ensuring that all users, regardless of language, can interpret the data accurately.

- **Tool Highlight:** Tableau and Power BI both offer localization features, allowing dashboard creators to tailor language, currency, time zones, and more. These tools also support custom themes to address color and design preferences across cultures.

***Case Study: Pharmaceutical Expansion in Latin America***

Consider a pharmaceutical company headquartered in Germany, preparing a data-driven presentation for local partners in Brazil and Mexico. The team uses Power BI to illustrate market trends, regulatory milestones, and distribution challenges.

Key adaptations include:

- **Narrative Structure:** Recognizing that Latin American business culture often values personal relationships and storytelling, the presenters begin with a brief narrative about the company's commitment to local healthcare, followed by data insights.
- **Visuals and Icons:** The dashboard uses universally recognized icons, such as pills or hospitals, and avoids metaphors or idioms that might not translate well.
- **Interactive Features:** Power BI's drill-down options allow local partners to explore state-level data, reinforcing transparency and collaboration.

By aligning the dashboard design and storytelling approach with local expectations, the company builds trust and ensures that insights lead to meaningful action.

### *Best Practices for Cross-Cultural Data Storytelling*

Successfully presenting data across cultures and regions involves thoughtful planning and ongoing feedback. Consider these strategies:

- **Research Audience Preferences:** Before presenting, learn about your audience's cultural norms, business etiquette, and communication styles.
- **Test and Iterate:** Share draft dashboards or visualizations with local stakeholders for feedback. Use this input to refine color schemes, formats, and narratives.
- **Leverage Visualization Tools:** Use features in Tableau, Power BI, or similar platforms to localize content and provide language options.
- **Build Flexibility:** Design modular dashboards or stories that can be easily adapted for different regions without starting from scratch each time.
- **Avoid Assumptions:** Never assume that visualizations or storytelling techniques are universally understood. Always provide context and explanations as needed.

Presenting data across cultures and regions is both a challenge and an opportunity. By respecting cultural differences and leveraging the localization capabilities of modern visualization tools, you can ensure your data stories make a lasting impact, regardless of geography.

## 8.5. Measuring Dashboard Effectiveness

As you move from crafting engaging data stories to building actionable dashboards, it is critical to evaluate whether your dashboards are genuinely serving their intended purpose. A dashboard's effectiveness is not determined by its visual appeal alone, but by how well it enables users to understand data, make informed decisions, and take timely action. To ensure your dashboards are more than just digital wallpaper, you need a structured approach to measuring their impact.

### *Defining Dashboard Effectiveness*

The effectiveness of a dashboard hinges on its alignment with business goals, its clarity, and its user experience. An effective dashboard answers key business questions, highlights critical metrics, and guides users toward actionable insights without overwhelming them with unnecessary details.

Key attributes of an effective dashboard include:

- **Relevance:** Displays the right metrics for the right audience.
- **Clarity:** Presents data in a way that is easy to interpret and digest.

- **Actionability:** Enables users to identify trends, anomalies, and next steps quickly.
- **Engagement:** Encourages regular use and exploration.

For instance, in a global sales organization, a dashboard should allow regional managers to instantly see sales performance by territory, identify underperforming products, and flag areas needing attention. In contrast, a marketing executive may need a dashboard that highlights campaign ROI, customer engagement rates, and lead conversion trends.

### *Key Metrics for Evaluating Dashboard Performance*

Measuring dashboard effectiveness involves both qualitative and quantitative approaches:

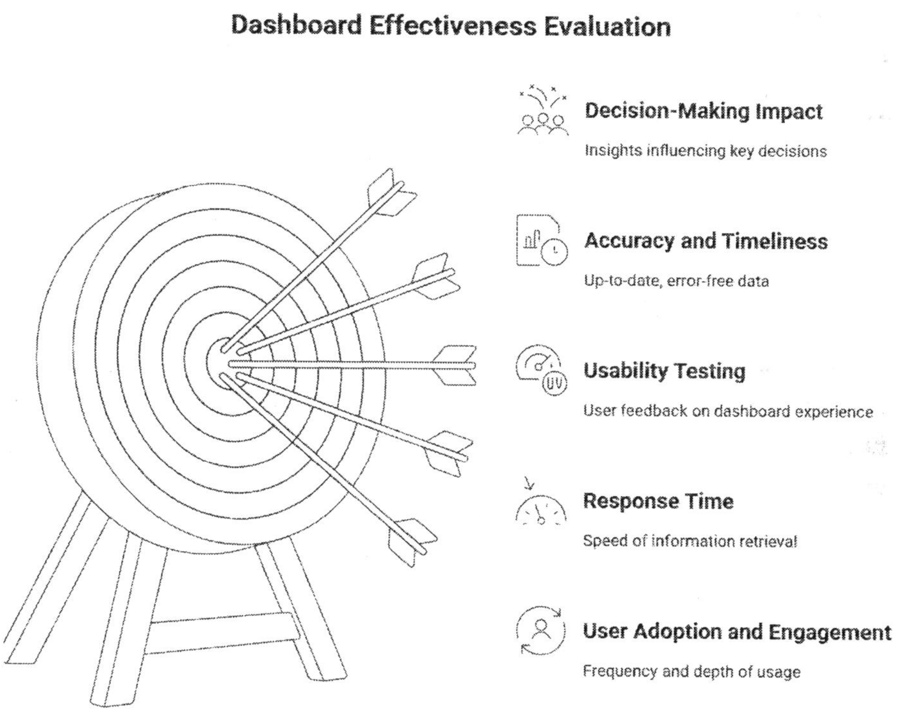


- **User Adoption and Engagement:** How often and how thoroughly do stakeholders use the dashboard? Tools like Power BI and Tableau provide usage analytics, highlighting feature engagement and time spent on visualizations.
- **Decision-Making Impact:** Are key business decisions being influenced by insights from the dashboard? This can be tracked through feedback surveys, meeting notes, or by observing changes in KPIs after dashboard deployment.

- **Accuracy and Timeliness:** Are the data sources up-to-date and free from errors? Timely, accurate data ensures credibility and trust.
- **Usability Testing:** Collect user feedback to uncover pain points, confusing elements, or missing functionality.
- **Response Time:** How quickly can users find answers to their questions? Fast, intuitive navigation is vital.

*Visualization Tool Examples: Tableau and Power BI*

Modern dashboard tools provide built-in features to help measure and enhance effectiveness:

**Tableau:** Offers 'Usage Analytics' dashboards that allow you to monitor how often users interact with specific views, which filters are most used, and where drop-offs occur. This data can reveal which parts of your dashboard are most valuable and where users may be struggling.

**Power BI:** With its 'Usage Metrics Report,' Power BI helps you identify usage patterns, report sharing frequency, and the most viewed pages or visuals. You can also set up alerts for key metric changes, ensuring stakeholders receive timely notifications.

Both platforms enable A/B testing of dashboard layouts or visualization types, allowing you to empirically determine which designs drive better comprehension and action.

*Real-World Use Cases*

Let's consider two business scenarios that highlight the importance of measuring dashboard effectiveness:

**1. Retail Performance Monitoring**

A multinational retail chain deploys a Power BI dashboard to track in-store and online sales across multiple regions. Initially, adoption is high, but weekly usage plummets after the first month. By examining the dashboard's usage metrics, the analytics team discovers that store managers find the interface cluttered and the key sales KPIs buried among less relevant data. A focused usability review leads to a dashboard redesign: redundant metrics are removed, and a clear hierarchy is established with critical sales figures front and center. Post-redesign, usage soars, and regional managers report greater confidence in making stock and staffing decisions, demonstrating the tangible impact of measuring and responding to dashboard effectiveness.

**2. Healthcare Operations Optimization**

A leading hospital in Southeast Asia implements a Tableau dashboard to monitor patient flow and resource allocation. The dashboard aggregates data from multiple departments, aiming to reduce wait times and optimize bed usage. After launch, the hospital gathers feedback from department heads and nurses. They learn that while the dashboard provides comprehensive data, users struggle to identify urgent bottlenecks due to information overload. The team introduces color-coded signals and drill-down capabilities focusing on key patient flow metrics. As a result, decision-makers react faster to surges in patient admissions, leading to a measurable reduction in wait times and improved patient satisfaction.

These examples demonstrate how measuring dashboard effectiveness—through both data analytics and user feedback—can drive iterative improvements that directly enhance business outcomes.

#### *Practical Steps for Measuring and Improving Dashboard Effectiveness*

To systematically assess and improve your business dashboards, follow these steps:

- **Define Success Criteria:** Start with clear objectives tied to specific business outcomes or user needs.
- **Monitor Usage:** Leverage built-in analytics in tools like Tableau and Power BI to observe engagement patterns.
- **Solicit Feedback:** Conduct regular surveys or interviews with users to capture qualitative insights.
- **Perform Usability Testing:** Observe how users interact with the dashboard and note challenges or areas for improvement.
- **Iterate and Refine:** Use insights from metrics and feedback to make targeted enhancements, then re-evaluate.

### 8.6. Reflection and Best Practices

As you move from traditional dashboards to dynamic data stories, it's essential to reflect on your evolving role as a communicator and the impact your visualizations can have within your organization. Mastering data storytelling is not just about selecting the right visuals, but about intentionally crafting experiences that drive action and insight. In this section, we'll distill best practices, highlight common pitfalls, and draw on real-world business scenarios to guide your journey from reporting to storytelling excellence.

#### *Recognizing the Shift: From Passive Dashboards to Engaged Audiences*

Dashboards have long served as the backbone of business reporting, providing real-time views of KPIs and operational metrics. However, static dashboards often leave stakeholders to interpret the data themselves, which can result in missed opportunities or misunderstood trends. Data stories, in contrast, actively guide your audience through a curated narrative, turning passive viewers into engaged decision-makers.

Consider the difference: a global retail company's dashboard in Tableau might display sales by region, inventory turnover, and customer satisfaction scores. While informative, it requires users to draw their own conclusions. Transforming this dashboard into a story—perhaps highlighting how a dip in customer satisfaction in Southeast Asia coincided with a supply chain disruption—enables the presenter to connect the dots, recommend strategies, and inspire action.

### *Best Practices for Evolving Your Presentations*

To ensure your transition from dashboards to data stories delivers maximum business impact, keep the following best practices in mind:

**Start with a Purposeful Question:**

Anchor your story around a central business question. For example, "Why did Q3 sales underperform in our European markets?" This sharpens your narrative and focuses stakeholder attention.

**Curate Visuals Thoughtfully:**

Instead of overwhelming viewers with every available metric, select visualizations that drive your narrative forward. In Power BI, use bookmarks or story points to sequence insights, revealing only the most relevant visuals at each stage of your presentation.

**Design for Clarity and Flow:**

Maintain a logical progression. Use consistent color palettes, clear labels, and intuitive layouts. Remember, every visual element should serve a purpose—avoid chartjunk and unnecessary complexity.

**Weave in Context and Action:**

Data alone rarely tells the whole story. Integrate qualitative context—such as customer feedback, market events, or operational changes—to enrich your narrative and suggest actionable next steps.

**Test and Iterate:**

Before presenting, seek feedback from a diverse group of colleagues or stakeholders. Does your story resonate? Are your visuals easy to interpret? Iterative refinement is key to impactful storytelling.

***Real-World Use Cases: Data Storytelling in Action***

To ground these best practices, let's explore two scenarios that demonstrate the power and nuance of advanced data storytelling.

### Case Study 1: E-Commerce Marketing Optimization

A multinational e-commerce company analyzed its digital marketing spend across continents using a standard dashboard in Tableau. Initially, executives saw only aggregated spend and ROI by region. The analytics team recognized that this view masked important trends. By evolving the dashboard into a data story, they highlighted a narrative: "Despite increased spend in South America, ROI dropped due to a shift to less effective ad formats." By layering in campaign-level detail, customer testimonials, and competitor benchmarks, the team persuaded leadership to pilot new ad formats, resulting in a 15% improvement in ROI the following quarter.

### Case Study 2: Healthcare Operations and Patient Outcomes

A regional hospital network tracked patient throughput and satisfaction using Power BI dashboards. When COVID-19 struck, the need for clear, actionable insights became urgent. Analysts moved beyond static dashboards, crafting data stories that showed how bottlenecks in triage correlated with spikes in patient wait times and lower satisfaction. By integrating patient narratives and real-time operational data, they built a compelling case for process redesign. Hospital leadership used these stories to secure funding for digital check-in systems, reducing wait times and improving patient experiences.

***Tool-Specific Best Practices***

Different visualization tools offer unique capabilities for storytelling. For example, Tableau's Story feature allows you to combine dashboards, text, and images into a guided narrative, while Power BI's PowerPoint export and bookmarks let you build sequenced, interactive presentations. Regardless of platform, focus on:

Using interactivity sparingly—too many filters or drill-downs can overwhelm the story.
Leveraging annotations and captions to clarify key points.
Ensuring accessibility, such as colorblind-friendly palettes and readable fonts.

*Reflecting on Pitfalls*

Transitioning to data storytelling is not without challenges. Common pitfalls include:

**Overloading with Data:** Too many metrics dilute your message.

**Neglecting Audience Needs:** Stories must be tailored; what resonates with executives may not work for front-line managers.

**Ignoring Cultural Context:** Global audiences interpret stories through different lenses. Adapt language, examples, and even color choices to ensure inclusivity.

Reflecting on your data storytelling approach—and applying these best practices—will elevate your presentations from static reports to memorable, actionable business narratives. By learning from real-world scenarios and leveraging the full capabilities of modern visualization tools, you'll drive greater understanding and influence across your organization.

In the next chapter, we'll dive deeper into advanced storytelling techniques, including integrating multimedia and real-time data, to further amplify your business impact and make your insights truly unforgettable.

# 9. PERSUASION AND INFLUENCE: DATA STORYTELLING STRATEGIES

In the modern business landscape, data alone rarely moves the needle—what truly drives action is the ability to persuade and influence through the stories we craft around that data. As organizations increasingly rely on analytics for critical decisions, the art of weaving data into compelling narratives has become indispensable. This chapter delves into the strategies and skills that transform data visualization from a tool for information sharing into a catalyst for business impact.

Here, you will explore the foundational principles of persuasive communication and discover how to create emotional resonance with your audience through thoughtfully designed visuals. We'll examine the psychological levers that help data stories not only inform but inspire decision-makers to act, whether you are presenting to an executive board, pitching to clients, or galvanizing a global team. Recognizing the diversity of today's business environments, this chapter also highlights how storytelling approaches can and should be adapted across cultures and markets, ensuring your message is both relevant and respectful.

Crucially, we'll address the responsibility that comes with influence, offering guidance on mitigating bias and maintaining objectivity to build trust and credibility. Throughout, you will find practical frameworks, real-world case studies, and a comprehensive persuasion checklist to help you apply these concepts with confidence.

By mastering these advanced storytelling strategies, you will elevate your data presentations beyond mere reporting, equipping yourself to shape conversations, drive innovation, and achieve meaningful business outcomes. Let's unlock the full persuasive power of your data stories together.

## 9.1. Principles of Persuasive Communication

In the digital age, information overload is a reality for organizations and professionals everywhere. Data alone does not drive decisions; it is the persuasiveness of the narrative built around the data that determines whether insights lead to meaningful action. Mastering the principles of persuasive communication is essential for transforming raw data into stories that inspire, convince, and mobilize stakeholders. This section explores the psychological, strategic, and visual elements that underpin persuasive data storytelling, equipping advanced practitioners with the tools to maximize their influence in any business context.

### *The Psychology of Persuasion in Data Storytelling*

Effective data storytelling transcends the mere presentation of facts. It leverages core psychological principles to resonate with audiences, foster trust, and drive alignment.

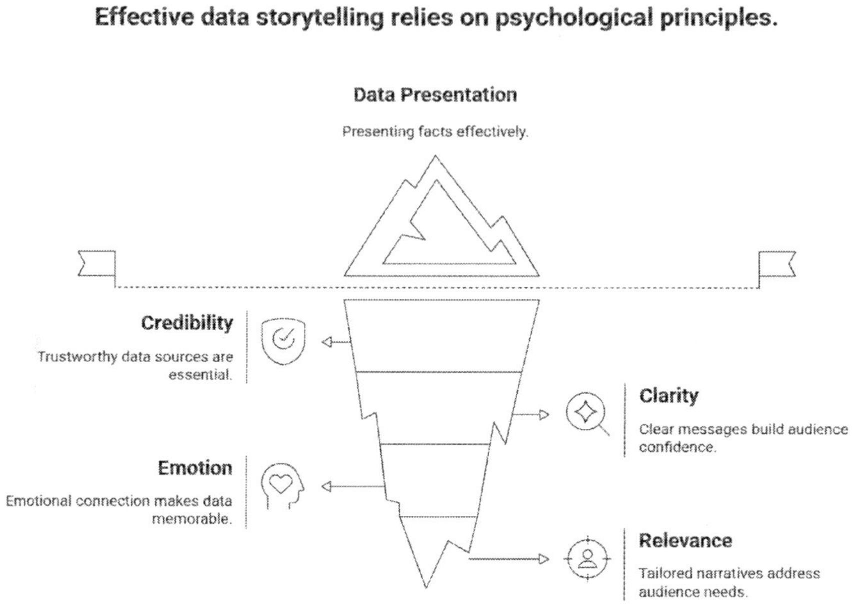


- **Credibility**: Audiences are more likely to accept data from sources they trust. Establishing credibility involves transparent sourcing, clear methodology, and demonstrating expertise with tools such as Tableau or Power BI.
- **Clarity**: Complex data must be distilled into clear messages. Ambiguity erodes confidence and can stall decision-making.
- **Emotion**: Data that connects on an emotional level is more memorable and motivating. Using relatable scenarios, such as customer success stories, makes data more impactful.
- **Relevance**: Tailoring narratives to audience needs ensures that the insights presented address real business challenges or opportunities.

### *Structuring Persuasive Data Narratives*

A persuasive data narrative is more than a sequence of charts; it is a structured journey that guides the audience from problem to resolution.

- **Context Setting**: Start by framing the business problem or opportunity. Use historical trends or industry benchmarks, visualized through tools like Power BI's KPI dashboards, to anchor your story.
- **Evidence Presentation**: Layer in your data, employing clear, context-specific visualizations. For example, Tableau's interactive maps can highlight regional sales disparities to make geographic trends tangible.
- **Insight Extraction**: Go beyond the numbers to extract actionable insights. Annotate line charts, add callouts to dashboards, or use color to spotlight anomalies or patterns.
- **Call to Action**: End with a compelling recommendation or decision point. Use summary dashboards or executive summaries to reinforce your message and prompt next steps.

*Visualization Tools and Dashboard Design for Persuasion*

The choice of visualization tools and dashboard design principles directly affects how persuasive your data story will be. Advanced tools like Tableau and Power BI offer features that support persuasive storytelling:

- **Interactive Dashboards**: Enable stakeholders to explore data themselves, increasing engagement and buy-in.
- **Drill-Down Capabilities**: Allow users to move from summary to detail, reinforcing transparency and credibility.
- **Strategic Use of Color**: Highlight key insights or urgent issues. For instance, using red to denote areas of concern on a sales performance dashboard can prompt immediate attention.
- **Adaptive Layouts**: Design dashboards that adjust to device or audience needs, ensuring clarity in all contexts.

### Example: Business Dashboard Illustration

Suppose a global retail chain wants to persuade regional managers to adopt a new inventory strategy. Using Power BI, the analyst creates a dashboard with the following elements:

```
- Regional map visualization: Highlights inventory turnover rates by
store.
- Time series chart: Shows reduction in stockouts after pilot
implementation in select regions.
- KPI cards: Compare sales growth in pilot versus control regions.
- Narrative text box: Summarizes key findings and recommends the
expansion plan.
```

By guiding viewers through a logical flow—problem (stockouts), evidence (pilot success), and action (rollout recommendation)—the dashboard becomes a persuasive tool rather than just an information repository.

*Real-World Use Cases*

### Case Study 1: Financial Services – Risk Mitigation Proposal

A multinational bank in Singapore needed to convince its executives to invest in advanced fraud detection. The analytics team used Tableau to integrate real-time transaction data, visualizing suspicious activity clusters through heatmaps and highlighting financial losses averted in pilot branches. By pairing these visuals with a concise narrative and a clear call to action, the team secured funding for a company-wide rollout.

### Case Study 2: Healthcare – Improving Patient Outcomes

A hospital network in Brazil sought to reduce readmission rates. Analysts built a Power BI dashboard tracking readmission trends by department and patient demographics. Color-coded alerts identified departments with the highest risk. By presenting this data alongside patient testimonials and benchmarking against national averages, the team persuaded leadership to invest in targeted care transition programs.

These examples underscore how persuasive communication is not about embellishing data, but about framing it in a way that aligns with business objectives and audience values.

Mastering the principles of persuasive communication empowers business professionals to transform complex analytics into compelling narratives that drive real-world results. By understanding audience psychology, structuring narratives effectively, and leveraging the right visualization tools, you can move stakeholders from insight to action with confidence.

## 9.2. Emotional Engagement through Visualization

To move beyond mere comprehension and into the realm of true influence, data storytelling must do more than present facts—it must evoke feeling. Emotional engagement is a critical lever in persuasive communication, transforming sterile numbers into narratives that inspire belief and action. When your audience connects emotionally to your data, they are more likely to internalize your message, remember your insights, and champion your recommendations.

### *The Science Behind Emotional Engagement*

Emotion shapes perception and decision-making. Research in neuroscience shows that information paired with emotion is more readily recalled and acted upon. In business contexts, this phenomenon is particularly powerful. When stakeholders feel a personal stake in the data—whether through empathy, urgency, or excitement—they are more inclined to support initiatives, allocate resources, or shift strategy.

Visualizations are uniquely positioned to foster this emotional engagement. By leveraging color, imagery, and storytelling structures, you can make abstract data personally relevant. For example, a simple line graph showing declining sales may not move an executive to action. However, framing the same trend within a narrative about lost opportunities for frontline employees, supplemented by impactful visuals, can ignite a sense of responsibility and urgency.

### *Designing for Emotional Impact*

Crafting emotionally resonant visualizations requires intention and sensitivity. Consider these core strategies:

- **Humanize Data**: Use icons, illustrations, or photographs to represent people or communities affected by the data. This fosters empathy and personal connection.
- **Leverage Color Psychology**: Colors evoke specific feelings. Warm tones like red and orange can signal urgency or opportunity, while cool tones like blue can communicate stability or calm.
- **Highlight Contrasts and Transitions**: Use visual cues to draw attention to key shifts or disparities in the data. Sudden drops, sharp increases, or marked differences between groups can all be accentuated to elicit emotional response.
- **Narrative Annotations**: Layer brief, human-centered stories or quotes onto your dashboards. A testimonial or a real-world scenario can make your data tangible.
- **Motion and Animation**: Animated transitions can create drama and guide the audience through a story arc, especially in digital dashboards and presentations.

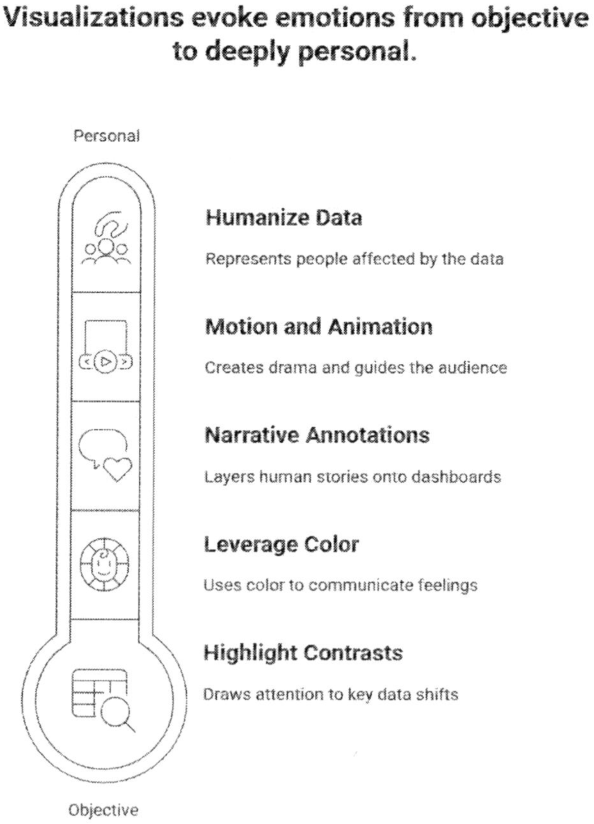

Advanced visualization tools like **Tableau** and **Power BI** offer features that make these techniques accessible. With Tableau, you can create interactive visuals that respond to user input, revealing layers of context as viewers explore. Power BI's integration of storytelling elements—such as bookmarks, custom tooltips, and image overlays—enables you to embed emotional cues directly within business dashboards.

### *Real-World Business Scenarios*

Consider a global healthcare provider faced with the challenge of reducing patient wait times across multiple regions. A standard dashboard might display wait time averages, but the data fails to inspire urgency. By redesigning the dashboard in Tableau, the analytics team overlays anonymized patient photos (with permission), includes interactive maps that highlight regions with the longest waits, and adds short patient testimonials. The result: the boardroom discussion shifts from operational statistics to the tangible impact on patient care, spurring a swift decision to invest in process improvements.

In another example, an international consumer goods company uses Power BI to visualize supply chain disruptions. Instead of relying solely on bar charts and line graphs, the dashboard features a timeline animation showing how delays ripple across continents, paired with stories from local managers about challenges faced on the ground. This approach not only clarifies the complexity of the issue but also evokes empathy and a sense of shared mission among executives, bridging cultural divides and accelerating cross-border collaboration.

### *Business Dashboard Illustrations*

Let's explore how emotional engagement can be directly embedded in dashboard design:

**Impactful Landing Page**: Start your dashboard with a summary visualization—a single, bold figure (such as "2,500 hours lost this quarter") overlaid on a relatable image. This immediately conveys significance and stakes.

**Progress Stories**: Use progress bars or milestone trackers that fill dynamically as goals are met. Pair these with short narratives or customer quotes that celebrate wins or highlight setbacks.

**Alerting and Urgency**: Integrate conditional formatting to shift colors or icons when key metrics surpass thresholds, signaling urgency and prompting immediate attention.

```
// Dynamic Card Visual for Urgency
IF([WaitTime] > 60,
   "CRITICAL: Average wait exceeds 1 hour!",
   "Wait times within target range")
```

Tableau enables similar interactivity with dashboard actions and parameter controls, allowing users to “drill down” into stories behind the numbers.

### *Cultural Nuances in Emotional Visualization*

Cultural context shapes emotional interpretation. A visualization that resonates in one region may fall flat—or even offend—in another. For instance, the color red might signify danger in North America but prosperity in parts of Asia. When building visual stories for global audiences, research local color symbolism, imagery, and storytelling conventions to ensure your designs evoke the intended emotions.

Harnessing emotion through visualization is not about manipulation; it is about making data meaningful and actionable. By grounding your visualizations in both cognitive and emotional engagement, you drive deeper understanding and lasting impact. As you master these techniques, remember to consider your audience’s cultural and contextual backgrounds to ensure your stories resonate universally.

## 9.3. Influencing Decision-Makers

To truly harness the power of data storytelling, business professionals must move beyond conveying information to actively influencing decision-makers. While crafting a compelling narrative is essential, the ultimate goal is to drive strategic action among those with the authority to shape an organization’s direction. This requires a sophisticated blend of analytical clarity, emotional resonance, and a deep understanding of stakeholders’ perspectives and priorities.

### *The Psychology of Persuasion in Data Storytelling*

Influencing decision-makers hinges on the principles of persuasion. Advanced data storytellers recognize that facts alone seldom sway opinions; instead, data must be contextualized within the decision-makers’ worldviews and business goals. Cognitive biases, organizational culture, and the individual’s risk appetite play significant roles in how information is received and acted upon.

Key psychological levers include:

- **Authority:** Referencing credible data sources and industry benchmarks enhances trust.
- **Social Proof:** Demonstrating alignment with peer organizations or market trends can reduce perceived risk.
- **Scarcity and Urgency:** Highlighting time-sensitive opportunities or threats can prompt quicker decisions.
- **Clarity:** Simplifying complex datasets into intuitive visuals fosters confidence and comprehension.

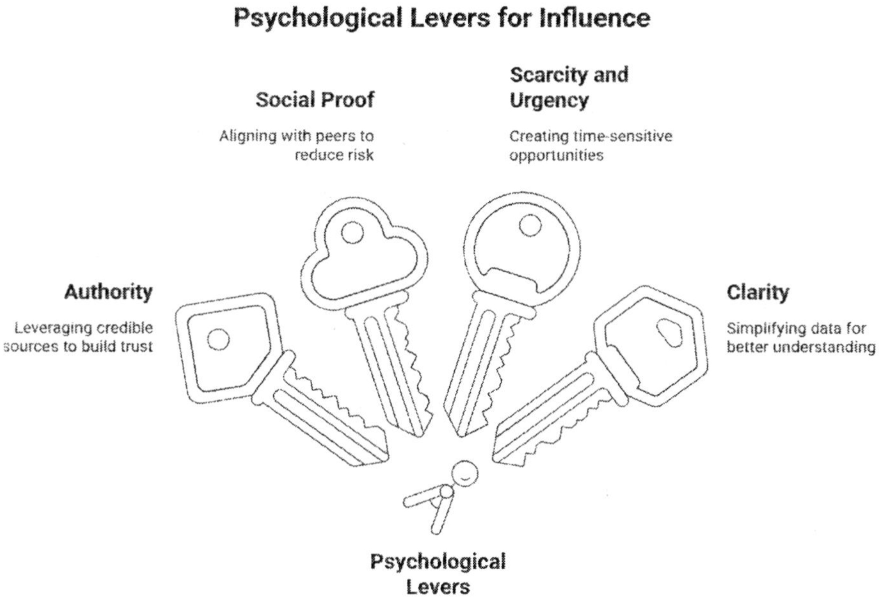


By integrating these elements, your data stories become not just informative, but transformative.

### *Strategic Framing: Aligning Data with Decision-Makers' Goals*

Effective data storytellers tailor their visualizations and narratives to the audience's strategic objectives. This alignment ensures your recommendations are perceived as enablers of business success, rather than abstract insights.

Consider the following process for strategic framing:

- **Understand Stakeholder Priorities:** Engage with decision-makers beforehand to identify their key performance indicators (KPIs), pain points, and strategic initiatives.
- **Select Relevant Data:** Filter and prioritize data that directly addresses these priorities.
- **Craft Targeted Visuals:** Use visualization tools such as Tableau or Power BI to create dashboards that spotlight the most pertinent metrics.
- **Narrate with Impact:** Build a story arc that connects the data to organizational goals, illustrating both the current state and the potential future impact of action or inaction.

For example, a marketing executive interested in customer acquisition may respond best to a Power BI dashboard that visualizes the cost per acquisition trend, segmented by campaign, overlaid with market benchmarks.

***Real-World Scenario: Driving Operational Change with Data Dashboards***

Let's examine a scenario within a global logistics company attempting to reduce delivery delays. The analytics team constructs a Tableau dashboard that visualizes real-time delivery performance across regions, highlighting bottlenecks and correlating them with weather patterns and resource allocation.

In presenting to the executive committee, the team:

- Opens with a story about a recent high-profile delivery failure, grounding the data in a relatable event.
- Demonstrates, through intuitive heat maps and trend lines, where delays cluster and how targeted interventions could improve performance.
- Offers a simulation within Tableau showing projected improvement if additional resources are allocated to specific regions.
- Frames recommendations in terms of potential revenue gains and risk mitigation, aligning with the executives' operational and financial priorities.

The result is a data-driven case for change that resonates emotionally and logically, prompting immediate action and resource reallocation.

***Visualization Tools for Persuasive Storytelling***

The choice of visualization platform significantly affects your ability to influence decision-makers. Advanced tools like Tableau and Power BI offer features that go well beyond static charts, enabling interactive, scenario-based narratives.

**Tableau:** Enables the creation of dynamic dashboards with drill-down capabilities, allowing executives to explore data at different levels of granularity. For example, a Tableau dashboard illustrating sales by region can empower leaders to simulate the impact of various investment scenarios in real time.

**Power BI:** Integrates seamlessly with Microsoft's ecosystem, allowing for real-time data refreshes and customizable alerts. Power BI's storytelling features, such as bookmarks and tooltips, can guide decision-makers through a structured narrative, focusing their attention on critical insights without overwhelming them with data.

Here is an example of a Power BI DAX formula used to create a dynamic KPI card for executive dashboards:

```
Total Sales Growth (%) =
VAR PrevPeriod = CALCULATE([Total Sales], PREVIOUSYEAR('Date'[Date]))
VAR CurrPeriod = [Total Sales]
RETURN
    DIVIDE(CurrPeriod - PrevPeriod, PrevPeriod)
```

This allows decision-makers to see at a glance whether sales growth aligns with strategic targets.

***Business Dashboard Illustration: Global Retail Expansion***

A multinational retailer evaluating expansion opportunities in Asia leverages a business dashboard built in Tableau. The dashboard visualizes:

- Market growth rates by country
- Competitor presence
- Regulatory risk scores
- Projected ROI scenarios

By layering interactive filters, executives can quickly compare markets and simulate outcomes. The presentation integrates narrative insights, such as consumer behavior trends and local partner testimonials, making the data story both persuasive and culturally attuned.

In summary, influencing decision-makers requires more than presenting accurate data; it demands a strategic blend of psychological insight, stakeholder alignment, and advanced visualization techniques. By employing tools like Tableau and Power BI, and by framing data in the context of organizational goals, you position your insights for maximum impact.

## 9.4. Global Perspectives: Storytelling in Diverse Markets

As organizations operate across borders and cultures, effective data storytelling must go beyond language and numeracy. Global markets vary in their expectations, visual literacy, and decision-making norms. To truly persuade and influence in diverse environments, data storytellers need to understand these nuances and adapt their approaches. This section explores how to craft data stories that resonate internationally, leveraging visualization tools and dashboard designs that accommodate cultural preferences and regulatory requirements.

***Navigating Cultural Contexts in Data Storytelling***

Business professionals often underestimate how culture shapes the way audiences interpret data visuals. Research in cross-cultural psychology and business communication reveals that factors such as color symbolism, information density, and storytelling structure differ significantly around the world.

For example, in many Western countries, audiences favor direct narratives and minimalistic visuals, expecting quick insights from dashboards. In contrast, East Asian markets may prefer holistic views and richer context, with visuals that allow for exploration and discovery. Recognizing these preferences is crucial for maximizing persuasion and ensuring that your data stories are both accessible and compelling.

***Visualization Tools for Global Audiences***

Modern business intelligence platforms like **Tableau** and **Power BI** offer extensive features for customizing dashboards and visualizations to suit diverse markets. These tools allow you to:

Localize number formats, currencies, and date conventions
Translate labels and tooltips for multilingual audiences
Adjust color palettes to respect cultural meanings (e.g., red for caution in Western markets, but prosperity in China)
Enable user-driven data exploration, catering to varying decision-making styles

By leveraging these capabilities, analysts and marketers can create dashboards that are not only technically accurate but also culturally sensitive.

***Business Use Case 1: Multinational FMCG Dashboard***

Consider a global fast-moving consumer goods (FMCG) company deploying a regional sales performance dashboard via **Power BI**. In designing this dashboard for both European and East Asian stakeholders, the analytics team faced several challenges:

**Color Selection**: The team avoided using red to denote negative trends in the China dashboard, as red carries positive connotations there. Instead, they used blue for declines and green for growth.

**Narrative Flow**: For the European version, the dashboard's homepage presented a single KPI headline with drill-downs available for detail—a direct, results-oriented approach. For East Asian users, the landing page displayed a broader overview, including context and trends, aligning with a preference for holistic information.

**Language and Metrics**: Power BI's dynamic localization features enabled seamless toggling between English, Mandarin, and French, as well as local currency conversions.

This tailored approach improved user adoption, facilitated cross-regional decision-making, and deepened engagement with the insights.

***Business Use Case 2: Global Health Initiative in Tableau***

A non-profit organization running a global vaccination campaign utilized **Tableau** to communicate program impact to donors and governments in North America, Africa, and the Middle East. Key adaptations included:

**Story Points for Regional Narratives**: Tableau's "Story Points" feature allowed the team to craft separate, interactive data stories for each region, emphasizing locally relevant outcomes.

**Visual Density**: North American dashboards prioritized simplicity and quick calls-to-action, while African and Middle Eastern versions incorporated narrative text boxes and richer annotation to provide necessary context, addressing varying levels of data literacy.

**Color and Symbolism**: Visualizations avoided culturally sensitive colors and iconography, opting for universally recognized symbols and neutral palettes.

The result was a set of dashboards that respected each region's communication style while maintaining consistent, credible messaging. Donor engagement and funding increased as a direct consequence of this tailored storytelling approach.

#### *Practical Tips for Adapting Data Stories Internationally*

To maximize persuasion and influence in global markets, consider the following strategies:

**Research Cultural Norms**: Before designing, engage with local experts or stakeholders to understand visual and narrative preferences.

**Leverage Tool Localization**: Use the internationalization features in Tableau, Power BI, or similar platforms to localize content without duplicating effort.

**Test with Target Users**: Conduct user testing with diverse audiences to ensure clarity and resonance.

**Emphasize Flexibility**: Design dashboards with optional levels of detail, allowing users to choose between summary and in-depth views depending on their preferences.

#### *Bridging Data Storytelling Across Borders*

Adapting your data storytelling for global markets is not merely about translation. It is about respecting and leveraging cultural diversity to maximize impact. When you align your stories with local expectations and norms, you build trust, enhance understanding, and increase the persuasive power of your insights.

In summary, mastering global data storytelling means combining technical proficiency with cultural empathy. As you refine your approach, you'll not only reach broader audiences but also drive more meaningful business results on the international stage.

## 9.5. Mitigating Bias and Ensuring Objectivity

As data storytellers, our power to persuade carries a profound responsibility: to ensure that the narrative we craft is both accurate and impartial. While compelling stories drive action, unchecked bias can erode trust, distort decision-making, and ultimately undermine business objectives. In this section, we delve into strategies for identifying, mitigating, and communicating bias, empowering you to present data with integrity and objectivity—no matter the audience or business context.

### *Recognizing Sources of Bias in Data Storytelling*

Bias can infiltrate data stories at any stage, from initial data collection to the final visualization shared in the boardroom. Advanced practitioners must develop a keen awareness of these entry points.

**Selection Bias:** Arises when certain data points are systematically excluded or favored, skewing the interpretation. For instance, a marketing dashboard that only displays data from top-performing regions might overlook critical challenges in underperforming markets.

**Confirmation Bias:** Occurs when analysts unintentionally seek out or emphasize data that supports preconceived beliefs. This often manifests in selective chart choices or color schemes that highlight desired outcomes.

**Visualization Bias:** Even the most objective data can be distorted through misleading scales, truncated axes, or inappropriate chart types. Overstating trends or compressing variance can subtly guide viewers toward a specific conclusion.

Understanding these biases is the first step in neutralizing their impact and maintaining credibility with stakeholders.

### *Practical Strategies for Ensuring Objectivity*

To foster transparency and trust in your data stories, consider the following advanced techniques and workflow enhancements:

- **Diverse Data Sourcing and Sampling**
    - Ensure datasets are representative of the entire business landscape, not just convenient or high-performing segments.
    - In Tableau or Power BI, leverage data blending features to incorporate multiple sources, providing a holistic view of performance indicators across demographics or regions.

- **Pre-Analysis Peer Review**

- Collaborate with cross-functional teams or external partners to review data selection and analysis methods.
- Implement workflow checkpoints where team members can interrogate assumptions and flag potential blind spots.

- **Visualization Audit Tools**

  - Use built-in audit features such as Tableau's "Explain Data" or Power BI's "Smart Narrative" to surface unexpected patterns and challenge initial interpretations.
  - Design dashboards with dual perspectives—for example, showing both absolute numbers and percentages—to encourage balanced, multifaceted insights.

- **Transparent Annotation and Metadata**

  - Clearly annotate visualizations with data sources, timeframes, and any known limitations. This transparency equips viewers to interpret findings within the correct context.
  - In Power BI, use the "Tooltip" and "Comment" features to embed explanations directly within charts, ensuring ongoing clarity.

***Business Scenario: Mitigating Bias in Global Sales Reporting***

Consider a multinational retail company using Tableau dashboards to drive quarterly sales strategy. Initially, the executive dashboard favors North American data, with charts prominently featuring growth in established markets. However, this selection bias masks declining sales in emerging regions.

To address this, the analytics team implements the following:

Integrates global sales data, applying robust sampling methods to ensure all regions are equally represented.

Adds filter controls allowing executives to toggle between regional and global views, reducing visualization bias.

Annotates dashboards with caveats about data collection periods and regional reporting discrepancies.

Schedules periodic cross-regional peer reviews to critique and refine the dashboard's story.

The result is a more nuanced, objective presentation—one that steers strategic investments toward areas of genuine opportunity rather than reinforcing existing perceptions.

***Business Scenario: Ensuring Objectivity in Marketing Campaign Analysis***

A digital marketing agency uses Power BI to report on the effectiveness of a multi-channel campaign for a European client. The initial dashboard highlights strong performance on social media platforms, aligning with the client's expectations. However, a peer review reveals that email channel data was underreported due to a technical integration issue—an example of selection bias.

To correct this:

The team corrects the data pipeline, ensuring all channels are included.

Visualization layouts are adjusted to give equal prominence to each channel, avoiding visual hierarchy bias.

Tooltips are added to each chart, explaining data limitations and the corrective actions taken.

The client receives a transparent report, including a section on methodology and data completeness, reinforcing the agency's commitment to integrity.

This approach builds client trust and ensures future decisions are based on a complete, accurate understanding of campaign performance.

***Tools and Dashboard Features for Bias Mitigation***

Modern visualization platforms offer advanced features to help teams proactively address bias:

**Tableau:** Data blending, "Explain Data" insights, customizable filters, and annotation tools to provide context.

**Power BI:** Integrated data lineage tracking, "Smart Narrative" for automatic explanations, and customizable tooltips for metadata transparency.

By leveraging these features, business professionals can enhance objectivity and invite constructive dialogue around the data.

Mitigating bias and ensuring objectivity are foundational to persuasive and ethical data storytelling. By proactively identifying potential sources of bias, leveraging collaborative review processes, and utilizing advanced visualization tools, you can build trust and drive more informed business decisions.

## 9.6. Summary and Persuasion Checklist

In the dynamic landscape of business communication, the power of persuasive data storytelling extends far beyond simply presenting information. As you've learned, effective data stories are crafted with intention, tailored for specific audiences, and delivered through thoughtfully designed visuals. This section distills the core strategies discussed in this chapter and provides you with a practical checklist for ensuring your data stories not only inform but inspire action and drive results.

### *The Essentials of Persuasion in Data Storytelling*

Mastering persuasion with data involves weaving together analytical rigor, audience insight, and narrative clarity. Before deploying your next visualization or dashboard, it's crucial to reflect on the following persuasion principles:

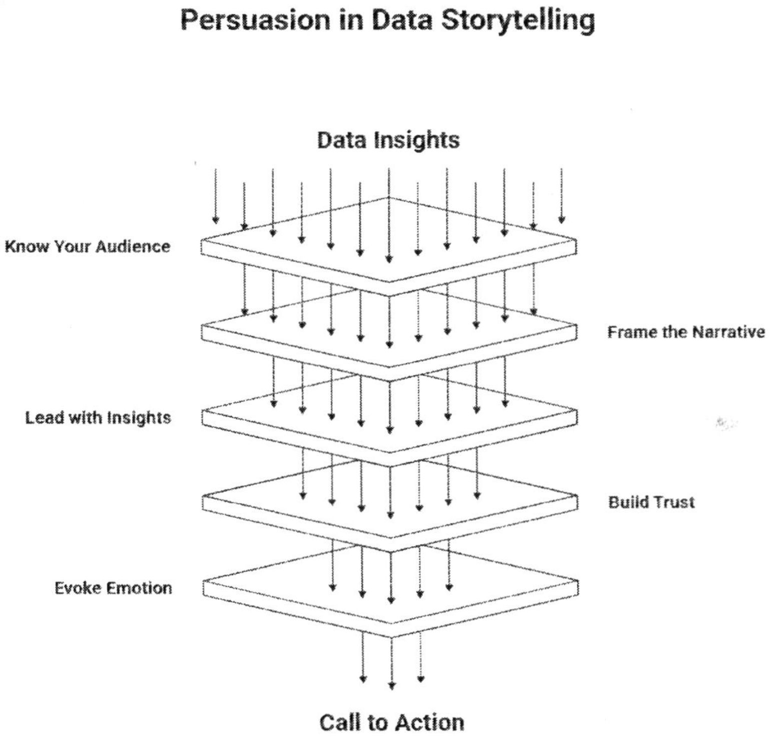


- **Know Your Audience:** Tailor your message to the knowledge level, cultural context, and business priorities of your stakeholders.
- **Frame the Narrative:** Choose a narrative arc—problem-solution, before-after, or cause-effect—that aligns with your objectives.

- **Lead with Insights:** Highlight actionable findings early to capture attention and set the agenda.
- **Build Trust:** Use clean, accurate data, cite sources, and avoid manipulative visuals or misleading scales.
- **Evoke Emotion:** Integrate relatable human elements or business outcomes to foster connection.
- **Call to Action:** Ensure your story concludes with a clear recommendation or next step.

#### *Persuasion Checklist for Data Storytelling*

To streamline your workflow and maximize business impact, apply this advanced checklist when preparing your data-driven presentations or dashboards:

- **Objective Alignment**
    - Have you clearly defined the business objective behind your data story?
    - Does every visualization contribute to this objective?

- **Audience Understanding**
    - Have you assessed your audience's background, expectations, and decision-making style?
    - Did you test the story's clarity with a peer or representative stakeholder?

- **Data Integrity and Preparation**
    - Are your data sources credible and up to date?
    - Have you pre-empted potential data challenges or stakeholder questions?

- **Visualization Selection and Design**
    - Did you select the most effective chart type for each insight? For example, use a **bar chart** in Tableau to compare sales across regions or a **line chart** in Power BI to illustrate trends over time.
    - Have you applied design principles such as color contrast, whitespace, and annotation to guide attention?

- **Narrative Structure**

- Is your data story cohesive, with a logical flow from context to conclusion?
- Did you intersperse data points with narrative commentary to maintain engagement?

- **Emotional and Rational Appeals**

  - Have you incorporated both quantitative evidence and qualitative context (e.g., customer testimonials, market anecdotes)?
  - Did you use visuals such as annotated business dashboards or infographics to bridge data and human impact?

- **Actionability**

  - Does your presentation end with a specific call to action or business recommendation?
  - Are stakeholders equipped with the necessary information to make informed decisions?

- **Feedback and Iteration**

  - Did you solicit feedback from a diverse group to check for clarity and resonance?

- Have you iterated on your visuals or narrative based on this feedback?

***Visualization Tools and Business Dashboard Examples***

The right visualization tool amplifies your persuasive power:

**Tableau:** Use dashboard storytelling features to combine maps, trend lines, and annotations that guide executive attention through complex healthcare or retail landscapes.

**Power BI:** Leverage the bookmarks and drill-through capabilities to allow stakeholders to explore different scenarios or outcomes interactively.

**Dashboard Illustration:** Consider a sales dashboard with a headline KPI card, segmented bar charts for region-wise performance, and a narrative text box highlighting key takeaways. This format ensures decision-makers grasp both the numbers and their implications at a glance.

```
# Example: Power BI DAX for Conditional Formatting of Sales
GrowthSalesGrowth =
VAR CurrentPeriod = SUM( 'Sales'[Amount])
VAR PreviousPeriod = CALCULATE(SUM( 'Sales'[Amount]), DATEADD(
```

```
'Sales'[Date], -1, MONTH))
RETURN
IF(CurrentPeriod > PreviousPeriod, "Positive", "Negative")
```

This conditional logic can visually cue executives to focus on areas of concern or opportunity in your dashboard.

By systematically applying this checklist and leveraging the capabilities of modern visualization tools, you can transform your data stories into persuasive narratives that drive action. Remember that persuasion is not about manipulation but about clarity, credibility, and connection.

# 10. ADVANCED VISUALIZATION TECHNIQUES

In today's data-driven business landscape, the ability to present information with clarity is no longer enough; true impact comes from uncovering hidden patterns and relationships that fuel innovation and strategic advantage. As organizations grapple with increasingly complex datasets, advanced visualization techniques have become essential tools for business professionals aiming to transform intricate data into actionable insights. This chapter delves into the cutting edge of data visualization, equipping you with the skills to decipher and communicate high-dimensional stories that conventional charts simply cannot reveal.

Building on the foundational principles explored earlier in this book, you will now discover how to visualize multiple variables simultaneously, map business dynamics across geographic regions, and illuminate connections within sprawling networks. The chapter introduces innovative approaches such as multivariate and high-dimensional plotting, geospatial mapping for regional analysis, and network charts that reveal relationships often overlooked in tabular reports. You'll also learn how to leverage predictive and prescriptive visuals to support forward-thinking decisions, and how animation can breathe life into your data stories, capturing attention and driving engagement.

To ground these concepts in practical reality, we'll examine their applications in global supply chain analytics—a field where advanced visualizations can spotlight inefficiencies, optimize logistics, and mitigate risk. Throughout, you'll encounter real-world examples and expert tips that bridge technical depth with business relevance, ensuring you can apply these techniques confidently within your organization. As you progress, you'll not only elevate your visualization toolkit but also amplify your influence as a data storyteller, prepared to meet the demands of today's competitive, data-rich world.

## 10.1. Multivariate and High-Dimensional Data

As data complexity grows, business decisions increasingly rely on understanding relationships among multiple variables simultaneously. Multivariate and high-dimensional data present unique challenges and opportunities for data storytellers. Unlike simple bar charts or line graphs, visualizing these intricate data structures demands advanced techniques that reveal meaningful patterns without overwhelming the audience.

### *The Challenge of Multivariate Data*

Multivariate data refers to datasets containing more than two variables. High-dimensional data takes this further, often involving dozens or even hundreds of variables, as seen in customer segmentation, market analysis, or risk assessment projects. Traditional visualization methods may obscure insights or lead to information overload in these scenarios.

To effectively communicate stories from such data, it is essential to use visualization strategies that clarify rather than complicate. The choice of technique and tool can make the difference between confusion and actionable insight.

### *Core Visualization Techniques*

Several visualization approaches are designed to handle multivariate and high-dimensional data. Each offers a distinct way to explore and present complex relationships:

**Scatterplot Matrix (SPLOM):** Displays pairwise relationships between variables in a grid of scatterplots. This is valuable for identifying correlations and outliers across many variables.

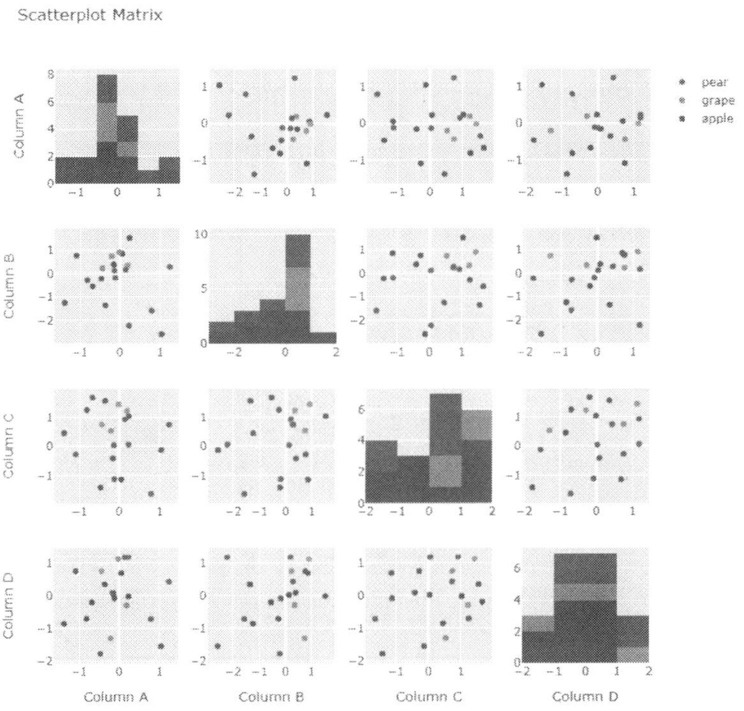

**Parallel Coordinates Plot:** Represents each variable as a vertical axis; data points are lines crossing the axes at corresponding values. This technique is powerful for highlighting clusters, trends, and anomalies in high-dimensional datasets.

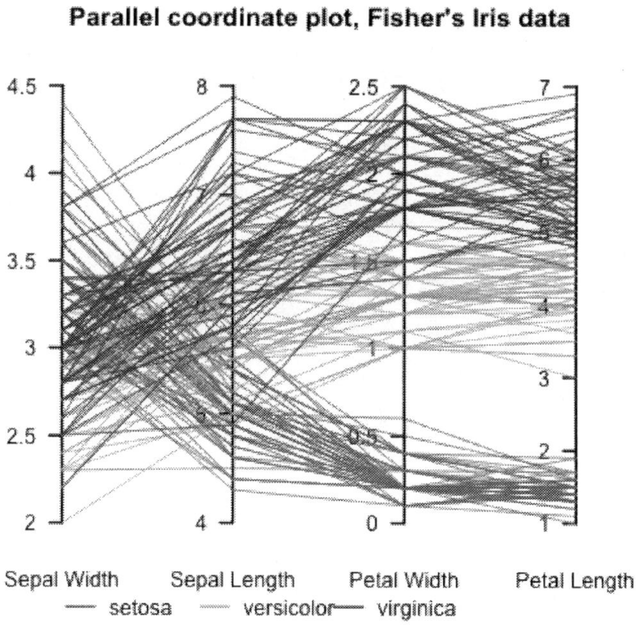


**Heatmaps:** Use color gradients to represent values in a matrix, often supplemented with hierarchical clustering. Heatmaps are effective in visualizing patterns in large datasets, such as product affinity or customer behavior matrices.

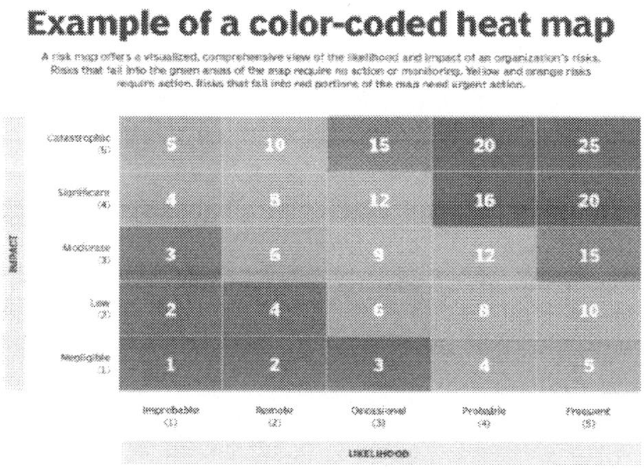

**Bubble Charts:** Extend scatterplots by encoding a third variable using the size of the data points, which helps in comparing three variables at once.

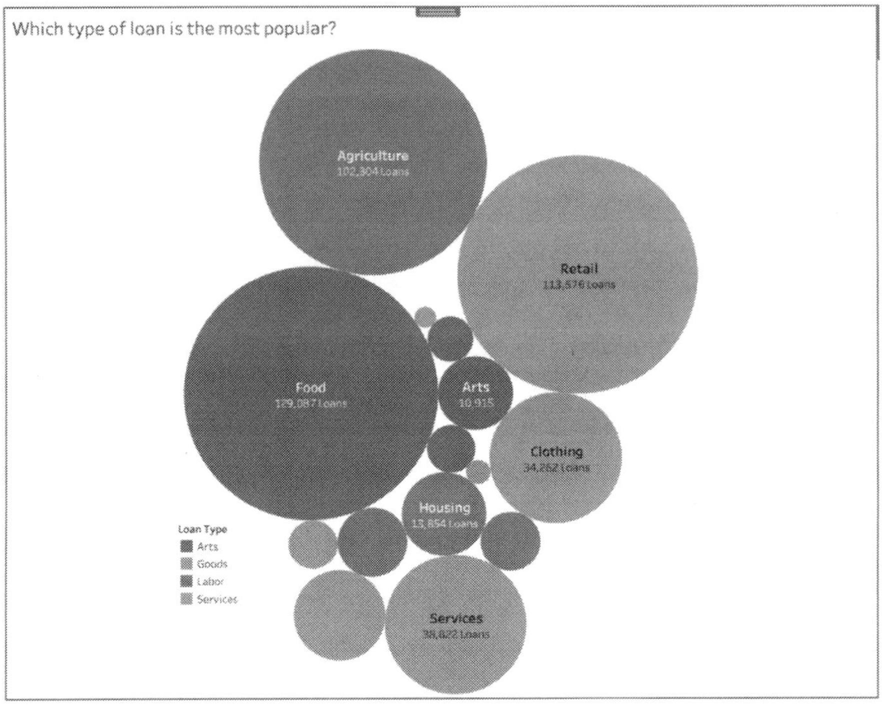


**Dimensionality Reduction (e.g., PCA, t-SNE):** Algorithms like Principal Component Analysis (PCA) or t-distributed Stochastic Neighbor Embedding (t-SNE) reduce the number of variables to two or three principal components, making it possible to visualize complex relationships in lower-dimensional plots.

### *Toolkits for Business Application*

Modern visualization tools such as Tableau and Power BI have robust support for multivariate analysis. These platforms enable users to create interactive dashboards that empower stakeholders to explore data from multiple perspectives.

For instance, in **Tableau**, users can easily construct scatterplot matrices or parallel coordinates plots by dragging multiple variables onto the visual canvas. Conditional formatting, tooltips, and dynamic filters further enhance exploration. **Power BI** offers similar flexibility, with customizable visuals and integration with Python or R scripts for advanced analytics.

#### Example: Customer Segmentation Dashboard

Consider a global retailer seeking to improve personalized marketing. Analysts compile a dataset with customer demographics, purchase history, web activity, and loyalty program status—each representing different variables.

Using Tableau, the team builds a dashboard featuring:

- A parallel coordinates plot illustrating how customer groups differ by age, spending habits, and loyalty engagement.
- A heatmap showing product affinity across segments, revealing untapped cross-selling opportunities.
- Interactive filters allowing marketing managers in different regions (e.g., North America, Asia-Pacific) to focus on local customer patterns.

This multivariate storytelling approach enables regional teams to tailor campaigns more precisely, boosting engagement and sales.

#### *Real-World Scenario: Financial Risk Analysis*

A multinational bank needs to assess credit risk across its diverse loan portfolio. The dataset includes variables such as borrower age, income, loan amount, repayment history, geographic location, and macroeconomic indicators.

The analytics team uses Power BI to create a dashboard featuring:

- A bubble chart comparing loan size, default probability, and borrower income, with color coding for geographic region.
- A scatterplot matrix to detect correlations among risk drivers.
- PCA to distill dozens of variables into two key risk dimensions, visualized as a 2D plot for executive review.

These visuals help risk officers quickly identify high-risk segments and allocate resources for further investigation, supporting data-driven decision-making across global markets.

#### *Best Practices for High-Dimensional Storytelling*

When working with multivariate and high-dimensional data, clarity is paramount. Keep these best practices in mind:

- **Avoid clutter:** Limit the number of variables shown at once, using interactivity or filters to manage complexity.
- **Explain your visuals:** Provide clear legends, labels, and tooltips to guide interpretation.
- **Tell a focused story:** Emphasize the variables and relationships most relevant to your business objective.

Effectively visualizing multivariate and high-dimensional data transforms overwhelming complexity into compelling, actionable stories. By leveraging advanced techniques and interactive tools, you empower stakeholders to uncover hidden insights and drive impactful business outcomes.

## 10.2. Geospatial Visualizations

As data storytelling matures, the ability to contextualize information in relation to geography becomes a critical differentiator. Geospatial visualizations empower business professionals to uncover patterns, trends, and insights that are often invisible in tabular data. By integrating location-based data into your visual narratives, you not only enhance clarity but also drive action rooted in real-world context.

Geospatial visualizations are particularly powerful in sectors such as retail, logistics, marketing, and public health. These techniques allow you to display data points geographically, revealing region-specific opportunities and challenges. When executed thoughtfully, geospatial visualizations can bridge the gap between abstract numbers and tangible business impact.

### *Fundamentals of Geospatial Visualization*

At its core, a geospatial visualization maps data to physical locations. This approach can range from simple point maps marking store locations to complex heatmaps illustrating customer density or sales performance by region. The choice of visualization depends on your data, narrative goals, and audience.

Key types of geospatial visualizations include:

**Choropleth Maps**: Display data aggregated by regions (e.g., countries, states, postal codes), using color intensity to represent value.

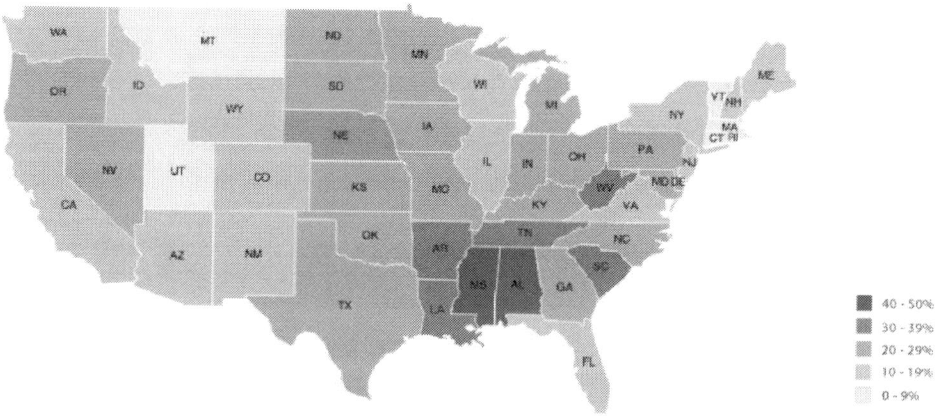

**Point Maps**: Plot individual data points (e.g., customer addresses, delivery sites) on a map.

**Heatmaps**: Show concentration or intensity of activity over a geographic area.

**Flow Maps**: Illustrate movement or migration, such as supply chain routes or commuter flows.

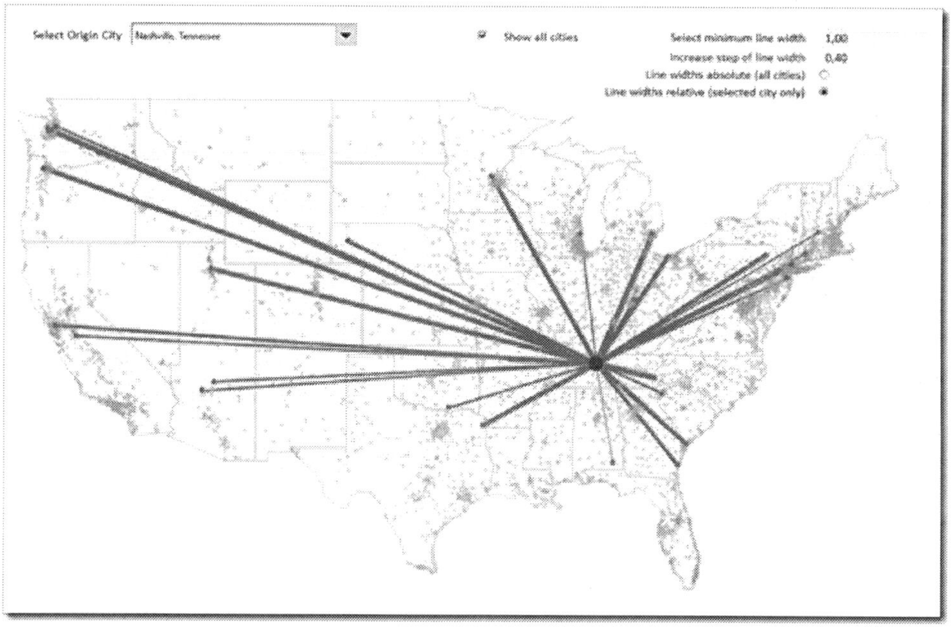


***Tools and Techniques for Creating Geospatial Visualizations***

Modern business intelligence platforms offer robust geospatial visualization capabilities. Notable examples include:

**Tableau**: Provides native geographic mapping, layered visualizations, and integration with external map sources. Tableau's drag-and-drop interface makes it accessible to both analysts and business users.

**Power BI**: Features customizable maps, integration with Bing Maps, and support for spatial data types. Power BI's dashboarding capabilities allow for seamless integration of geospatial visuals with other business metrics.

**QGIS**: An open-source GIS tool for advanced spatial analysis, suitable for organizations requiring in-depth geographic capabilities.

**Google Maps Platform**: Enables custom map creation and integration into web-based dashboards, ideal for real-time or location-aware business applications.

Here's a sample Power BI code snippet to plot store locations and sales volumes on a map:

```
Map.Visualize(
    Data: StoreLocations,
    Latitude: "Lat",
    Longitude: "Long",
    Size: "SalesVolume"
)
```

### *Business Dashboards: Bringing Geospatial Data to Life*

Effective geospatial dashboards combine interactive maps with supporting charts and KPIs, allowing users to explore data from multiple angles. For example, a retail dashboard might integrate a choropleth map of sales by region with a bar chart of top-performing stores, enabling quick identification of geographic strengths and weaknesses.

Consider these dashboard design tips:

**Contextual Filters**: Allow users to zoom in on specific locations or filter by business unit.

**Layered Data**: Combine multiple map layers (e.g., customer demographics and competitor locations) for richer insights.

**Responsive Interaction**: Ensure maps update dynamically when other dashboard elements are selected.

### *Real-World Use Cases*

To illustrate the transformative power of geospatial visualizations, let's examine two business scenarios:

**1. Retail Market Expansion**

A multinational retailer in Southeast Asia used Tableau to analyze sales performance across cities. By overlaying sales data with population density maps, the company pinpointed high-potential areas for expansion. The visualization revealed underserved neighborhoods near major transport hubs, leading to strategic site selection and a 15% increase in new store profitability.

**2. Logistics Optimization**

A European logistics firm leveraged Power BI's mapping features to monitor delivery routes and identify bottlenecks. By visualizing shipment delays and route efficiency on a flow map, the firm discovered that certain urban zones consistently experienced traffic-related slowdowns. This insight prompted route adjustments and improved on-time delivery rates, enhancing customer satisfaction.

These cases demonstrate how geospatial storytelling not only clarifies the "where" but also guides impactful, data-driven decisions.

#### *Best Practices and Considerations*

As you integrate geospatial visualizations into your business narratives, keep these principles in mind:

- **Simplicity**: Avoid clutter. Only display geographic detail relevant to your story.
- **Accessibility**: Use colorblind-friendly palettes and clear legends for broader inclusivity.
- **Cultural Sensitivity**: Ensure maps respect political boundaries and local naming conventions, especially for global organizations.

Concluding this section, geospatial visualizations bridge the abstract and the concrete, translating data into actionable insights anchored in location. As you master these techniques, your data stories become more persuasive and actionable, driving strategic decisions across your organization.

### 10.3. Network and Relationship Charts

In the evolving landscape of data storytelling, understanding the intricate web of relationships within your data is a powerful way to reveal hidden insights and strategic opportunities. Network and relationship charts are advanced visualization tools that move beyond linear or unidimensional representations, enabling you to map connections, dependencies, and influences among entities. Unlike traditional charts that focus on numeric trends or categorical comparisons, these visualizations illuminate the complex interplay between people, organizations, products, or even abstract concepts.

#### *Fundamentals of Network and Relationship Charts*

At their core, network charts (often called graph visualizations) represent data as nodes (entities) and edges (relationships). Each node signifies an actor—such as a customer, department, or asset—while edges illustrate the interactions or relationships linking these actors. Relationship charts can take multiple forms, including force-directed graphs, chord diagrams, and matrix visualizations, each suited to different types of relational data.

The value of these visualizations lies in their ability to:

- Uncover clusters or communities within large datasets
- Identify influential nodes (such as key decision-makers or central products)

- Detect bottlenecks, redundancies, or vulnerabilities in processes or communication flows

When crafted thoughtfully, network charts do not just map relationships, they tell stories about influence, collaboration, risk, and opportunity.

#### *Business Applications: Real-World Scenarios*

To appreciate the practical impact of network and relationship charts, consider these business scenarios:

### 1. Global Supply Chain Optimization (Manufacturing Sector)

A multinational electronics manufacturer uses network graphs in Tableau to visualize its supplier ecosystem. Each node represents a supplier, and edges denote supply dependencies. By filtering by region, procurement managers identify clusters of suppliers at risk due to geopolitical disruptions. The visualization highlights over-reliance on a single supplier in Southeast Asia, prompting the company to diversify sourcing and mitigate potential production delays.

### 2. Customer Journey Mapping (Retail and E-commerce)

A leading e-commerce platform leverages Power BI to construct a network chart mapping customer interactions across multiple touchpoints—website visits, social media engagement, and in-store purchases. Nodes depict individual customers, while edges show shared behaviors or referrals. By spotting highly connected clusters, marketing teams identify brand advocates and design targeted loyalty programs, enhancing customer retention and cross-sell opportunities.

These examples illustrate how network charts bring relational data to life, helping businesses make smarter, more informed decisions rooted in the structure of their own ecosystems.

#### *Visualization Tools and Techniques*

Modern BI tools like **Tableau** and **Power BI** offer robust options for building network and relationship charts, though their complexity often requires intermediate to advanced proficiency. For more intricate or interactive needs, open-source libraries such as D3.js or Gephi provide additional flexibility.

**Tableau** supports network graph creation through custom calculations and extensions, allowing users to import edge and node lists. **Power BI** uses custom visuals—like the Network Navigator chart—to render interactive networks for business dashboards.

Here's a simplified example of how a node-edge list might be structured for importing into a visualization tool:

```
Source, Target, Relationship, Strength
SupplierA, ManufacturerX, Supplies, 0.8
SupplierB, ManufacturerX, Supplies, 0.5
ManufacturerX, RetailerZ, ShipsTo, 1.0
```

This list can be visualized to instantly reveal supplier dependencies and the flow of goods.

When designing network charts:

- Limit visual clutter by filtering for key nodes or relationships
- Use color and size to emphasize node importance or connection strength
- Provide interactive options (such as zoom or filter) in dashboards to help users explore details relevant to their role

#### *Integrating Network Charts into Business Dashboards*

Embedding network and relationship charts into executive dashboards adds context and depth to standard KPIs. For example, a sales dashboard might include a network view of top clients and their referral trees, revealing which relationships drive the most business. Similarly, an IT risk dashboard could map system dependencies, highlighting critical nodes where outages would cascade.

Always pair network charts with succinct annotations or narrative cues to guide interpretation. By doing so, you bridge the gap between sophisticated data structures and actionable business insights.

Network and relationship charts unlock a new dimension of data storytelling by visualizing the connections that underpin business dynamics. As you integrate these advanced charts into your toolkit, you empower stakeholders to see patterns and opportunities that static tables or simple bar charts might miss.

### 10.4. Predictive and Prescriptive Visuals

Building on our understanding of narrative-driven design, advanced data storytelling often demands more than describing what has happened or is happening. To truly elevate your business impact, you must guide your audience toward actionable decisions by visualizing what is likely to happen next, and what actions should be taken. This is where **predictive and prescriptive visuals** come into play, transforming static dashboards into dynamic decision-support systems.

*Demystifying Predictive and Prescriptive Visuals*

**Predictive visuals** leverage historical and real-time data to forecast future outcomes. These charts and dashboards often incorporate statistical models, machine learning outputs, or trend analyses to provide a glimpse into what may occur if current conditions persist.

**Prescriptive visuals** go a step further by not only forecasting possible outcomes but also recommending specific actions based on those predictions. They integrate optimization models or scenario analyses, helping users evaluate the impact of different decisions.

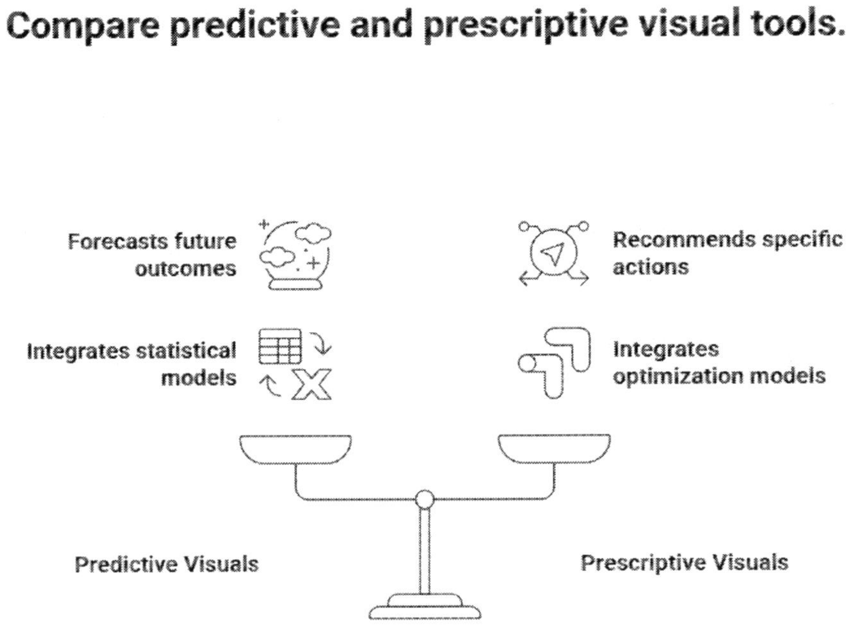


Both types of visuals empower business leaders to move from descriptive analytics ("What happened?") to forward-thinking analytics ("What should we do next?").

*Key Visualization Techniques*

Effective predictive and prescriptive visuals require thoughtful design choices and tool selection. Let's explore several foundational approaches:

- **Forecasting Charts**
  - Line and area charts are frequently used to project trends. Adding confidence intervals (shaded regions) helps illustrate prediction uncertainty.

- **Tool Example**: In Tableau, you can add a forecasting model to a time series, which automatically displays predicted values and confidence bands.
- **Business Application**: A retail company forecasts weekly sales using historical purchase data, with the dashboard highlighting likely peaks and troughs to optimize inventory.

- **What-If Analysis Dashboards**

  - Interactive dashboards enable users to manipulate variables (like pricing or marketing spend) and instantly see potential outcomes.
    - **Tool Example**: Power BI's "What-If" parameters allow users to adjust inputs and visualize how those changes affect forecasted results.
    - **Business Application**: A global telecommunications provider models the impact of different pricing strategies on customer churn rates, displaying optimal combinations for retention.

- **Scenario Planning Visuals**

  - Decision trees, Sankey diagrams, or scenario matrices help visualize the outcomes of multiple choices under varying conditions.
    - **Tool Example**: Python libraries such as Plotly or D3.js are often used for highly customized scenario trees.
    - **Business Application**: An energy company uses scenario matrices to present the financial and environmental impact of adopting renewable energy sources under different regulatory futures.

- **Prescriptive Model Outputs**

  - Optimization dashboards display recommended actions, often using color-coded indicators or ranked lists.
    - **Tool Example**: Tableau's integration with Python (TabPy) enables real-time optimization outputs to be visualized alongside business data.
    - **Business Application**: A manufacturing firm uses prescriptive dashboards to recommend daily production schedules, factoring in demand forecasts, resource constraints, and operational costs.

### *Real-World Business Scenarios*

Let's examine how advanced organizations leverage predictive and prescriptive visuals to drive meaningful outcomes:

#### Scenario 1: Healthcare Resource Planning

A hospital system in Singapore implemented predictive dashboards to forecast patient inflow during flu season. By visualizing predicted admission spikes and overlaying recommended staffing levels, administrators proactively adjusted shift schedules and resource allocation, improving patient care and reducing overtime costs.

#### Scenario 2: E-commerce Personalization

A European e-commerce retailer uses Power BI to visualize customer lifetime value predictions, segmenting users by expected future purchases. The dashboard presents prescriptive recommendations for targeted offers and personalized marketing campaigns. By acting on these insights, the business increased repeat purchases and customer satisfaction.

### *Best Practices for Maximum Impact*

To ensure predictive and prescriptive visuals drive action and clarity:

- Clearly indicate **forecasted vs. historical data** using distinct colors or line styles.
- Visually communicate **uncertainty** with confidence intervals, error bars, or scenario bands.
- Enable **interactivity** so users can explore different scenarios and inputs.
- Provide concise **narrative context**—explain what the predictions mean and why recommended actions matter.
- Regularly validate and update models to maintain trust and relevance.

Predictive and prescriptive visuals represent the pinnacle of data storytelling, turning insight into foresight and strategy. By mastering these techniques, you empower stakeholders to not only understand potential futures but to act decisively.

## 10.5. Animation and Storytelling

Building on the advanced visualization techniques discussed earlier, animation emerges as a dynamic tool for bringing data stories to life. While static charts and dashboards lay the foundation, animation infuses movement, guiding the viewer's attention, emphasizing trends, and connecting data points over time. When used effectively, animation can transform even the most complex analytics into engaging, persuasive business narratives that drive decisions and inspire action.

#### *Why Animation Matters in Data Storytelling*

Animation is far more than a cosmetic feature. It supports cognitive processing by:

- Demonstrating change over time, which is crucial for time-series analysis or tracking progress toward goals.
- Highlighting cause-and-effect relationships, making it easier to trace the impact of business decisions or external factors.
- Directing focus to key insights through controlled sequencing, reducing information overload.
- Fostering emotional engagement, as viewers are more likely to remember moving visuals than static ones.

For business professionals, these capabilities mean your message is not just seen, but truly understood.

#### *Practical Applications in Business Contexts*

To illustrate the power of animation in data storytelling, consider the following real-world scenarios:

### 1. Sales Performance Dashboards

A multinational retailer uses Tableau to animate quarterly sales data across regions. By animating a map, stakeholders can observe how a new marketing campaign influences sales progression from one quarter to the next. The animation not only highlights surges in specific regions but also makes the tempo and scale of change visually intuitive.

### 2. Financial Forecasting Presentations

A global bank leverages Power BI's "Play Axis" to animate year-over-year changes in loan portfolios. As the animation advances, viewers see how different risk categories expand or contract, making it easy for executives to pinpoint when and why risk levels shifted—information that would be difficult to discern in static tables or charts.

These examples demonstrate how animation can clarify trends, spotlight turning points, and narrate the story behind the numbers in a compelling, business-relevant way.

### *Implementing Animation in Visualization Tools*

Most leading data visualization platforms offer built-in animation features. Understanding how to deploy them effectively is crucial for advanced practitioners.

#### Tableau

Tableau's "Pages" shelf allows users to animate data across dimensions such as time or categories. By dragging a dimension (like date) onto Pages, the visualization progresses through each period, showing the evolution of metrics.

Example: Animate a scatter plot to show how product profitability shifts each month, making it easy to correlate performance with marketing activities or external events.

#### Power BI

Power BI's "Play Axis" custom visual animates data along a chosen axis, such as time or category. This is especially powerful for dashboards tracking metrics like customer acquisition, inventory levels, or campaign performance.

Example: Create an animated bar chart race comparing market share among competitors over several years, emphasizing competitive dynamics and strategic inflection points.

#### Practical Code Example: Animated Line Chart in Python (Plotly)

For teams preferring custom solutions, libraries like Plotly enable interactive, animated charts. Consider this simplified Python example:

```
import plotly.express as px
df = px.data.gapminder()
fig = px.line(df, x="year", y="gdpPercap", animation_frame="year",
color="continent",
              line_group="country", hover_name="country")
fig.show()
```

This code animates GDP per capita trends by continent and country, reinforcing how movement can make complex global patterns accessible and memorable.

### *Best Practices for Animated Storytelling*

While animation captivates, it must be purposeful. To maximize impact:

- **Define the narrative arc**: Use animation to support a clear beginning, middle, and end, guiding the audience through the story.
- **Control pacing**: Allow viewers enough time to absorb each stage but avoid unnecessary delays that can distract or frustrate.

- **Emphasize key transitions**: Use pauses, highlights, or callouts to draw attention to pivotal moments or outliers.
- **Test accessibility**: Ensure that animations are not overwhelming and are accessible to audiences with varying abilities.

Animation elevates data storytelling by transforming static insights into kinetic narratives, making trends, patterns, and relationships both visible and memorable. As you incorporate animation into your advanced visualization toolkit, remember its power lies in clarity and intent, not mere spectacle.

## 10.6. Practical Application: Supply Chain Analytics

Supply chain analytics offers fertile ground for advanced visualization techniques, where dynamic data flows, multifaceted relationships, and time-sensitive decisions demand clarity and precision. For business professionals, transforming supply chain data into compelling visual stories is crucial to optimize processes, manage risk, and fuel strategic growth. Leveraging modern tools and thoughtful design, advanced learners can build dashboards and narratives that not only inform but also inspire decisive action across global operations.

### *Contextualizing Supply Chain Data for Storytelling*

Before diving into visualization, consider the unique storytelling opportunities within supply chain analytics. Data points—such as inventory levels, shipment status, supplier reliability, and demand forecasts—can be overwhelming in raw form. By contextualizing these figures within a narrative, you empower stakeholders to quickly grasp bottlenecks, anticipate disruptions, and identify growth opportunities.

For instance, a global manufacturer might face delays due to port congestion in Asia. A well-crafted visualization reveals not only the where and when but also the domino effect on distribution centers in Europe and North America. This narrative approach helps shift supply chain conversations from reactive troubleshooting to proactive strategy.

### *Building Advanced Dashboards: Tools and Techniques*

Today, tools like **Tableau** and **Power BI** enable the creation of sophisticated supply chain dashboards. These platforms support multi-layered visualizations that can display real-time updates, interactive filters, and drill-down capabilities. Here's how advanced learners can approach building a supply chain analytics dashboard:

#### Identify Key Metrics and Questions

Start by collaborating with stakeholders to determine which metrics matter most—such as lead times, fill rates, transportation costs, and supplier performance. Frame these metrics around critical business questions: Where are delays most frequent? Which suppliers are most reliable? How do inventory levels align with sales forecasts?

### Select Appropriate Visualization Types

Advanced techniques might include:

- **Network diagrams:** Map supplier-customer relationships to highlight dependencies.
- **Sankey diagrams:** Visualize the flow of goods and information through the supply chain, pinpointing inefficiencies.
- **Heatmaps:** Identify regions or time periods with high levels of stockouts or disruptions.
- **Animated timelines:** Show the evolution of shipments, orders, or disruptions over time for trend analysis.

### Design for Actionability

Integrate interactive elements, such as filters for regions, products, or suppliers. Use color strategically—for example, highlighting at-risk shipments in red or on-time deliveries in green. Ensure the dashboard guides the user's attention from high-level overviews to granular details.

### Embed Narrative Elements

Incorporate annotations, tooltips, or embedded text summaries that provide context, highlight anomalies, or suggest next steps. This ensures that even non-technical stakeholders can quickly interpret the data story.

#### Example: Multinational Retailer Dashboard in Power BI

Consider a multinational retailer facing fluctuating demand and volatile shipping costs. Using Power BI, the analytics team constructs a dashboard featuring:

- An interactive map displaying real-time shipment status across continents
- A Sankey diagram tracing product flow from suppliers to distribution centers to retail outlets
- A heatmap overlay pinpointing regions with high transportation costs
- Trend lines forecasting inventory levels against sales projections

By weaving together these advanced visuals, the dashboard tells a vivid story: it not only shows where bottlenecks exist but also uncovers why they happen and how they impact profitability. This empowers executives to prioritize urgent shipments, renegotiate with underperforming suppliers, or adjust inventory strategies in near real-time.

**Example: Pharmaceutical Supply Chain Scenario in Tableau**

A pharmaceutical company navigating global vaccine distribution uses Tableau to create a dashboard that:

Animates shipment timelines from production sites to clinics worldwide
Uses color-coded risk indicators for countries experiencing customs delays
Embeds narrative commentary explaining regulatory hurdles and mitigation strategies

This approach transforms abstract logistics data into a human-centric story: it highlights the critical path vaccines travel, the potential impact of delays, and the collaborative efforts needed to ensure timely delivery. Such visualization facilitates cross-functional alignment and rapid response in a high-stakes environment.

Advanced visualization techniques in supply chain analytics elevate simple data reporting into strategic storytelling, empowering organizations to act swiftly and confidently. By leveraging tools like Tableau and Power BI, and by designing dashboards that blend interactivity with narrative, business professionals can translate complexity into clarity.

## 10.7. Reflection and Advanced Tips

As you advance your data storytelling skills, it's essential to step back and critically reflect on your visualizations. Mastery comes not just from technical proficiency, but from a deep understanding of how visuals impact business decisions, influence stakeholders, and adapt to diverse audiences. This section synthesizes advanced strategies and offers actionable insights for refining your practice, ensuring your data stories achieve their maximum business impact.

***The Power of Iterative Refinement***

Advanced data storytellers recognize that the first draft of any visualization is rarely the best. The process of iterative refinement — revisiting your visual, gathering feedback, and optimizing for clarity — is crucial in transforming good stories into great ones. This approach is especially vital in high-stakes business environments, where small improvements can have significant consequences.

**Solicit Stakeholder Feedback:** Share preliminary dashboards or visuals with a representative slice of your intended audience. Ask for specific feedback on clarity, relevance, and emotional resonance.

**A/B Test Variations:** In tools like Tableau or Power BI, create multiple versions of a chart or dashboard. Test which version drives better comprehension or action within your team.

**Revisit Your Narrative:** As new data emerges or business priorities shift, update your story. A living dashboard should evolve alongside business objectives.

### *Tool-Specific Tips for Advanced Users*

With experience, leveraging the full power of visualization platforms becomes second nature. Here are some advanced tips for getting the most out of leading tools:

**Tableau:** Use calculated fields to create dynamic annotations, parameter controls for user-driven scenarios, and story points to guide viewers through a sequential narrative.

**Power BI:** Implement bookmarks to toggle between different analytical views, leverage DAX for complex business logic, and use Power BI's natural language Q&A feature to allow non-technical users to interact with data.

**Cross-Platform Integration:** Consider embedding dashboards directly into business applications (such as Salesforce or custom portals) to bring insights closer to daily workflows.

### *Beyond the Visual: Storytelling as an Ongoing Dialogue*

Advanced data storytelling is not a one-way broadcast. Treat every dashboard or data narrative as the beginning of a conversation with your audience. Foster a culture where stakeholders feel comfortable asking questions, challenging assumptions, and suggesting new perspectives. This ongoing dialogue not only leads to better data quality but also ensures your insights remain relevant and actionable.

In mastering advanced visualization techniques, you evolve from simply presenting data to orchestrating impactful business stories that drive real outcomes. Whether refining dashboards for global teams or tailoring financial visuals for investors, your role as a data storyteller is never static.

# 11. AVOIDING PITFALLS AND ENSURING DATA INTEGRITY

In the fast-paced world of business, a single misleading chart or inaccurate data point can erode trust, derail decision-making, and undermine even the most compelling story. As organizations increasingly rely on data-driven narratives to influence strategy and engage stakeholders, the stakes for getting it right have never been higher. This chapter serves as your essential guide to navigating the most common pitfalls in data visualization and storytelling, empowering you to deliver insights with confidence, clarity, and integrity.

Building on the skills and principles introduced throughout this book, you will explore the subtle yet critical errors that can occur when visualizing and communicating data, from misrepresenting trends to overlooking data quality issues. You'll learn proven strategies for ensuring data accuracy and transparency, laying the foundation for trustworthy analysis that stands up to scrutiny in any boardroom or client meeting.

Ethics and inclusivity take center stage as we examine how to tell stories that are not only compelling but also fair, responsible, and accessible to diverse audiences. Through real-world business case studies—including both successes and instructive failures—you'll discover how organizations across industries and cultures have navigated challenges, learned from mistakes, and elevated their data storytelling practices.

This chapter concludes with practical tools and a reflection checklist to help you embed integrity into your workflow. By mastering these principles, you'll not only avoid costly errors but also strengthen your reputation as a thoughtful, ethical data storyteller. Let's dive in and ensure every story you tell with data is accurate, inclusive, and impactful.

## 11.1. Common Visualization Mistakes

As business leaders and data professionals become adept at leveraging data visualization, the risk of falling into common traps increases. Even seasoned analysts and executives can inadvertently undermine their message by misrepresenting data, overwhelming audiences, or neglecting context. Recognizing and avoiding these visualization mistakes is essential for maintaining credibility, ensuring data integrity, and maximizing business impact.

### *Misleading Visual Encodings*

One of the most damaging errors is using visual elements that distort the underlying data. This often happens when scales, axes, or proportions are manipulated, intentionally or not, leading to misinterpretation.

For example, truncating the y-axis on a bar or line chart can artificially exaggerate differences, making minor changes appear dramatic. While tools like Tableau and Power BI allow customization of axes, they also provide warnings and options to default to zero-based axes—best used unless a compelling reason exists otherwise.

Consider a global marketing team presenting quarterly sales growth. If the y-axis starts at 90 instead of 0, a modest 2% sales increase might appear as a steep surge, prompting misplaced urgency or celebration. Maintaining proportional scaling preserves trust and analytical integrity.

### *Overloading with Information*

Another frequent mistake is cramming dashboards or reports with excessive metrics, colors, or chart types. Overly dense visuals hinder comprehension and dilute key messages.

A case in point: a retail operations team in Southeast Asia builds a Power BI dashboard to track store performance. In an effort to be comprehensive, they include 15 metrics, four chart types, and a color-coded map—all on a single screen. The result is cognitive overload, with decision-makers struggling to discern priorities or actionable insights.

The remedy is thoughtful curation. Focus each visualization on a single business question, and present only the most relevant metrics. Use white space and grouping to guide the viewer's attention, and resist the temptation to showcase every available data point.

### *Inappropriate Chart Selection*

Choosing the wrong chart type for your data can obscure key findings or even mislead the audience. For instance, using a pie chart to represent trends over time, or a stacked bar chart for unrelated categories, can confuse stakeholders.

A multinational logistics company illustrated this when they used a 3D pie chart to show shipment delays by region. Not only did the 3D effect make it hard to compare slices, but the pie format itself was ill-suited for highlighting trends or patterns. A simple bar chart would have provided clearer, more actionable insight.

Visualization platforms like Tableau offer recommendations for chart types based on the data's structure, but advanced users should always consider the nature of their audience and the story they're trying to tell. Ask: Does this chart make the comparison easy and intuitive?

### *Ignoring Context and Annotations*

Charts and dashboards divorced from context are vulnerable to misinterpretation. Failing to define axes, units, or data sources leaves audiences guessing and can erode confidence in the analysis.

In a business intelligence dashboard designed for a European fintech startup, a line chart showed "User Growth" over time. However, the axis was unlabeled, and it was unclear whether the figures represented thousands, millions, or percentages. This omission led to confusion and skepticism among investors.

Effective data storytellers use annotations, legends, and clear titles to provide essential context, ensuring that all viewers—regardless of background—can interpret visualizations accurately.

### *Aesthetic Issues: Color, Font, and Visual Clutter*

Visual polish matters. Misusing color, font, or shape can distract, mislead, or even exclude viewers. Common pitfalls include:

Overusing bright or similar colors, which can hinder readability or accessibility for color-blind users.
Employing decorative fonts or excessive italics/bold, which can reduce clarity.
Adding unnecessary graphics or 3D effects, which may obscure the data itself.

Visualization tools like Power BI now offer colorblind-friendly palettes and font guidelines. When designing for a multicultural, global audience, it's wise to test visuals for accessibility and clarity across diverse user groups.

### *Real-World Business Use Cases*

## Pharmaceutical Product Launch (Tableau Dashboard)

A global pharmaceutical company launched a new medication and used a Tableau dashboard to visualize early sales data. Eager to impress, the marketing team presented a dashboard cluttered with sales by region, demographic breakdowns, and competitor analysis—using a mix of treemaps, pie charts, and bubble charts. Executives struggled to discern the product's actual launch trajectory. By refocusing on a simple line chart comparing sales to target and annotating with key milestones, the team clarified the narrative and drove strategic alignment.

### Financial Services Customer Retention (Power BI Report)

A financial services firm in Latin America visualized customer retention rates using a stacked area chart. However, the chart's color scheme used nearly indistinguishable shades, and the legend was missing. As a result, regional managers misread retention trends, leading to misguided outreach strategies. After revising the chart with a distinct color palette and detailed annotations, the team improved understanding and decision-making across regions.

Avoiding common visualization mistakes is crucial for maintaining both data integrity and audience trust. By being mindful of visual encodings, information density, chart selection, context, and design details, business professionals can ensure their data stories are both compelling and credible. As you refine your approach, remember that the goal is not just to display data, but to drive meaningful action.

## 11.2. Ensuring Data Accuracy and Transparency

Building on our discussion of validation best practices, it's crucial to recognize that even the most visually stunning data stories can lose credibility if the underlying data is inaccurate or lacking transparency. As advanced practitioners, your responsibility extends beyond aesthetic design to include rigorous data stewardship. This commitment not only upholds ethical standards but also ensures your insights drive informed and confident business decisions.

#### *The Pillars of Data Accuracy*

Data accuracy is the foundation of impactful data storytelling. Inaccurate or outdated data can lead to misinformed strategies, loss of stakeholder trust, and, in some cases, significant financial or reputational damage. Ensuring accuracy involves a systematic approach, integrating both technical checks and business context.

To maintain data accuracy, consider the following:

- **Data Source Integrity:** Always verify the credibility and currency of your data sources. Whether data is extracted from internal databases or third-party providers, traceability is key.
- **Consistent Data Cleaning:** Develop repeatable processes for handling missing values, duplicates, and anomalies.

- **Automated Validation:** Leverage features in visualization tools like Tableau's Data Interpreter or Power BI's Query Editor to automate error detection and correction.
- **Collaborative Review:** Cross-functional validation with business stakeholders ensures that numbers align with business realities, not just technical correctness.

#### *Transparency in Data Storytelling*

Transparency is about making your data processes, assumptions, and limitations visible to your audience. In practice, this means documenting your methods and being upfront about uncertainties or potential biases. Transparent communication fosters trust and allows stakeholders to make decisions with a full understanding of the data's strengths and constraints.

##### Techniques for Enhancing Transparency

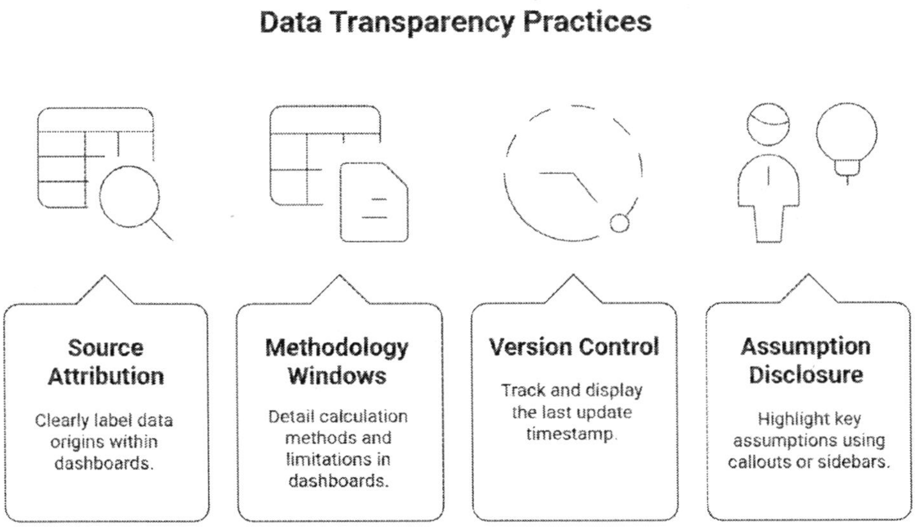


**Source Attribution:** Clearly label the origins of your data within dashboards or reports. For example, Tableau allows you to add footnotes or info icons linking to source documentation.

**Methodology Windows:** Incorporate expandable sections or tooltips in Power BI dashboards detailing calculation methods, data refresh schedules, and known limitations.

**Version Control:** Track and display the last update timestamp and dataset version, which is particularly important for rapidly evolving business environments.

**Assumption Disclosure:** Use callouts or sidebars to highlight key assumptions, such as market segmentation criteria or forecasting models.

***Real-World Scenario: Financial Services Dashboard***

A global bank headquartered in Singapore rolled out a Tableau-based executive dashboard to track loan performance across multiple regions. Initially, regional managers reported discrepancies between dashboard figures and local accounting records. Investigation revealed that different data refresh cycles were causing temporary mismatches.

To address this, the team implemented the following:

Automated data refresh schedules synchronized with regional closing times.
A visible timestamp on every dashboard page indicating the last update.
A tooltip explaining data aggregation logic, enabling users to understand how regional numbers rolled up to the global view.

This commitment to accuracy and transparency not only resolved confusion but also increased executive confidence in the dashboard's insights. As a result, the dashboard became a trusted tool for strategic decision-making, accelerating loan portfolio optimization across regions.

***Business Dashboard Illustration: Retail Sales Performance***

Imagine a multinational retail company using Power BI to visualize weekly sales performance. To ensure accuracy and transparency:

- The dashboard includes a data quality indicator, flagging when data feeds are incomplete or delayed.
- A sidebar documents the business rules applied, such as how sales returns are handled or how online and in-store channels are merged.
- Users can drill down to the raw transaction data for auditing, increasing confidence in the summarized insights.

By embedding these transparency features, the dashboard not only informs but also reassures users about the reliability of the reported figures.

***Visualization Tools: Built-in Features for Accuracy and Transparency***

Modern data visualization platforms offer robust tools to support your data integrity efforts:

**Tableau:** Data Source Filters, Data Quality Warnings, and built-in Lineage Tracking help maintain both accuracy and transparency.
**Power BI:** Dataflows for centralized cleaning, Data Profiling tools, and Auditing Logs enable thorough data governance.

**Qlik Sense:** Integrated data lineage and data quality dashboards allow users to trace data from source to visualization.

Each tool provides mechanisms to document, audit, and communicate the path data takes from source to story, ensuring stakeholders have both the insights and the context needed for action.

Ensuring data accuracy and transparency is not a one-time task but an ongoing discipline that underpins every effective data story. By embedding checks, documentation, and clear communication within your visualization processes, you safeguard your credibility and empower your audience to trust and act on your insights.

### 11.3. Ethical Storytelling with Data

Ethical storytelling with data is the compass that guides persuasive narratives away from manipulation and toward trust and transparency. As business professionals, your influence hinges not just on the clarity of your visualizations, but also on the integrity with which you present your insights. In the realm of advanced data storytelling, ethical considerations become even more critical: subtle choices in design, selection, and context can profoundly sway interpretation and business outcomes.

#### *Defining Ethical Data Storytelling*

Ethical storytelling means honoring the truth of your data while conveying it in a manner that is accessible, honest, and actionable. At its core, it involves:

**Accurate Representation:** Visual elements should reflect the underlying data faithfully, without exaggeration or omission.

**Transparency:** Clearly communicate sources, methodologies, and any limitations or assumptions.

**Audience Respect:** Recognize diverse backgrounds and avoid cultural bias or language that may mislead or exclude.

**Intentional Design:** Every visual choice should serve the narrative ethically, avoiding manipulative tactics such as truncated axes or misleading color schemes.

Ethical storytelling is not merely about avoiding falsehoods; it is about fostering informed decision-making and sustaining organizational credibility.

#### *Common Pitfalls and How to Avoid Them*

Advanced practitioners must be vigilant against subtle pitfalls that compromise ethical standards. These include:

**Cherry-Picking Data:** Selecting only data points that support a predetermined conclusion undermines the integrity of the narrative.

**Misleading Visuals:** Using disproportionate scales, omitted baselines, or ambiguous labels can distort meaning.

**Excessive Simplification:** Over-summarizing data can erase nuance and mask important trends or outliers.

**Cultural Insensitivity:** Icons, colors, or symbols may carry different meanings across cultures, risking misinterpretation.

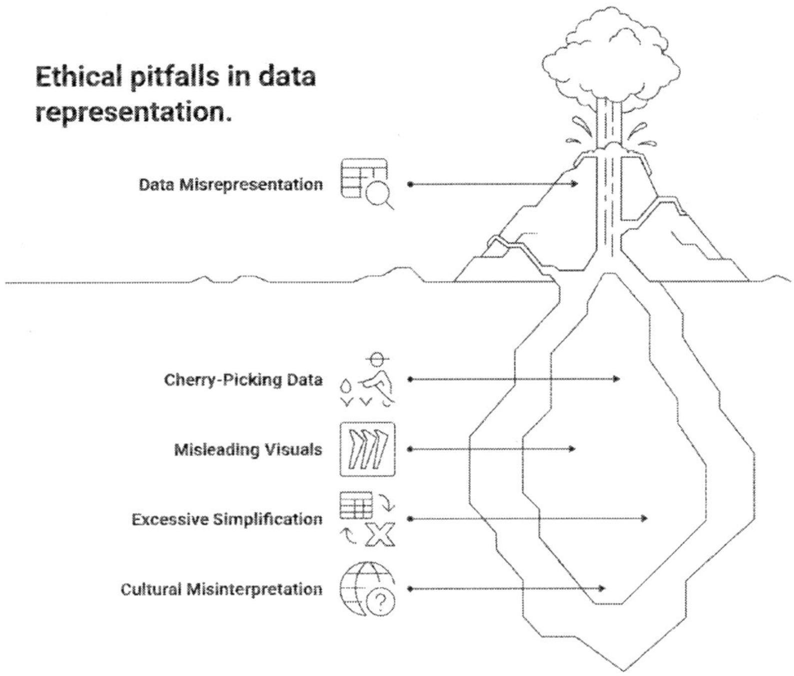


To avoid these pitfalls, always review your work with a critical eye and seek feedback from diverse stakeholders. When in doubt, err on the side of over-communication and transparency.

*Implementing Ethical Principles with Visualization Tools*

Modern visualization platforms like Tableau and Power BI offer powerful capabilities, but they also make it easy to inadvertently (or deliberately) mislead. Let's explore how to harness these tools ethically:

**Tableau:**

- Use **reference lines and annotations** to clarify context, such as historical baselines or forecast ranges.
- Ensure **axis scales** start at zero where appropriate to avoid amplifying differences.
- Leverage Tableau's **dashboard actions** to enable viewers to drill down into the data, promoting transparency and self-discovery.

**Power BI:**

- Apply **data tooltips** to offer additional context or definitions for metrics.
- Clearly label filters and slicers so users understand what subset of data they are viewing.
- Use **custom visuals** responsibly, ensuring they adhere to established best practices for clarity and accuracy.

**Business Dashboard Illustration:**

Consider a dashboard tracking global sales performance. An ethical approach would include:

- A **clearly indicated time range** and geographic scope.
- Visual cues (such as warning icons) if data for certain regions is incomplete.
- Contextual footnotes explaining currency conversions or market anomalies.
- A toggle or filter allowing users to compare normalized values, avoiding distortion due to currency fluctuations.

```
# Example: Adding a reference line in Tableau to indicate sales target

worksheet = Dashboard.add_worksheet( "Global Sales")
worksheet.add_bar_chart(data=sales_data, x= "Region", y= "Sales")
worksheet.add_reference_line(y=target_sales, label= "Target")
```

By embedding such features, you reinforce transparency and empower audiences to interpret the data responsibly.

***Real-World Use Cases***

Let's examine how ethical storytelling plays out in practice:

**Scenario 1: Pharmaceutical Launch Dashboard**

A European pharmaceutical firm preparing to launch a new drug used Power BI to visualize clinical trial results for executive decision-makers. The initial dashboard omitted data from a trial site with inconclusive results, leading to an overly optimistic narrative. After a peer review, the team restored this data and added clear annotations explaining its limitations. This ethical correction built executive trust and influenced a more cautious, phased launch strategy, ultimately protecting patient safety and corporate reputation.

**Scenario 2: Diversity Metrics in Technology Hiring**

A global technology company's HR analytics team used Tableau to present diversity hiring trends. Recognizing the potential for cultural insensitivity, the team engaged local stakeholders to review visual symbols and language. They also included context for regional hiring laws and socio-economic factors, ensuring the dashboard reflected not just numbers, but the nuanced realities of each market. This approach fostered candid dialogue and informed, culturally sensitive policy adjustments.

These cases underscore the business value of ethical storytelling: not only do you protect stakeholder interests, but you also enhance your credibility as a trusted advisor.

In summary, ethical storytelling with data is the foundation for sustainable business influence. By prioritizing accuracy, transparency, and cultural sensitivity, you transform data visualizations from persuasive tools into vehicles for truth and trust. As you advance in your data storytelling journey, keep ethics at the forefront—your reputation and business impact depend on it.

## 11.4. Designing for Inclusivity and Accessibility

As we move from auditing frameworks to the broader impact of our data visualizations, it is essential to address a critical aspect often overlooked: designing for inclusivity and accessibility. Creating visual stories that resonate across diverse audiences not only broadens your reach but also upholds ethical standards and strengthens your business case. In today's interconnected world, business decisions are made by teams with varied abilities, cultural backgrounds, and technological access. By ensuring that your data stories are inclusive and accessible, you empower every stakeholder to engage with your insights meaningfully.

### *Why Inclusivity and Accessibility Matter in Data Storytelling*

Inclusive and accessible design goes beyond compliance; it is a strategic advantage. When data visualizations are accessible to people with disabilities, adaptable to different cultural contexts, and considerate of technological constraints, your message gains clarity and credibility. In global organizations or markets, failing to address these factors can inadvertently exclude key decision-makers or customers, resulting in missed opportunities and reputational risks.

### *Key Principles of Inclusive and Accessible Data Visualization*

To design for all, consider the following foundational principles:

- **Clarity and Simplicity**: Avoid clutter and prioritize clarity. Simple layouts with clear hierarchies guide users' attention and reduce cognitive load.
- **Color Accessibility**: Use color palettes that are distinguishable by people with color vision deficiencies. Tools like Tableau's built-in color-blind palettes or Power BI's high-contrast themes can help.
- **Alternative Text and Descriptions**: Provide text alternatives for all visual elements. This supports screen readers and ensures understanding even if visuals cannot be seen.
- **Scalability and Device Responsiveness**: Ensure that visualizations remain legible across different screen sizes and devices, from laptops to smartphones.
- **Language and Cultural Sensitivity**: Use language and symbols that are culturally neutral or appropriately localized, avoiding idioms or icons that may not translate well globally.

### *Implementing Accessibility in Visualization Tools*

Modern business intelligence platforms offer features to support inclusive design, but thoughtful implementation is key. Here's how you can leverage popular tools:

**Tableau**:

- Use Tableau's "Color Blind" color palette to enhance color accessibility.
- Add descriptive captions and tooltips for charts and data points, supporting screen reader compatibility.
- Structure dashboards with logical tab orders for keyboard navigation.

**Power BI**:

- Apply high-contrast themes to improve visibility for users with low vision.
- Use the "Alt Text" field for each visual, providing a concise explanation of the data being shown.
- Power BI's accessibility checker can highlight issues and suggest improvements.

**Practical Example: Global Sales Dashboard**

Consider a multinational company presenting quarterly sales performance to regional managers in Europe, Asia, and North America. The dashboard, built in Power BI, incorporates:

- High-contrast themes for easy viewing in brightly lit conference rooms.
- Color palettes tested for color vision deficiencies.
- All visuals equipped with alt text, such as:

"Bar chart showing Q2 sales by region: Europe leads with $12M, followed by Asia at $9M, North America at $8M."

Filters and slicers accessible via keyboard navigation for those unable to use a mouse.

This approach ensures that every manager, regardless of ability or device, can interpret and act on the sales data.

*Case Study: Making Financial Reports Accessible*

A leading Singaporean bank, aiming to make its quarterly financial reports more inclusive, revamped its Tableau dashboards. The team consulted with accessibility experts and stakeholders with visual impairments. Key improvements included:

Switching to a color palette distinguishable by users with red-green color blindness.
Adding data labels and tooltips with plain-language explanations.
Offering downloadable text summaries for each dashboard.

The result was a marked increase in report engagement, with feedback highlighting improved clarity and a stronger sense of inclusion among employees.

*Steps to Audit Your Visualizations for Inclusivity and Accessibility*

- **Run Accessibility Checks**: Use built-in tools (e.g., Power BI's Accessibility Checker) or browser extensions to flag potential barriers.
- **Test with Assistive Technologies**: Ensure compatibility with screen readers and keyboard navigation.
- **Solicit Diverse Feedback**: Share prototypes with colleagues from varied backgrounds and abilities for real-world usability insights.
- **Iterate and Document**: Implement feedback, document accessibility features, and provide guidance for end users.

*Business Impact of Accessible Data Storytelling*

Investing in inclusive design is not merely a legal or ethical obligation. It expands your audience, enhances stakeholder trust, and can reveal insights that may otherwise remain hidden. In competitive markets, the ability to communicate clearly and inclusively can be the differentiator that drives consensus and action.

In summary, designing for inclusivity and accessibility transforms your data storytelling into a powerful, unifying business tool. By making your visualizations usable for everyone, you ensure your insights reach their full impact, fostering informed decisions and organizational alignment.

### 11.5. Learning from Failure: Business Case Studies

Learning from the mistakes of others can be as valuable—if not more so—than studying their successes. In the realm of data storytelling, failed projects, misinterpreted dashboards, and visualization mishaps offer rich lessons on both the technical and human aspects of presenting data. Advanced practitioners who wish to avoid costly missteps must examine these failures with a critical eye, asking not just what went wrong, but why, and how similar challenges can be prevented in their own organizations.

#### *When Dashboards Deceive: The Financial Firm's Cautionary Tale*

A leading multinational financial institution implemented a series of Power BI dashboards to monitor real-time trading performance across global markets. Their goal was to centralize complex data streams, offer executives a high-level view, and flag anomalies for risk management.

At launch, the dashboards dazzled with interactive features and vibrant visuals. However, within months, the firm suffered a high-profile trading loss linked to a misinterpretation of dashboard signals. An internal review exposed several underlying causes:

- **Overloaded Visuals:** The dashboards featured dense clusters of line and bar charts, with multiple y-axes and overlapping colors. While intended to provide a comprehensive view, the design overwhelmed users and obscured critical trends.
- **Inconsistent Data Sources:** Integrations pulled real-time data feeds from disparate systems, some of which lagged by several hours. This created a false sense of timeliness and accuracy.
- **Lack of User Training:** Executives and analysts received minimal onboarding, leading to varying interpretations of the same data points.

The aftermath prompted the firm to re-evaluate its approach to data storytelling:

- They simplified dashboards, using clearer color hierarchies and limiting views to the most actionable metrics.
- They implemented automated data validation scripts in Power BI, flagging discrepancies before publication.

- Regular training sessions were introduced to align users around dashboard intent and interpretation.

This experience underscores the importance of **clarity, consistency, and communication**—pillars that must underpin any data storytelling initiative. Even the most sophisticated tools can lead to misjudgment if foundational principles are ignored.

***The Global Retailer: When Visualization Breeds Bias***

A prominent European retailer sought to optimize its supply chain by leveraging Tableau dashboards to visualize sales, inventory, and logistics performance across continents. The project's ambition was matched by its technical complexity, integrating data from hundreds of stores and distribution centers.

Despite the technical prowess, the project faltered. Executives made a series of poor inventory decisions that led to both stockouts and costly overstocking. A root cause analysis revealed:

- **Selective Storytelling:** The dashboard design team, influenced by regional leadership, chose to highlight only positive trends, minimizing visibility into underperforming locations.
- **Inadequate Segmentation:** Aggregated sales data masked local anomalies. Filtering options were available, but buried, and few users had the expertise or incentive to dig deeper.
- **Cultural Disconnects:** Visualizations used color schemes and iconography familiar to the dashboard creators but confusing to non-European users, leading to misinterpretation in Asian and African markets.

The retailer responded with a comprehensive overhaul:

Dashboard templates were re-designed to surface negative trends as prominently as positive ones, fostering a culture of transparency.

Drill-down features were made prominent and intuitive, encouraging exploration of granular data.

Color palettes and iconography were adapted for cultural sensitivity, ensuring inclusiveness and clarity.

This scenario highlights the risks of **confirmation bias** and the critical need for diversity in dashboard design—not only in the data presented, but also in consideration of a global user base.

### *Tool-Specific Reflections and Practical Reminders*

Both case studies reveal that the choice of visualization tool, while important, is secondary to the design and governance processes surrounding it. Power BI, Tableau, and similar platforms offer immense flexibility, but this very freedom can amplify the impact of poor design or insufficient oversight.

For advanced practitioners, consider these guiding questions when building or auditing business dashboards:

Are visualizations designed with the end-user and their business context in mind?
Is data provenance and timeliness clearly indicated, especially when integrating multiple sources?
Do dashboards provide balanced views, surfacing risks as well as opportunities?
Are cultural and regional differences respected in color, language, and iconography choices?

Technical safeguards, such as automated data integrity checks, and governance practices, like regular cross-functional reviews, can bolster confidence in your visual stories.

These case studies illustrate that failure in data storytelling is rarely due to technical limitations alone. Instead, pitfalls arise from overlooked human factors, unclear communication, and the temptation to present overly optimistic or complex narratives. Mastering data storytelling means learning from these failures, embedding lessons of clarity, inclusivity, and integrity into every visualization.

## 11.6. Reflection and Integrity Checklist

After exploring actionable frameworks for resilient data stories, it's crucial to pause and systematically assess the integrity of your data storytelling process. Reflection is not a mere afterthought; it's a deliberate step that ensures your insights, visuals, and narratives are not only compelling but also accurate, ethical, and trustworthy. This section presents a practical checklist for advanced practitioners to audit their data storytelling workflows, accompanied by real-world business scenarios and tool-specific guidance.

### *The Mindset of Reflection: Why It Matters*

The most impactful data storytellers are those who habitually question their assumptions, review their methods, and strive for continuous improvement. Reflection is the linchpin that connects technical rigor with business credibility. When you take time to review your approach, you minimize the risk of misinterpretation, reinforce stakeholder trust, and position your insights for meaningful action.

Integrity, meanwhile, forms the ethical backbone of your work. It's not enough for a visualization to be visually appealing; it must also be a faithful representation of reality, free from distortion or manipulation. Together, reflection and integrity elevate your data stories from informative to transformative.

### *The Data Storytelling Integrity Checklist*

Before sharing your next dashboard, report, or presentation, work through this integrity checklist. Think of it as your final quality gate, ensuring your data stories are robust, reliable, and ready for high-stakes business decision-making.

- **Data Source Validation**
  - Have you verified the credibility and recency of your data sources?
  - Are all sources clearly documented within your analysis or dashboard?
  - For tools like Tableau or Power BI, is the data connection live or static, and are there potential issues with refresh or synchronization?

- **Data Transformation Transparency**
  - Did you document all data cleaning, filtering, or transformation steps?
  - Are any assumptions, imputations, or aggregations clearly explained to your audience?

- **Visualization Accuracy**
  - Are chart types appropriately matched to the data and business question?
  - Have you avoided misleading scales, truncated axes, or other forms of visual distortion?
  - For example, in Power BI, have you used the "Show Data Table" feature to allow users to verify the underlying numbers?

- **Context and Annotation**
  - Are key insights and outliers effectively annotated?
  - Did you provide necessary business context, including relevant benchmarks or historical comparison?

- **Bias and Objectivity Review**
  - Have you checked for cognitive or confirmation bias in your visual or narrative choices?

- Did you consider alternative explanations or viewpoints, especially if your story will influence significant business decisions?

- **Accessibility and Inclusivity**

  - Are your visuals colorblind-friendly and readable for all audiences?
  - Have you used descriptive titles and labels, and, in tools like Tableau, leveraged "Tooltip" or "Narrative" features to enhance understanding?

- **Confidentiality and Compliance**

  - Have you protected sensitive data and complied with privacy regulations such as GDPR?
  - Is confidential or proprietary information appropriately masked or aggregated before sharing externally?

- **Stakeholder Feedback Integration**

  - Have you solicited review and feedback from cross-functional team members or impacted business units?
  - Did you incorporate this feedback to improve clarity or address potential misinterpretations?

***Tool-Specific Tips: Putting the Checklist to Work***

Each visualization tool offers features to support integrity checks:

**Tableau**: Use "Data Source" and "Data Details" panes to document sources; apply "Annotations" directly on charts for context; employ "Custom Color Palettes" to ensure accessibility.

**Power BI**: Leverage "Q&A" and "Explain the Increase/Decrease" features for transparency; use "Bookmarks" to present multiple viewpoints; export data tables for stakeholder review.

When developing business dashboards, incorporate a visible "Info" or "About" section summarizing your data sources, key assumptions, and methodology. This not only demonstrates diligence but also invites constructive feedback and dialogue—key ingredients for business trust.

***Reflection: Building a Culture of Data Integrity***

Integrating this checklist into your workflow fosters a culture where data-driven decisions are not only innovative but also ethical and reliable. Encourage your teams to make integrity checks a standard project milestone, not an afterthought. By reflecting on both the technical and human dimensions of your work, you lay the groundwork for sustainable business impact.

As you master these habits, you'll find your data stories not only resonate more deeply but also withstand scrutiny from the most discerning audiences. This diligence is what distinguishes effective data storytellers in today's complex business environment.

In summary, embracing a structured reflection and integrity process transforms your data storytelling from good to exceptional, reinforcing trust, transparency, and ethical leadership.

# 12. ELEVATING YOUR BUSINESS WITH STORYTELLING

In today's high-velocity business landscape, the organizations that thrive are those able to transform raw data into stories that inspire, persuade, and lead to meaningful action. By now, you've acquired the foundations of effective data visualization and storytelling—skills that empower you to turn complex analytics into compelling narratives. Yet, real impact is achieved when these skills transcend individual presentations and become ingrained in your company's culture. This chapter is your guide to scaling data storytelling beyond personal mastery, embedding it as a core business capability that drives strategic advantage.

Here, you'll explore how to foster a culture that champions data storytelling at every level, ensuring your insights consistently resonate with diverse audiences. You'll learn practical methods for measuring the true business impact of your data-driven narratives, moving from anecdotal wins to quantifiable results that influence decision-making. We'll examine strategies for deploying data storytelling across departments and borders, drawing lessons from global organizations that set the benchmark for excellence.

As data visualization continues to evolve, staying ahead of emerging trends and innovations is crucial. This chapter highlights the latest developments shaping the future of data storytelling, preparing you to lead with confidence. Finally, you'll be equipped to chart your own course—developing a personalized roadmap to advance your skills and amplify your influence.

Whether you're a marketer aiming for greater audience engagement, an executive driving organizational change, or an analyst seeking wider impact, this chapter brings together the insights and strategies needed to elevate your business with masterful data storytelling. Prepare to move from competence to leadership, and from insight to sustained business value.

## 12.1. Building a Data Storytelling Culture

Cultivating a robust data storytelling culture is essential for organizations striving to become truly data-driven. While individual mastery of visualization and storytelling is valuable, the most significant impact comes when these skills are embedded across teams, workflows, and leadership mindsets. A culture that supports and celebrates data storytelling empowers everyone—from marketers to executives—to communicate insights, challenge assumptions, and drive innovation.

### *Defining a Data Storytelling Culture*

A data storytelling culture extends beyond technical proficiency. It is characterized by:

- **Curiosity:** Teams ask questions, seek patterns, and approach data with a desire to understand the "why" behind the numbers.
- **Accessibility:** Insights are democratized; data and visualizations are available and understandable to a broad audience, not just analysts or data scientists.
- **Collaboration:** Cross-functional teams co-create narratives, combining business context with analytical rigor.
- **Feedback and Iteration:** Storytelling is a dynamic process—stories are refined based on stakeholder feedback and evolving business needs.

Organizations with these traits are better positioned to unlock the full value of their data assets.

### *Strategies to Embed Data Storytelling in Your Organization*

Developing a data storytelling culture requires intentional actions at multiple levels. Consider the following strategies:

#### Executive Sponsorship and Modeling

Leadership must champion data storytelling, exemplifying best practices in meetings and communications. When executives use compelling dashboards or narrative-driven presentations, they set expectations and inspire others to follow suit.

#### Training and Upskilling

Invest in regular workshops and hands-on sessions using visualization tools like Tableau and Power BI. Tailor training for different business units, ensuring marketers, finance teams, and operations staff are comfortable crafting and interpreting data narratives.

#### Standardization of Tools and Templates

Establish a common set of visualization tools and branded templates. For example, create standardized dashboard layouts in Power BI that highlight key performance indicators (KPIs), trend analyses, and contextual commentary. This fosters consistency and accelerates adoption.

```
   # Example: Power BI Dashboard Layout
   - KPI Tiles (Top Row): Sales Growth, Customer Churn Rate, Campaign
ROI
```

```
   - Trend Line Visualization (Center): Monthly Sales Over 24 Months
   - Segmentation Breakdown (Left): By Region, Product, or Demographic
   - Narrative Panel (Right): Key Insights, Recommendations, Action
Items
```

## Recognition and Rewards

Acknowledge individuals and teams who excel in communicating insights. Celebrate impactful data stories in company-wide meetings or internal newsletters, reinforcing the value placed on clear, persuasive communication.

## Integration with Business Processes

Embed data storytelling in recurring business activities, such as quarterly reviews, project kickoffs, and strategic planning. Require teams to present insights with narrative context, not just raw charts or tables.

### *Real-World Business Scenarios*

To illustrate how a data storytelling culture transforms organizations, consider these scenarios:

## Global Retail Expansion:

A multinational retailer uses Tableau dashboards to unify sales data from dozens of countries. By implementing a shared data storytelling framework, local managers interpret performance variances in a global context, using annotated trend lines and region-specific narratives. This approach highlights successes in emerging markets and surfaces supply chain risks in real time, resulting in faster, more informed decisions across continents.

## Healthcare Operations Optimization:

A hospital system in Southeast Asia incorporates Power BI dashboards into daily operational meetings. Clinicians and administrators co-create data stories that connect patient wait times, staffing levels, and treatment outcomes. Visual timelines and annotated scatter plots make it simple to spot bottlenecks and propose targeted interventions, leading to measurable improvements in patient satisfaction and resource utilization.

### *Overcoming Common Barriers*

Challenges in building a data storytelling culture often include:

- Siloed data and expertise
- Resistance to change

- Overemphasis on technical detail at the expense of narrative clarity

Address these by fostering open data sharing, providing ongoing support, and consistently emphasizing the business impact of strong data communication.

Establishing a data storytelling culture transforms how organizations learn from, act on, and share insights. By aligning tools, training, and leadership behaviors, businesses empower every contributor to become a persuasive storyteller.

## 12.2. Measuring the Business Impact

In the pursuit of driving business transformation, the ultimate measure of data storytelling's success lies in its tangible impact. Advanced practitioners know that a compelling narrative alone is not enough—data stories must deliver measurable business outcomes. To elevate your practice, it is essential to develop rigorous approaches for assessing how your data storytelling initiatives influence decision-making, operational efficiency, and strategic direction.

### *Defining Business Impact in Data Storytelling*

Business impact manifests in multiple forms, from increased revenue and cost savings to improved customer satisfaction and market agility. In data storytelling, impact can be observed in:

- Accelerated decision-making cycles
- Enhanced stakeholder alignment and engagement
- Higher adoption rates of recommended actions or strategies
- Improved performance metrics directly linked to data-informed decisions

To systematically measure these outcomes, advanced storytellers integrate key performance indicators (KPIs) into their visualization and reporting strategies, ensuring that every story is tied to clearly defined business objectives.

### *Building Impact Measurement into Your Workflow*

Assessing the influence of your data stories involves both quantitative and qualitative metrics. Begin by aligning your storytelling goals with the strategic aims of your organization. Consider the following process:

### Define Success Criteria

Collaborate with stakeholders to establish what success looks like. This could include faster project delivery, increased sales conversions, or reduced operational risks.

### Select Relevant KPIs

Identify metrics directly affected by your data story. For a marketing campaign dashboard, this might be lead conversion rates, customer acquisition cost, or net promoter score.

### Leverage Visualization Tools for Monitoring

Platforms like Tableau and Power BI excel at creating dynamic dashboards that track these KPIs in real time. For instance, configure a Power BI dashboard to visualize sales pipeline velocity before and after a major data storytelling initiative, providing clear evidence of narrative influence.

### Gather Stakeholder Feedback

Supplement quantitative analysis with qualitative insights. Surveys, interviews, and anonymous polls can reveal how data stories have shifted perceptions, increased confidence in data-driven decisions, or clarified complex issues.

### Iterate and Optimize

Use your findings to refine future storytelling efforts, ensuring each narrative is more impactful than the last.

***Real-World Business Scenarios***

To illustrate these principles, consider the following examples from different industries and regions:

#### Global Retail Chain: Enhancing Supply Chain Efficiency

A multinational retailer implemented a Tableau dashboard, visualizing inventory turnover rates, supplier lead times, and out-of-stock trends across regions. By embedding interactive data stories directly into their weekly management briefings, they identified bottlenecks in the Asia-Pacific supply chain. Over the next quarter, the company observed a 12 percent reduction in stockouts and a significant uptick in on-time deliveries, demonstrating direct business impact.

#### Financial Services: Strengthening Stakeholder Buy-In

A leading European bank sought to accelerate the adoption of a new risk assessment model. Using Power BI, analysts crafted a narrative dashboard that blended risk scores, historical loss events, and scenario simulations. Executives, many of whom were initially skeptical, reported increased understanding and trust in the model. The result was a smoother rollout and a measurable decrease in regulatory incidents in the following year.

Measuring business impact transforms data storytelling from an art into a disciplined, results-driven practice. By embedding KPIs and leveraging visualization tools, you can provide stakeholders with clear evidence of your stories' effectiveness, driving organizational buy-in and continuous improvement.

## 12.3. Scaling Data Storytelling Across the Organization

To truly realize the transformative power of data storytelling, organizations must move beyond isolated efforts and embed these practices at scale. This involves equipping teams across departments with the skills, tools, and frameworks necessary to consistently craft and share compelling data-driven narratives. By scaling data storytelling, businesses foster alignment, drive informed decision-making, and create a shared language around insights, regardless of geography or function.

### *Building a Scalable Foundation*

Scaling data storytelling requires a robust foundation that encompasses technology, process, and culture. While technology platforms such as Tableau, Power BI, and Looker provide the infrastructure for visualization, success hinges equally on standardized processes and an organizational mindset that values narrative-driven insights.

Consider a multinational retail corporation that leverages Power BI dashboards to unify sales data from regional branches. By standardizing reporting templates and storytelling frameworks, the company ensures every sales manager, from Singapore to São Paulo, can interpret and communicate performance metrics in a consistent manner. This aligns strategy across continents and empowers local teams to act on insights confidently.

### *Key Enablers for Scaling*

To achieve widespread adoption and impact, organizations should focus on several critical enablers:

- **Centralized Data Governance:** Establish clear data definitions, quality controls, and access protocols to ensure consistent and trustworthy narratives.
- **Reusable Templates and Storytelling Frameworks:** Develop branded visualization templates and narrative structures that can be easily adapted by teams with varying analytical expertise.
- **Training and Enablement:** Offer ongoing workshops, e-learning, and peer mentoring to build data storytelling fluency at every organizational level.

- **Integrated Collaboration Platforms:** Utilize shared workspaces, such as Microsoft Teams or Slack integrated with Tableau, to facilitate feedback, iteration, and cross-functional collaboration.

### *Visualization Tools for Enterprise Storytelling*

Visualization platforms play a pivotal role in scaling data storytelling. Tools like Tableau and Power BI offer enterprise features designed for large-scale dissemination and adoption:

**Tableau:** Enables the creation and distribution of interactive dashboards, supports governance with user permissions, and integrates with collaboration tools for real-time feedback.

**Power BI:** Provides robust integration with Microsoft Office, allowing business users to embed data stories directly into presentations and documents. Its dashboard sharing capability ensures that insights are accessible to decision-makers at every level.

**Looker:** Built for cloud scalability, Looker allows organizations to define data models centrally, ensuring consistency across hundreds of self-service dashboards.

For example, a global logistics firm implemented Tableau across its operations, creating a centralized dashboard for shipment tracking and performance analytics. By assigning role-based permissions, regional teams could tailor the dashboard's narrative elements to local needs while maintaining a unified story structure. This not only improved operational visibility but also empowered teams to surface region-specific insights without sacrificing global consistency.

### *Illustrative Business Dashboard Example*

To bridge the gap between technical tools and business impact, consider the following illustration of a scalable business dashboard:

```
- Executive Summary Tab: High-level KPIs (Revenue, Customer Retention,
NPS)
- Regional Performance Tab: Interactive map with drill-down
capabilities by country or state
- Trend Analysis Tab: Line charts highlighting year-over-year growth
with annotated storytelling points
- Action Items Tab: Automatically updated recommendations generated
from data insights
```

Such a dashboard, built in Power BI or Tableau, can be shared organization-wide. Customizable views ensure relevance for C-suite executives, regional managers, and front-line teams alike, while embedded commentary guides users through the narrative behind the numbers.

#### *Global Use-Case: Scaling Data Storytelling in a Financial Institution*

A leading European bank sought to harmonize risk reporting across dozens of subsidiaries. By deploying Power BI dashboards anchored in a unified data model, the central analytics team provided local offices with self-service storytelling tools. Each branch could supplement core risk metrics with region-specific context, such as market trends or regulatory changes, all while adhering to a consistent narrative structure defined by headquarters. This approach not only improved compliance and risk awareness, but also fostered innovation as local teams shared best practices through dashboard storyboards.

#### *Reflecting on Organizational Impact*

Scaling data storytelling is not simply about wider adoption—it's about transforming how organizations think, communicate, and act on data. When every team member can translate insights into action using a shared narrative language, data becomes a catalyst for alignment and innovation.

## 12.4. Staying Ahead: Trends and Innovations

Staying agile in the dynamic world of data storytelling requires more than mastering today's best practices; it demands a keen awareness of emerging trends and the foresight to leverage innovations. As organizations collect data at unprecedented volumes and velocities, the tools and techniques we use to extract value from this data must also evolve. Let's explore how forward-thinking professionals are adopting new technologies and methodologies to ensure their data stories remain influential and relevant.

#### *Embracing Augmented Analytics*

Augmented analytics is reshaping the way businesses approach data storytelling by integrating artificial intelligence (AI) and machine learning (ML) into their analytics processes. These technologies enhance human capabilities, automating data preparation, insight discovery, and even narrative generation. Instead of manually sifting through data, analysts can now use tools like Tableau's Explain Data or Microsoft Power BI's AI Insights to surface key trends and anomalies instantly.

For example, a global consumer goods company might leverage augmented analytics to analyze customer feedback from multiple markets. By using NLP (natural language processing) within Power BI, the team can quickly identify emerging sentiment trends, allowing them to tailor product launches and marketing campaigns for different cultural contexts.

### *Interactive and Real-Time Dashboards*

Static reports are rapidly giving way to interactive dashboards that empower users to explore data on their own terms. Modern visualization platforms such as Tableau, Power BI, and Looker enable the creation of dynamic dashboards that respond to user input, filter data in real-time, and provide personalized insights.

Consider a scenario in a multinational logistics firm: Managers rely on a real-time Tableau dashboard that visualizes shipment statuses, route efficiencies, and bottlenecks across continents. With interactive filters, regional managers can drill down to local operations, compare performance, and immediately act on insights, thus optimizing delivery networks and enhancing customer satisfaction globally.

### *Data Storytelling with Embedded Analytics*

Business value is maximized when insights are delivered where decisions are made. Embedded analytics integrates dashboards and visualizations directly into business applications, removing the friction of toggling between platforms. This trend is gaining momentum as organizations seek to democratize data and empower frontline workers with actionable insights.

For instance, a retail chain might embed Power BI visualizations within its inventory management system. Store managers can instantly view sales performance, stock levels, and predictive restock alerts, all within their daily workflow. This not only accelerates decision-making but also ensures that data-driven action is woven into the fabric of day-to-day operations.

### *Advanced Visualization Types and Storytelling Formats*

The evolution of visualization tools has expanded the palette of options available for telling compelling stories. Animated charts, network graphs, and geospatial visualizations are increasingly accessible, allowing storytellers to present complex relationships and trends with clarity.

**Animated time-series**: Tools like Flourish and Tableau offer animated charts that reveal how metrics evolve over time, making trends and turning points more intuitive.

**Network diagrams**: Platforms such as Gephi or Power BI's custom visuals help map relationships in social networks, supply chains, or organizational structures.

**Geospatial mapping**: Tableau's Mapbox integration or Google Data Studio's geo tools make it easier to visualize data by region, city, or even specific store locations.

***Practical Use-Case: Healthcare Operations Dashboard***

A large hospital group in Southeast Asia implemented an interactive Power BI dashboard to monitor patient flow, resource utilization, and care outcomes across multiple facilities. By embedding AI-driven anomaly detection and real-time data feeds, administrators could identify capacity issues or operational bottlenecks as they emerged. The result was a measurable improvement in patient wait times and resource allocation, demonstrating how innovative data storytelling directly impacts business performance and community well-being.

***Preparing for the Future***

Staying ahead demands continuous curiosity and investment in new skills. Forward-thinking organizations encourage their data teams to experiment with emerging tools, participate in global data visualization communities, and regularly review the latest research in data storytelling. By fostering a culture of innovation, businesses remain competitive, agile, and ready to seize new opportunities as they arise.

## 12.5. Global Leaders in Data Storytelling

Around the globe, organizations that have mastered data storytelling stand out as innovators, influencing their industries and shaping decision-making processes at the highest levels. By blending sophisticated data analysis with compelling narratives, these global leaders move beyond static reporting, leveraging advanced visualization platforms to drive business transformation. Their strategies and successes provide valuable blueprints for professionals aiming to elevate their own practice.

***Lessons from the Pioneers: Real-World Business Use-Cases***

Examining how leading organizations deploy data storytelling reveals commonalities in approach and the transformative effect on business outcomes. Consider the following scenarios:

### 1. Unilever's Sustainability Dashboard Initiative

Unilever, a multinational consumer goods company, faced the challenge of communicating progress on sustainability initiatives to stakeholders across continents. By developing interactive dashboards in **Tableau**, Unilever was able to distill massive, complex datasets into clear, actionable stories. These dashboards combined regional performance metrics, trend analyses, and scenario modeling, empowering local managers to track their environmental impact in real time.

The dashboard's design utilized color-coded indicators and intuitive filtering, allowing users to explore data relevant to their market. The narrative thread emphasized not only current achievements but also projected outcomes, making the sustainability journey tangible and motivating. This approach helped align Unilever's global workforce around shared goals and enhanced transparency with investors and the public.

### 2. DBS Bank's Data-Driven Customer Experience

DBS Bank, headquartered in Singapore, is renowned for its innovative use of data storytelling to enhance customer engagement. By deploying **Power BI** dashboards, DBS enabled its relationship managers to visualize customer journeys, segment behaviors, and identify upsell opportunities. Instead of static reports, advisors received interactive storyboards that combined quantitative trends with qualitative insights.

For example, a dashboard might depict a customer's product adoption path, highlight key moments of engagement, and suggest personalized next steps. This narrative approach fostered deeper customer relationships, improved service delivery, and led to measurable growth in cross-selling rates. DBS's experience illustrates the value of integrating data storytelling into client-facing roles, reinforcing trust and driving business impact.

#### *Visualization Tools Powering Data Storytelling Excellence*

Global leaders rely on a suite of advanced visualization tools to bring their data stories to life. Selecting the right platform is essential for translating raw data into engaging, actionable narratives.

**Tableau:** Known for its intuitive interface and robust analytical capabilities, Tableau is often the choice for large enterprises needing to develop interactive dashboards that scale across departments and geographies.

**Power BI:** Microsoft's Power BI excels in integrating with enterprise systems and delivering real-time data insights through customizable visualizations, making it ideal for operational dashboards and executive overviews.

**Qlik Sense:** Favored for its associative data model and self-service analytics, Qlik Sense empowers business users to explore data freely, uncovering stories that might otherwise remain hidden.

#### *Cross-Cultural and Industry Adaptations*

While the fundamentals of data storytelling are universal, their application varies across cultures and sectors. Japanese manufacturing firms such as Toyota, for instance, emphasize continuous improvement (kaizen) by embedding data narratives into daily operational routines. Their dashboards focus on incremental changes and collective performance, using simple, culturally resonant visuals to drive alignment.

In contrast, American healthcare organizations like Kaiser Permanente often employ data storytelling to communicate complex patient outcomes and regulatory compliance. Here, visualizations must balance clarity with regulatory precision, ensuring narratives support both clinical decisions and public transparency.

## 12.6. Your Next Steps: Developing Your Personal Roadmap

Having explored strategies for evaluating your data storytelling impact, it's time to chart your path forward. Advanced business professionals must transform insights into action by developing a personal roadmap for mastering data storytelling. This roadmap is not a static document but a living framework, designed to evolve as your skills, business objectives, and organizational needs change. By intentionally planning your growth, you ensure that data storytelling becomes an integral, sustainable pillar of your business influence.

### *Assessing Your Current Position*

Begin with an honest assessment of where you stand in your data storytelling journey. This requires reflecting on your technical proficiency, narrative capabilities, and the business outcomes your visualizations have driven so far. Consider the following dimensions:

**Technical Skills:** Are you comfortable with tools like Tableau, Power BI, or Python's visualization libraries? Can you create interactive dashboards or automate recurring reports?

**Narrative Craft:** Do you weave data into compelling, audience-centric stories, or do your presentations remain purely analytical?

**Business Impact:** Have your data stories influenced strategic decisions, sparked innovation, or driven measurable results such as increased revenue or cost savings?

Mapping your strengths and gaps in these areas will help you set realistic, targeted goals for advancement.

### *Setting SMART Goals for Growth*

A roadmap without clear milestones is little more than a wish list. Apply the **SMART** framework—Specific, Measurable, Achievable, Relevant, Time-bound—to shape your objectives. For example:

- **Specific:** "Develop an executive dashboard in Power BI for quarterly sales performance."
- **Measurable:** "Increase stakeholder engagement with data presentations by 30% over the next six months."

- **Relevant:** "Align visualization projects with the organization's strategic priorities."
- **Time-bound:** "Complete advanced Tableau certification within four months."

These goals keep you accountable and motivated, while ensuring your efforts align with broader business objectives.

***Bridging Skills with Tools and Practice***

To actualize your roadmap, you must blend upskilling with practical application. Advanced learners benefit most from hands-on projects that mirror real business challenges.

Consider a scenario at a multinational retail chain. The analytics team, seeking to optimize inventory levels, leverages Tableau to visualize real-time sales and supply chain data. By integrating geospatial mapping, the team uncovers regional demand patterns, enabling local managers to adjust orders dynamically. The story crafted from these visuals, presented in executive meetings, leads to a 15% reduction in stockouts and improved profitability.

Alternatively, in a fintech startup, analysts use Python and Power BI to build an investor dashboard, tracking key performance indicators such as user growth, churn rates, and transaction volumes. By employing narrative techniques—highlighting anomalies with color, annotating trends, and embedding "what-if" scenario sliders—the team secures additional funding by clearly illustrating growth potential to stakeholders.

These examples highlight the importance of:

- Selecting the right tool for your business context
- Customizing dashboards for different audiences
- Iterating visuals based on feedback and results

***Building Your Personal Dashboard Portfolio***

A compelling way to demonstrate your evolving expertise is by curating a portfolio of business dashboards and data stories. This collection becomes both a tangible record of your progress and a showcase for internal leadership or external opportunities.

When building your portfolio, focus on:

- Variety: Include dashboards for sales, marketing, operations, or finance.
- Interactivity: Showcase dynamic filters, drilldowns, and scenario analysis.

- Annotation: Document the business problem addressed, data sources used, and the impact achieved.

For example, you might include a **Tableau dashboard** visualizing marketing campaign ROI by region, annotated with a narrative on how insights drove reallocation of advertising budget. Or a **Power BI report** tracking supply chain performance, with embedded commentary on how visualizations informed vendor negotiations.

#### *Continuous Learning and Feedback Loops*

Data storytelling mastery is a journey, not a destination. Foster a habit of regular reflection, peer review, and stakeholder feedback. Join professional communities, attend workshops, and stay abreast of emerging tools and techniques. As you iterate, revisit your roadmap to adjust goals and strategies.

Developing your personal roadmap is essential for elevating your business impact through masterful data storytelling. By assessing your current skills, setting SMART goals, practicing with real-world projects, and building a portfolio, you ensure sustained growth and relevance.

### 12.7. Final Reflection and Book Summary

As we reach the close of this chapter and the culmination of your journey through masterful data storytelling, it is essential to pause and reflect on the transformative power that effective data visualization and narrative can wield within a business context. The advanced techniques, strategic frameworks, and practical applications explored throughout this book are not just tools—they are catalysts for organizational growth, agility, and influence.

#### *Synthesizing Key Lessons*

Throughout this guide, you've learned that data storytelling is far more than aesthetics or technical prowess. It is about forging meaningful connections between complex datasets and the decisions that shape business futures. By integrating robust visualization tools like Tableau and Power BI, you have gained the capability to move beyond static reporting, embracing dynamic dashboards and interactive experiences that empower stakeholders at every level.

Consider the following core principles reinforced in this final chapter:

**Narrative Structure Enhances Comprehension:** Crafting a clear beginning, middle, and end transforms scattered data into a cohesive message, guiding your audience through insights and implications.

**Visual Design Drives Engagement:** Strategic use of color, hierarchy, and layout ensures that your message is not just seen, but truly understood and remembered.

**Audience-Centric Storytelling Fuels Impact:** Tailoring your story to the cultural, regional, and professional context of your audience ensures resonance and relevance, breaking down barriers to action.

### *Visualization Tools and Dashboard Strategies*

Whether you are using Tableau, Power BI, or another visualization platform, the key is not simply to display data, but to **guide your audience**. Techniques such as:

**Drill-down capabilities** for exploring details without overwhelming the initial view

**Dynamic filtering and segmentation** to personalize insights for different departments or geographies

**Integrated annotations and callouts** to highlight pivotal moments or changes in the data narrative

enable business professionals to move fluidly between high-level strategy and granular detail. These capabilities are essential for fostering an environment where data-driven decisions become the norm, not the exception.

### *Looking Ahead: Sustaining a Data Storytelling Culture*

As you reflect on the journey so far, it's clear that mastering data storytelling is not a one-time achievement but an ongoing commitment. The most successful organizations embed these practices into their daily operations, encouraging cross-functional collaboration and continuous learning. By championing data storytelling, you become an agent of change—bridging technical expertise and business strategy to create lasting value.

In summary, the mastery of data storytelling empowers you to surface hidden insights, inspire confidence, and drive organizational momentum. As you prepare to institutionalize these skills within your teams, remember that the true impact lies in your ability to unite data with purpose and vision.

# GLOSSARY OF KEY TERMS

**Accessibility**

The design of data visualizations and storytelling elements to be usable and understandable by people with diverse abilities. This includes considerations for color blindness, screen readers, and cognitive load, ensuring that insights are available to all stakeholders regardless of physical or cognitive differences.

**Annotation**

Text, symbols, or visual markers added to charts or graphs to provide context, highlight important data points, or clarify trends. Annotations help guide the audience's interpretation of data and can emphasize critical insights within a visualization.

**Bar Chart**

A common chart type that uses rectangular bars to represent categorical data with lengths proportional to the values they represent. Bar charts are widely used to compare quantities across different categories or groups in a clear, straightforward manner.

**Bias (in Data)**

A systematic error or distortion in data collection, analysis, or presentation that can mislead interpretation and decision-making. Recognizing and addressing bias is essential for ensuring the accuracy and fairness of data-driven stories.

**Big Data**

Extremely large and complex datasets that traditional data processing tools cannot efficiently manage or analyze. Big data often requires specialized technologies and analytical methods to extract meaningful insights and inform business strategy.

**Brand Consistency**

The practice of aligning data visualizations with an organization's established visual identity, including colors, fonts, and logo usage. Maintaining brand consistency in data storytelling reinforces trust and professionalism during communication.

**Bubble Chart**

A type of scatter plot that displays three dimensions of data. Each point is represented by a bubble, where the position indicates two variables and the bubble size represents a third. Bubble charts are useful for visualizing relationships between multiple quantitative variables.

**Business Intelligence (BI)**

The process and technologies involved in collecting, analyzing, and presenting business data to support decision-making. BI often relies on dashboards and data visualization to make complex information accessible to business users.

**Categorical Data**

Data that represents distinct groups or categories, such as product types, regions, or customer segments. Categorical data is often visualized using bar charts, pie charts, or heatmaps to compare values across different groups.

**Chartjunk**

Unnecessary or distracting visual elements in a chart or graph that do not improve, and may even obscure, the understanding of the data. Examples include excessive colors, decorative graphics, or overly complex design details.

**Choropleth Map**

A thematic map where regions are shaded or colored according to the value of a variable, such as sales by country or population density by state. Choropleth maps are effective for visualizing geographic patterns and spatial data.

**Color Theory**

The study of how colors interact and the psychological effects they have on viewers. In data visualization, color theory is applied to select palettes that improve readability, highlight key insights, and evoke intended emotions.

**Correlation**

A statistical measure indicating the relationship between two variables. In data visualization, correlation is often shown through scatter plots or line charts, helping viewers identify patterns or potential causation.

**Dashboard**

An interactive interface that consolidates multiple data visualizations and metrics in a single view. Dashboards allow decision-makers to monitor key performance indicators (KPIs) and track business trends in real time.

**Data Cleaning**

The process of identifying and correcting errors, inconsistencies, and inaccuracies in a dataset. Data cleaning ensures that visualizations and analyses are based on reliable, high-quality information.

**Data Democratization**

Making data and analytical tools accessible to a wide range of employees within an organization, regardless of technical expertise. This approach empowers more individuals to make data-informed decisions and participate in storytelling.

**Data Ethics**

The principles and standards governing the collection, analysis, and presentation of data. Data ethics ensures that data storytelling is conducted responsibly, respecting privacy, consent, and fairness.

**Data Granularity**

The level of detail or depth represented in a dataset. High granularity means detailed, fine-level data, while low granularity refers to more aggregated or summarized information. Choosing the right granularity is critical for effective storytelling.

**Data Literacy**

The ability to read, understand, create, and communicate data as information. Data literacy enables business professionals to interpret visualizations accurately and engage meaningfully with data-driven stories.

**Data Pipeline**

A series of processes that move and transform raw data from its source to its final destination, such as a dashboard or report. Data pipelines often include extraction, cleaning, transformation, and loading steps.

**Data Storytelling**

The art and science of using narrative techniques combined with data visualization to communicate insights and drive action. Data storytelling bridges the gap between complex analytics and business decision-making by making data relatable and compelling.

**Data Visualization**

The graphical representation of data and information using charts, graphs, maps, and other visual formats. Data visualization helps uncover patterns, trends, and insights that may be difficult to discern from raw numbers alone.

**Dashboarding**

The creation and management of dashboards for monitoring, analyzing, and presenting key business metrics. Dashboarding involves selecting relevant data, designing intuitive layouts, and ensuring that information is updated in real time.

**Decision Intelligence**

An emerging field that combines data science, artificial intelligence, and behavioral science to improve the quality of business decisions. Decision intelligence leverages advanced analytics and visualization to guide strategic choices.

**Descriptive Analytics**

The analysis of historical data to understand what has happened in the past. Descriptive analytics provides context and baseline insights, often communicated through dashboards and summary visualizations.

**Dimensionality Reduction**

A process in data analysis and visualization that reduces the number of variables under consideration, simplifying complex datasets. Techniques such as principal component analysis (PCA) help make patterns more apparent and visualizations more interpretable.

**Drill-Down**

A feature in interactive data visualizations or dashboards that allows users to explore data at more detailed levels. Drill-downs enable stakeholders to move from high-level summaries to granular insights with a few clicks.

**Exploratory Data Analysis (EDA)**

A set of techniques for examining and summarizing datasets prior to formal modeling or hypothesis testing. EDA often uses visualizations to reveal trends, detect outliers, and generate hypotheses.

**Funnel Chart**

A visualization that represents the progressive reduction of data as it passes through stages in a process, such as sales pipelines or customer journeys. Funnel charts help identify bottlenecks and drop-off points.

**Heatmap**

A graphical representation of data where values are depicted by color intensity. Heatmaps are commonly used to show relationships between two variables or to visualize activity patterns, such as website clicks or sales by region.

**Histogram**

A chart that displays the distribution of a continuous variable by grouping data into bins and showing the frequency of values in each bin. Histograms help identify patterns, such as skewness or the presence of outliers.

**Infographic**

A visual representation that combines data, graphics, and narrative elements to communicate complex information quickly and engagingly. Infographics are often used in marketing, reporting, and executive summaries.

**Insight**

A clear, actionable understanding derived from data analysis or visualization. Insights help inform business decisions, spark innovation, and drive measurable outcomes.

**Interactive Visualization**

A dynamic data visualization that allows users to manipulate variables, filter data, or explore different perspectives. Interactivity enhances engagement and enables deeper exploration of complex datasets.

**Key Performance Indicator (KPI)**

A quantifiable metric used to assess progress toward a specific business objective. KPIs are often visualized in dashboards and reports to provide at-a-glance performance tracking.

**Line Chart**

A chart that displays data points connected by straight lines, typically used to show trends over time. Line charts are effective for illustrating changes, comparisons, and patterns in continuous data.

**Misleading Visualization**

A chart or graph that distorts data, intentionally or unintentionally, through poor design choices such as truncated axes, disproportionate scaling, or inappropriate chart types. Misleading visualizations can result in misinterpretation and flawed decision-making.

**Narrative Arc**

The structure of a story, including the setup, conflict, and resolution. In data storytelling, a narrative arc helps organize insights and guides the audience through the journey from data discovery to business impact.

**Normalization**

The process of adjusting data values to a common scale, making it easier to compare across different categories or time periods. Normalization is vital for clear, fair visualizations and accurate analysis.

**Outlier**

A data point significantly different from others in a dataset. Outliers can indicate errors, unique cases, or important trends and should be carefully analyzed to understand their cause and business implications.

**Pie Chart**

A circular chart divided into slices to illustrate numerical proportions. Each slice represents a category's contribution to the whole, making pie charts suitable for showing simple part-to-whole relationships.

**Predictive Analytics**

The use of statistical models and machine learning to forecast future outcomes based on historical data. Predictive analytics is increasingly visualized to inform strategic planning and risk management.

**Qualitative Data**

Non-numeric information, such as opinions, descriptions, or categories, often collected through interviews, surveys, or observations. Qualitative data adds context and depth to data stories, complementing quantitative analysis.

**Quantitative Data**

Numeric information that can be measured and analyzed statistically. Quantitative data forms the backbone of most business analytics and data visualizations, enabling objective comparisons and trend analysis.

**Real-Time Data**

Information that is updated instantly or with minimal delay from its source. Real-time data visualization is essential for monitoring operations, tracking KPIs, and making timely business decisions.

**Scatter Plot**

A chart that displays individual data points plotted on two axes, used to show the relationship between two variables. Scatter plots help identify correlations, clusters, and trends in data.

**Storyboarding**

The process of planning the structure and key elements of a data story before creating the final visualization. Storyboarding involves outlining the narrative flow, selecting visuals, and defining key messages for clarity and impact.

**Sunk Cost Fallacy**

A cognitive bias where decision-makers continue investing in a course of action due to previously invested resources, rather than evaluating current data. Recognizing this fallacy is crucial for objective, data-driven storytelling.

**Time Series**

A sequence of data points collected or recorded at regular time intervals. Time series analysis and visualization help track trends, seasonality, and cycles in business performance.

**Tooltip**

A small, interactive box that appears when hovering over a data point in a visualization. Tooltips provide additional information or context without cluttering the main chart, enhancing user experience and understanding.

**Trend Line**

A line added to a chart, often a scatter plot or line chart, that shows the general direction or pattern of the data. Trend lines help highlight underlying movements and support predictive analysis.

**User Experience (UX)**

The overall experience users have when interacting with data visualizations or dashboards. Good UX ensures that visualizations are intuitive, engaging, and support the audience's needs, increasing the effectiveness of data storytelling.

**Visual Hierarchy**

The arrangement of elements in a visualization to guide the viewer's attention in order of importance. Effective visual hierarchy highlights key insights, ensures clarity, and supports the logical flow of the data story.

**Wireframe**

A basic, low-fidelity sketch or blueprint of a data visualization or dashboard layout. Wireframes are used in the early design stages to plan structure, placement, and user flow before full development.

**Zero Baseline**

A principle in chart design where the y-axis starts at zero, ensuring that visual comparisons are accurate and not exaggerated. Adhering to a zero baseline prevents misleading visualizations, especially in bar and column charts.

# ANNEXURE 1: DATA VISUALIZATION TEMPLATES

## Purpose and Connection

This annexure provides readers with ready-to-use data visualization templates specifically tailored for common business scenarios. These templates are designed to bridge the gap between raw data and compelling visual storytelling, supporting the book's core message that effective visualization enhances communication, drives decisions, and delivers measurable business outcomes. By offering practical, adaptable templates, this section empowers business professionals to present complex insights with clarity, whether they are marketers, analysts, or executives.

## Introduction to Visualization Templates

A well-structured visualization template saves time, ensures consistency, and amplifies the impact of your data story. Templates act as blueprints, guiding your chart selection, layout, and messaging. The following templates are customizable and rooted in best practices discussed throughout the book. Each template includes suggested use cases, design notes, and global business examples to demonstrate their application.

## Template 1: The Executive Dashboard

### *Overview*

The Executive Dashboard template distills key performance indicators (KPIs) and high-level metrics into a single, intuitive view. It enables quick decision-making by providing at-a-glance insights into business health, trends, and emerging issues.

### *Key Features*

- Modular layout for 3-5 core KPIs
- Consistent use of color and iconography
- Clear trend lines, targets, and variance indicators
- Minimal text, maximum clarity

### *Application Example: Retail Chain Performance*

Imagine a multinational retail chain with stores across North America and Europe. The executive team needs to monitor sales performance, customer satisfaction, inventory turnover, and online engagement. Using this template, the dashboard displays:

- A line chart showing monthly sales trends with year-over-year comparison
- A gauge chart for customer satisfaction (Net Promoter Score)

- A bar chart indicating inventory turnover across regions
- A sparkline for online engagement rates

Consistent colors distinguish regions (e.g., blue for North America, green for Europe), while icons reinforce metrics (shopping cart for sales, smiley face for satisfaction).

***Design Notes***

Maintain white space to avoid clutter. Use annotations sparingly to highlight significant changes or anomalies. Tailor the dashboard to the executive audience by focusing only on actionable metrics.

### Template 2: The Comparative Analysis Chart

***Overview***

Comparative analysis is central to business storytelling—whether evaluating product lines, market segments, or campaign effectiveness. This template uses a combination of grouped bar charts and highlight tables to showcase differences and trends.

***Key Features***

- Side-by-side bar or column charts for direct comparison
- Color emphasis for best and worst performers
- Optional small multiples to show sub-group details

***Application Example: Marketing Campaign Performance in Asia-Pacific***

A software company runs simultaneous digital campaigns in Japan, India, and Australia. The marketing team needs to compare campaign reach, conversion rates, and cost per acquisition (CPA).

The template arranges three grouped bar charts—one for each metric—side by side. Each country is represented by a distinct color, with the highest performer highlighted in a bold shade. A below-the-charts highlight table summarizes key takeaways (e.g., “India: Highest reach, lowest CPA”).

***Design Notes***

Choose colors that are culturally appropriate and accessible for colorblind users. When presenting in multicultural contexts, localize chart titles and labels to ensure clarity for all stakeholders.

## Template 3: The Change Over Time Storyboard

### *Overview*

Understanding trends and forecasting future outcomes is critical for business planning. The Change Over Time Storyboard template leverages connected line graphs and annotation layers to narrate the story of change, pinpointing inflection points and causal events.

### *Key Features*

- Line or area charts with annotated milestones
- Vertical bands for notable events (e.g., product launches, regulatory changes)
- Forward-looking projections with dashed lines

### *Application Example: Financial Services Growth in Africa*

A pan-African bank tracks the adoption rate of its mobile banking app over five years. The visualization displays:

- A line chart of monthly active users
- Vertical bands marking major app updates and marketing pushes
- An annotated note when a competitor entered the market
- A dashed line projecting growth based on current trends

This storyboard helps the executive team connect strategic actions with user adoption, enabling data-driven resource allocation.

### *Design Notes*

Use subtle color gradients for projection areas to differentiate actuals from forecasts. Keep annotation text concise but informative.

## Summary

These templates provide a foundation for transforming business data into persuasive visuals. By customizing the layouts and content to specific audiences and objectives, professionals can elevate their data storytelling and drive meaningful business outcomes. As you adapt these templates in your organization, remember to iterate based on feedback and evolving business needs.

# ANNEXURE 2: BUSINESS CASE STUDIES IN DATA STORYTELLING

## Purpose and Connection

This annexure presents real-world case studies illustrating how organizations across industries and cultures have leveraged data storytelling and visualization to achieve significant business impact. These examples serve as practical inspiration, reinforcing the book's central thesis that effective data communication catalyzes action and drives results. Each case study details the challenge, approach, visualization techniques used, and the resulting business outcomes.

## Case Study 1: Reducing Churn in a Telecom Operator (Europe)

### *Background*

A large European telecom provider faced rising customer churn, threatening revenue and market share. Despite collecting vast customer data, the company struggled to identify actionable insights for retention strategies.

### *Approach*

The business analytics team consolidated customer data from CRM, billing, and network usage systems. They developed an interactive dashboard using heatmaps and cohort analysis charts to visualize churn rates by customer segment, contract type, and service usage.

### *Visualization Techniques*

- **Heatmaps** showed churn concentration by age group and region.
- **Line charts** tracked churn trends over time.
- **Cohort tables** revealed long-term retention patterns.

### *Business Impact*

By visualizing churn drivers, the company identified high-risk segments (e.g., young urban customers with short-term contracts). Targeted retention offers and service improvements led to a 15 percent reduction in churn within six months, saving millions in potential lost revenue.

### Case Study 2: Optimizing Inventory for a Global Apparel Brand (Asia & North America)

#### *Background*

A global apparel company operating in Japan and the United States faced challenges with inventory stockouts and overages. The supply chain team needed a way to visualize inventory dynamics to balance supply and demand across regions.

#### *Approach*

Data was aggregated from point-of-sale systems, warehouse logs, and e-commerce platforms. The team used layered bar charts and geospatial maps to pinpoint stock imbalances and identify high-performing SKUs.

#### *Visualization Techniques*

**Stacked bar charts** compared inventory levels versus sales by region and product category.

**Geospatial heatmaps** identified regions with frequent stockouts or surplus.

**Pareto (80/20) charts** highlighted the top-selling products contributing to most revenue.

#### *Business Impact*

Improved visualization enabled dynamic inventory reallocation, reducing stockouts in Tokyo stores by 25 percent and decreasing surplus inventory in California by 18 percent. The result was increased sales and reduced holding costs.

### Case Study 3: Financial Inclusion in Microfinance (Africa)

#### *Background*

A microfinance institution in Kenya sought to expand financial inclusion among rural women entrepreneurs but struggled to communicate impact to donors and stakeholders.

#### *Approach*

Survey and transaction data were visualized using human-centric storytelling. Infographics, before-and-after charts, and photo overlays showcased not just numbers but individual success stories.

#### *Visualization Techniques*

**Infographic-style dashboards** combined key metrics (loans distributed, repayment rates) with beneficiary quotes and photos.

**Before-and-after bar charts** illustrated business growth for selected entrepreneurs.

**Map visualizations** showed geographic expansion over time.

***Business Impact***

The storytelling approach resonated with international donors, resulting in a 30 percent increase in funding. Local stakeholders also gained a clearer understanding of impact, fostering community trust and engagement.

## Summary

These case studies illustrate the transformative power of data storytelling across regions and industries. By contextualizing data within relatable narratives and culturally relevant visuals, organizations can bridge the gap between analytics and actionable business outcomes. Readers are encouraged to adapt these approaches to their unique business challenges, considering both the technical and human elements of effective data communication.

# ANNEXURE 3: TECHNICAL RESOURCES AND TOOLS

## Purpose and Connection

For business professionals seeking to deepen their data visualization practice, selecting the right tools and resources is crucial. This annexure provides an overview of recommended software, libraries, and learning platforms, aligned with the principles and techniques discussed in the book. It aims to empower readers to translate theory into practice, regardless of technical background.

## Selecting the Right Visualization Tool

The choice of tool depends on several factors:

- **Audience:** Will the visuals be interactive or static? Is the audience internal or external?
- **Data Complexity:** Are you working with simple summaries or large, multi-dimensional datasets?
- **Collaboration Needs:** Do you require cloud-based sharing and real-time updates?
- **Technical Expertise:** Is coding required, or will a drag-and-drop interface suffice?

## Popular Visualization Tools

### *1. Tableau*

Widely used in business environments, Tableau offers a drag-and-drop interface, extensive chart options, and robust connectivity to various data sources. It is suitable for both analysts and executives.

**Example Application:**

A marketing manager uses Tableau to create interactive dashboards tracking campaign performance, enabling real-time exploration in client meetings.

### *2. Microsoft Power BI*

Power BI integrates seamlessly with Microsoft products, making it ideal for organizations already using the Office suite. It offers strong data modeling capabilities and easy sharing within enterprise environments.

**Example Application:**

A finance team builds monthly P&L reports with drill-down capabilities, allowing executives to explore variances by business unit.

### *3. Google Data Studio (Looker Studio)*

This free, web-based tool is excellent for collaborative reporting and integrates well with Google Analytics and other cloud services.

**Example Application:**

A digital agency creates live reports for clients, visualizing web traffic, conversions, and SEO performance.

### *4. Python & R Visualization Libraries (matplotlib, seaborn, ggplot2, plotly)*

For data scientists and technical analysts, coding libraries offer maximum flexibility and customization. They are ideal for advanced analytics or embedding visuals in applications.

```
import matplotlib.pyplot as plt

# Example: Simple line chartmonths = [ 'Jan', 'Feb', 'Mar', 'Apr']
sales = [1000, 1200, 1100, 1500]
plt.plot(months, sales)
plt.title( 'Monthly Sales Trend')
plt.xlabel( 'Month')
plt.ylabel( 'Sales')
plt.show()
```

## Learning Platforms and Resources

**Coursera, edX, Udemy:** Offer courses on data visualization, analytics, and storytelling, ranging from beginner to advanced.

**The Data Visualization Society:** A global community for sharing best practices, case studies, and networking.

**Books and Blogs:**

- *Storytelling with Data* by Cole Nussbaumer Knaflic
- *The Big Book of Dashboards* by Steve Wexler et al.
- Blogs by FlowingData, Information is Beautiful, and Tableau Public

## Data Sources for Practice

To hone your skills, use publicly available datasets:

**World Bank Open Data:** Economic, social, and development indicators worldwide.

**Kaggle:** A platform for data competitions and datasets across industries.
**UN Data Portal:** Global statistics on demographics, trade, and more.

## Summary

Equipped with the right tools and resources, business professionals can elevate their data storytelling practice from static charts to interactive, persuasive narratives. This annexure encourages ongoing learning and experimentation, underscoring the principle that effective data storytelling is both an art and a science.

# ANNEXURE 4: CHART SELECTION GUIDE

## Purpose and Connection

Choosing the appropriate chart type is fundamental to effective data storytelling. This annexure serves as a quick-reference guide, helping business professionals align their visualization choices with the story they need to tell. It supports the book's emphasis on clarity, relevance, and audience engagement.

## Chart Types and When to Use Them

### *1. Comparison*

**Best for:** Comparing values across categories (e.g., sales by region, product performance).

**Bar chart:** For discrete categories.
**Column chart:** For time-based or ordinal data.
**Bullet chart:** For performance against a target.

*Application Example:*

A sales executive compares quarterly revenue across four regions using a grouped column chart, instantly highlighting the top-performing area.

### *2. Distribution*

**Best for:** Showing the spread or concentration of data (e.g., customer age, product ratings).

**Histogram:** For continuous data distributions.
**Box plot:** For comparing distributions between groups.

*Application Example:*

An HR manager visualizes employee age distribution to inform recruitment and retention strategies.

### *3. Trend Over Time*

**Best for:** Displaying changes, seasonality, or long-term trends (e.g., website traffic, stock prices).

**Line chart:** For continuous time series.
**Area chart:** For cumulative totals or emphasizing volume.

*Application Example:*

A marketing analyst tracks weekly email open rates over a year using a line chart, identifying seasonal peaks.

#### *4. Part-to-Whole Relationship*

**Best for:** Showing proportions within a whole (e.g., market share, budget allocation).

**Pie chart:** For simple, few categories (use sparingly).
**Stacked bar chart:** For detailed part-to-whole breakdowns.

*Application Example:*

A nonprofit visualizes funding sources using a stacked bar, making it easy to compare government, private, and public contributions.

#### *5. Correlation and Relationship*

**Best for:** Exploring relationships between two variables (e.g., advertising spend vs. sales).

**Scatter plot:** For patterns, clusters, or outliers.
**Bubble chart:** Adds a third variable (size).

*Application Example:*

A product manager investigates correlation between product ratings and return rates using a scatter plot.

### Cultural and Accessibility Considerations

Use culturally neutral colors or localize palettes for international audiences.
Avoid red-green combinations for colorblind accessibility.
Always provide labels, legends, and context for non-technical stakeholders.

### Summary

Selecting the right chart type transforms data from confusion to clarity. This guide equips you to match your message with the most effective visual form, ensuring your data stories resonate with diverse business audiences and drive informed decisions.

# FURTHER READING

**1. Visualising Information for Advocacy: An Introduction to Information Design**

Tactical Tech Collective (Guide, Free Download)

Focused on advocacy and social impact, this guide offers practical advice on using visuals to influence and inform. It's particularly valuable for readers interested in communication that transcends business, including nonprofit, public sector, or global development contexts. The guide broadens the book's perspective on the power of data storytelling for change.

**2. The Big Book of Dashboards: Visualizing Your Data Using Real-World Business Scenarios**

Steve Wexler, Jeffrey Shaffer, Andy Cotgreave (Book)

A must-have resource for those building business dashboards, this book presents dozens of dashboard examples across industries and functions. It provides actionable advice on choosing the right visuals and overcoming common challenges, including international perspectives. It pairs well with this guide by offering hands-on, scenario-based insights that help readers translate theory into business impact.

**3. Data Visualisation: A Handbook for Data Driven Design**

Andy Kirk (Book)

Kirk's handbook is an accessible introduction to data visualization, covering both conceptual frameworks and practical techniques. Its comprehensive structure—exploring form, function, and design—supports business professionals in mastering fundamentals and refining their visual storytelling skills. This resource extends the book's coverage of design principles and expands on effective communication through visuals.

**4. Good Charts: The HBR Guide to Making Smarter, More Persuasive Data Visualizations**

Scott Berinato (Book)

Targeted at business leaders and communicators, this Harvard Business Review guide breaks down the psychology and mechanics of persuasive data visuals. Berinato explains how to create charts that drive decision-making and action. The book's rich business cases and clear frameworks deepen readers' understanding of how narrative and design combine to influence outcomes.

**5. Data Story: Explain Data and Inspire Action Through Story**

Nancy Duarte (Book)

Duarte's expertise in corporate storytelling shines in this book, which equips professionals to bridge the gap between data analysis and persuasive business narratives. It offers tools for structuring stories, understanding audiences, and designing visuals that resonate. This resource amplifies the book's focus on emotional connection and practical storytelling.

**6. Information Dashboard Design: Displaying Data for At-a-Glance Monitoring**

Stephen Few (Book)

A classic in the field, this book covers the principles of dashboard design for business environments. Few's practical advice on clarity, simplicity, and actionable insights aligns with the book's emphasis on business impact. Readers will appreciate its actionable frameworks and real-world critiques, applicable whether working in finance, marketing, or operations.

**7. Makeover Monday: Improving How We Visualize and Analyze Data, One Chart at a Time**

Andy Kriebel, Eva Murray (Book)

Based on the global data visualization community's weekly project, this book offers a collection of before-and-after chart makeovers, with explanations for each transformation. It provides hands-on practice and diverse examples, encouraging readers to develop their own style. This resource is especially useful for readers seeking to refine their visual skills through iteration and feedback.

**8. The Functional Art: An Introduction to Information Graphics and Visualization**

Alberto Cairo (Book)

Cairo explores the intersection of function, design, and storytelling in information graphics. Combining theory with practical case studies, this book helps readers think critically about visual communication. Its insights into international news graphics and cross-cultural storytelling enrich the book's global perspective and practical application.

**9. Effective Data Storytelling: How to Drive Change with Data, Narrative and Visuals**

Brent Dykes (Book)

Dykes delivers a comprehensive guide to blending narrative structure with data and visuals for business communication. He outlines a repeatable process for building persuasive data stories that inspire action, making it highly relevant to business professionals. The book's actionable templates and real-world examples reinforce this guide's core themes.

**10. Data Visualization: A Practical Introduction**

Kieran Healy (Book)

Focusing on practical skills, Healy introduces readers to modern data visualization tools using R and ggplot2. While technical, it's approachable for non-coders, providing reproducible examples relevant to business analytics. This resource extends the book's practical toolkit for readers seeking hands-on experience in building effective visualizations.

**11. Visualising Data (Blog)**

Andy Kirk (Website/Blog)

This long-standing blog curates articles, resources, and examples on data visualization for all skill levels. Regularly updated, it includes tool reviews, expert interviews, and visualization critiques. It's a dynamic complement to the book, offering ongoing learning and exposure to global trends and best practices.

**12. Tableau Public Gallery**

Tableau Software (Website)

A showcase of interactive visualizations created by the global Tableau community, this gallery provides inspiration and practical examples across industries and cultures. Exploring these dashboards helps readers see real-world applications of design and storytelling concepts, complementing the book's emphasis on actionable data communication.

**13. Fundamentals of Data Visualization**

Claus O. Wilke (Book, Open Access)

Wilke's open-access book is a clear, example-driven introduction to the craft of visualization. Covering key principles, pitfalls, and design choices, it's suitable for business professionals seeking technical fluency without overwhelming detail. The resource is especially helpful for those who want to deepen their understanding of chart types and clarity.

**14. Harvard Business Review: Data & Visuals**

Harvard Business Review Editors (Articles/Website)

HBR's collection of articles on data visualization and storytelling addresses the unique needs of business professionals. Topics include visual persuasion, dashboard design, and effective communication in global organizations. These timely, research-backed insights align with the book's business focus and provide ongoing professional development.

**15. Datawrapper Academy**

Datawrapper (Online Tutorials)

Datawrapper offers free, beginner-friendly tutorials for creating accessible, professional charts and maps. Its Academy covers both the "how" and the "why" behind visualization choices, making it ideal for business users with limited technical backgrounds. The platform's emphasis on clarity and inclusivity matches the book's principles.

**16. Nightingale: The Journal of the Data Visualization Society**

Data Visualization Society (Magazine/Website)

Nightingale publishes diverse, global perspectives on data storytelling, design, and ethics. Articles range from technical tutorials to cultural critiques, offering a rich resource for professionals seeking to understand the broader impact of data visualization. It extends the book's coverage of cultural context and ethical communication.

**17. Google Data Studio Help Center**

Google (Online Documentation)

For business professionals using Google's free data visualization tool, this comprehensive help center offers guides, templates, and troubleshooting tips. It empowers users to create interactive reports and dashboards, supporting the book's focus on practical, scalable business solutions.

**18. Visual Vocabulary**

Financial Times Visual Journalism Team (Reference Guide)

This downloadable resource provides a taxonomy of chart types with clear examples and guidance on appropriate uses. It's invaluable for professionals seeking to match business questions to effective visual formats, reinforcing the book's chart selection frameworks.

**19. Introduction to Data Visualization with Python**

DataCamp (Online Course)

A hands-on, business-focused course for those looking to use Python for data visualization. It covers basic to intermediate skills, including chart creation and customization. This resource extends the book's toolkit for readers interested in automating or scaling their visualizations programmatically.

**20. LinkedIn Learning: Data Visualization for Data Analysis and Analytics**

Bill Shander (Online Course)

This course explores how to communicate insights visually for business stakeholders. Shander emphasizes storytelling, audience needs, and actionable outcomes, aligning closely with the book's themes. The course format offers interactive learning and practical exercises for immediate application.

**21. The Truthful Art: Data, Charts, and Maps for Communication**

Alberto Cairo (Book)

A follow-up to The Functional Art, this book dives deeper into the ethics and accuracy of data communication. Cairo's focus on "truthfulness" is essential for building trust and credibility, a key business concern discussed throughout this book.

**22. One Chart at a Time (YouTube Series)**

Andy Cotgreave (Video Series)

Each episode explores a different chart type, with business context and design tips. The series is concise and approachable, making it easy for busy professionals to pick up new skills and ideas. It complements the book's practical approach to chart selection.

**23. Data Visualization Society Resources**

Data Visualization Society (Website/Community)

This global professional community offers curated resources, networking, events, and best practices for business communicators and analysts. Membership and active participation help readers stay current with emerging trends and connect with peers worldwide.

**24. The Guardian Datablog**

The Guardian (Blog)

This influential news blog features innovative data journalism and visual storytelling on global topics. Its diverse examples demonstrate how data can be used to engage broad audiences, providing business professionals with inspiration for impactful communication in multicultural contexts.

These resources collectively support the journey from foundational understanding to advanced mastery in data storytelling and visualization, ensuring readers of all backgrounds and business needs can find guidance, inspiration, and practical tools to amplify their professional impact.

# BIBLIOGRAPHY

Azzam, T. (2020). Data visualization in evaluation: New directions for evaluation, number 158. Jossey-Bass.

Berinato, S. (2016). Good charts: The HBR guide to making smarter, more persuasive data visualizations. Harvard Business Review Press.

*Berinato's book is a practical guide for business professionals seeking to create persuasive data visualizations. It offers actionable advice, real-world examples, and emphasizes the importance of clarity and narrative in data-driven communication, aligning well with the book's focus on storytelling.*

Bigman, C. A., & Anker, A. E. (2017). Using narrative communication as a tool for promoting health behavior change: A conceptual, theoretical, and empirical overview. Health Education & Behavior, 44(5), 823-832.

Börner, K. (2015). Atlas of knowledge: Anyone can map. MIT Press.

Boukhelifa, N., & Duke, D. J. (2020). Uncertainty visualization: Why might it fail? Computers & Graphics, 91, 1-12.

Cairo, A. (2019). How charts lie: Getting smarter about visual information. W. W. Norton & Company.

*This book exposes common misinterpretations and manipulations in charts, teaching readers to critically analyze visual data. Cairo's insights are essential for both creating honest visualizations and helping readers avoid common pitfalls.*

Cairo, A. (2016). The truthful art: Data, charts, and maps for communication. New Riders.

Cleveland, W. S. (2013). Visualizing data. Hobart Press.

Cukier, K., & Mayer-Schoenberger, V. (2014). The rise of big data: How it's changing the way we think about the world. Foreign Affairs, 92(3), 28-40.

Dykes, B., & Allsopp, J. (2020). Effective data storytelling: How to drive change with data, narrative and visuals. Wiley.

*Dykes and Allsopp provide a comprehensive framework for integrating narrative and visualization to drive business change. Their emphasis on actionable insights and organizational impact makes this source particularly relevant for business professionals.*

Few, S. (2012). Show me the numbers: Designing tables and graphs to enlighten (2nd ed.). Analytics Press.

Few, S. (2018). Data visualization effectiveness profile. Perceptual Edge.

Fry, B. (2018). Visualizing data: Exploring and explaining data with the processing environment. O'Reilly Media.

Google. (2022). Data Studio Help. https://support.google.com/datastudio/?hl=en#topic=6267740

Healy, K. (2018). Data visualization: A practical introduction. Princeton University Press.

Knaflic, C. N. (2015). Storytelling with data: A data visualization guide for business professionals. Wiley.

*Knaflic's widely acclaimed book is foundational for understanding how to blend data visualization with storytelling techniques. It offers step-by-step examples, practical tips, and best practices, making it an excellent resource for both novices and experts.*

Knaflic, C. N. (2019). Storytelling with data: Let's practice! Wiley.

Krum, R. (2013). Cool infographics: Effective communication with data visualization and design. Wiley.

Lankow, J., Ritchie, J., & Crooks, R. (2012). Infographics: The power of visual storytelling. Wiley.

Lindquist, E., & Copeland, D. (2020). Data storytelling: The essential data science skill everyone needs. Harvard Business Review. https://hbr.org/2020/03/data-storytelling-the-essential-data-science-skill-everyone-needs

*This HBR article highlights the growing importance of data storytelling in business, advocating for a blend of analytical rigor and narrative skill. It underlines key skills and strategies that align directly with the goals of this book.*

Miller, J. (2017). The data storytelling workbook: Using data to inspire action. DataStory Academy Press.

Miller, S. (2019). Data storytelling for marketers: How to tell compelling stories with data. Kogan Page.

Murray, S. (2017). Interactive data visualization for the web (2nd ed.). O'Reilly Media.

Nussbaumer Knaflic, C. (2022). Beyond dashboards: Enabling data-driven decisions throughout your organization. Wiley.

OECD. (2022). Data-driven innovation in business. OECD Digital Economy Papers, No. 341. https://doi.org/10.1787/4ffebf55-en

Pandey, A. (2021). Visualizing data with Microsoft Power BI. Packt Publishing.

Qlik. (2020). The business value of data storytelling. Qlik Whitepaper. https://www.qlik.com/us/resource-library/the-business-value-of-data-storytelling

*This industry report explores how organizations use data storytelling to drive business value, with case studies from various sectors. It provides a business-focused perspective that bridges technical visualization with measurable impact.*

Rowell, J., & Ouellette, J. (2020). Visual storytelling with D3: An introduction to data-driven graphics and visualization on the web. Addison-Wesley.

SAS. (2019). Data visualization: What it is and why it matters. https://www.sas.com/en_us/insights/big-data/data-visualization.html

Schwabish, J. A. (2021). Better data visualizations: A guide for scholars, researchers, and wonks. Columbia University Press.

*Schwabish offers a comprehensive overview of visualization types and how to choose the right one for any data story. His guidance is especially useful for professionals who need to communicate complex information with clarity.*

Segel, E., & Heer, J. (2010). Narrative visualization: Telling stories with data. IEEE Transactions on Visualization and Computer Graphics, 16(6), 1139-1148.

Smith, S., & MacGregor, J. N. (2019). Using data visualization to make better decisions faster. MIT Sloan Management Review, 60(2), 1-7.

Tableau. (2022). Data storytelling: What it is, why it matters, and how to do it. https://www.tableau.com/learn/articles/data-storytelling

Tufte, E. R. (2013). The visual display of quantitative information (2nd ed.). Graphics Press.

Tufte, E. R. (2006). Beautiful evidence. Graphics Press.

Wexler, S., Shaffer, J., & Cotgreave, A. (2017). The big book of dashboards: Visualizing your data using real-world business scenarios. Wiley.

*This book provides practical dashboard and visualization solutions for a wide variety of business challenges, using case studies from different industries. Its pragmatic approach is ideal for readers looking to apply concepts directly to their own organizations.*

Yau, N. (2016). Visualize this: The FlowingData guide to design, visualization, and statistics. Wiley.

Yau, N. (2017). Data points: Visualization that means something. Wiley.

Yoon, A. (2021). Data storytelling in business: How to communicate with data and drive better decision making. Routledge.

Zhao, J., & Vande Moere, A. (2021). Embodiment in data storytelling: A survey of the literature. IEEE Transactions on Visualization and Computer Graphics, 27(2), 1116-1134.

**Annotations for Key Sources**

**Berinato, S. (2016). Good charts: The HBR guide to making smarter, more persuasive data visualizations. Harvard Business Review Press.**

This book bridges the gap between data analysis and business communication. Berinato demystifies visualization by focusing on clarity, persuasion, and narrative, making it a key resource for business professionals aiming to make data impactful.

**Cairo, A. (2019). How charts lie: Getting smarter about visual information. W. W. Norton & Company.**

Cairo's work provides a critical perspective on interpreting data visualizations, discussing how charts can mislead and how to avoid these pitfalls. This is essential for professionals to develop both critical consumption and creation skills in data storytelling.

**Dykes, B., & Allsopp, J. (2020). Effective data storytelling: How to drive change with data, narrative and visuals. Wiley.**

Dykes and Allsopp's book is a practical manual for using narrative and visuals to influence business outcomes. It offers actionable frameworks and case studies, directly supporting the book's goal of integrating data and storytelling for business impact.

**Knaflic, C. N. (2015). Storytelling with data: A data visualization guide for business professionals. Wiley.**

This foundational text provides step-by-step instructions for creating effective, accessible, and persuasive data visualizations. Knaflic makes complex concepts approachable, ensuring readers can immediately apply techniques in their own business contexts.

**Lindquist, E., & Copeland, D. (2020). Data storytelling: The essential data science skill everyone needs. Harvard Business Review.**

This article emphasizes the critical role of storytelling in translating data insights into actionable business decisions. It aligns with the book's focus on the intersection of technical skills and persuasive communication.

**Qlik. (2020). The business value of data storytelling. Qlik Whitepaper.**

Qlik's industry report provides a business-oriented view on how data storytelling drives value. It includes case studies and practice-oriented insights, demonstrating the tangible impact of good data communication in organizations.

**Schwabish, J. A. (2021). Better data visualizations: A guide for scholars, researchers, and wonks. Columbia University Press.**

Schwabish compiles a comprehensive toolkit for choosing and designing effective visualizations. His focus on matching the right chart to the data story enhances the practical approach of the book.

**Wexler, S., Shaffer, J., & Cotgreave, A. (2017). The big book of dashboards: Visualizing your data using real-world business scenarios. Wiley.**

This book presents real-world dashboard solutions for varied business challenges, illustrating how visualization can be tailored for different audiences and objectives. Its case studies make it highly relevant for practitioners.

**Tableau. (2022). Data storytelling: What it is, why it matters, and how to do it. https://www.tableau.com/learn/articles/data-storytelling**

Tableau's resource provides up-to-date industry practices, tools, and techniques for applying data storytelling in business. Its practical guidance and examples support readers in implementing concepts using modern visualization platforms.

**OECD. (2022). Data-driven innovation in business. OECD Digital Economy Papers, No. 341.**

This report offers a global perspective on how data-driven practices, including storytelling and visualization, are transforming business innovation. Its cross-cultural approach makes it particularly relevant for readers in diverse markets.

# AFTERWORD: BEYOND THE CHART—SHAPING THE FUTURE

As we reach the close of this journey through the art and science of data storytelling, it's worth pausing to reflect on how far we've come—and how far you, as a business professional, can go by harnessing the power of data visualization. The chapters preceding this epilogue have equipped you with practical frameworks, design principles, and communication strategies to transform raw numbers into narratives that inform, inspire, and influence. Yet, beyond the techniques and tools, the true value of mastering data storytelling lies in its capacity to bridge the gap between data and decision-making, between insight and action, and ultimately, between organizations and the people they serve.

## Synthesizing the Journey: From Data to Lasting Impact

Throughout this book, we began with the foundational belief that data is not just a collection of numbers—it is a language, a potential story waiting to be told. We explored the importance of clarity in visualization, the psychology of color and design, and the necessity of context when presenting insights. You learned how to select the right chart for your data, how to employ visual hierarchy to guide your audience's attention, and how to weave facts and figures into narratives that resonate at both intellectual and emotional levels.

These skills are not theoretical—they are essential. In today's global business environment, where information overload is the norm and attention spans are fleeting, clear and compelling data storytelling can be the differentiator that sets your message, your idea, or your initiative apart. The ability to communicate data-driven insights effectively is now among the most sought-after competencies in business, transcending roles, industries, and cultures.

## The Transformative Power of Applied Data Storytelling

To fully appreciate the potential of these techniques, let's revisit how they come alive in the real world. Consider the following examples from diverse business contexts:

### *Case Study 1: Unifying Global Teams at a Multinational Tech Company*

A leading technology firm headquartered in Germany faced a challenge common to many global organizations: siloed data and fragmented narratives across regional offices. Quarterly business reviews had devolved into a barrage of dense spreadsheets and inconsistent charts, leaving executives confused and disengaged.

With the adoption of a unified data storytelling approach, the company's analytics team began crafting interactive dashboards that combined key metrics with succinct narrative summaries and intuitive visual cues. By standardizing color palettes and applying consistent design principles, they created a common visual language that transcended linguistic and cultural barriers. The results were immediate: greater engagement in meetings, faster consensus-building, and a measurable improvement in cross-regional collaboration. Instead of data being a source of confusion, it became a catalyst for global alignment.

***Case Study 2: Driving Social Impact in Southeast Asia***

In Indonesia, a non-profit organization dedicated to improving public health needed to communicate the urgency of childhood vaccination rates to government officials and rural community leaders. Raw statistics alone failed to convey the real-world consequences of inaction.

By partnering with local data visualization experts, the organization developed story-driven infographics that mapped vaccination gaps alongside personal stories and regional health outcomes. The combination of emotionally resonant narratives and clear visuals empowered officials to prioritize resources and inspired community buy-in. Within a year, vaccination rates increased by 20 percent in targeted districts—a testament to the persuasive power of well-crafted data stories.

***Case Study 3: Marketing Innovation in the United States***

A midsize retail brand in the United States sought to revitalize its marketing strategy in the face of declining customer engagement. Traditional campaign reports, filled with pie charts and tables, failed to tell a compelling story about shifting consumer preferences.

The marketing team embraced data storytelling techniques learned from this book: they began framing campaign results within the context of evolving customer journeys, using annotated line charts and customer persona illustrations. By focusing on trends and cause-and-effect relationships, they communicated not just what happened, but why it mattered. The impact was striking—executive buy-in increased, budgets were reallocated to high-performing channels, and the brand's share of voice grew in a competitive market.

## The Broader Implications for Business Communication

These stories, drawn from different sectors and continents, highlight a universal truth: data storytelling is not merely a technical skill, but a strategic capability that can transform organizations. At its core, it is about making data human, relatable, and actionable. Whether you're a marketer in New York, an analyst in Mumbai, or an executive in São Paulo, the principles of effective data communication can bridge cultural divides and unify teams around shared goals.

Moreover, as organizations become more data-driven, the stakes for clear communication rise. Misinterpreted data can lead to costly missteps, while well-told data stories can inspire innovation, foster trust, and drive growth. In a world where business decisions are increasingly scrutinized by diverse stakeholders—investors, customers, regulators, and the public—the ability to communicate with precision and empathy is not just an asset, but a necessity.

### Looking Forward: The Future of Data Storytelling

As you look to apply these lessons in your own professional context, it's worth considering the trends and challenges that will shape the future of data storytelling.

First, the democratization of data is accelerating. Advances in self-service analytics tools and platforms mean that more people across organizations can access and visualize data than ever before. This democratization brings opportunity and risk: while it empowers individuals, it also increases the likelihood of miscommunication and misinterpretation. The need for clear, ethical, and context-rich storytelling will only grow.

Second, new forms of data—such as unstructured text, geospatial data, and real-time streams—are expanding the boundaries of what can be visualized. The future will demand fluency not only in traditional charts and dashboards, but also in emerging modalities like interactive storytelling, augmented reality, and data-driven video.

Third, cultural and ethical considerations will become increasingly pivotal. As data stories reach broader audiences, it is essential to ensure that visualizations are accessible, inclusive, and sensitive to local contexts. The responsibility to avoid misleading representations and to communicate uncertainty transparently will rest on the shoulders of every data storyteller.

Finally, artificial intelligence and automation are poised to play a growing role in the creation and interpretation of data stories. While AI can suggest visualizations or surface insights, the uniquely human ability to craft context, empathy, and narrative will remain irreplaceable. The future of data storytelling lies in partnership—where technology augments, but does not replace, human judgment and creativity.

### Your Call to Action: Become a Data Storyteller

With these insights in mind, consider where you stand today. Are you still presenting data as static tables and generic charts, or are you seizing the opportunity to shape perceptions and decisions through storytelling? Are you empowering your colleagues to see not just the "what" but the "why" behind your numbers? Are you using visualization to build bridges across teams, markets, and cultures?

The journey does not end with the last page of this book. The tools, principles, and strategies you've learned are only as powerful as the actions you take next. Challenge yourself to:

Apply the visualization best practices in your next presentation, report, or meeting.
Seek feedback from colleagues outside your immediate domain to ensure your data stories resonate broadly.
Stay curious about new tools, methods, and cultural perspectives that can enrich your storytelling.
Advocate for a culture of data literacy within your organization, where every team member feels empowered to communicate insights effectively.

Remember, data storytelling is not about embellishing the truth—it's about illuminating it. It's about making the invisible visible, the complex comprehensible, and the abstract actionable. In doing so, you have the power to inspire trust, drive innovation, and create lasting impact in your organization and beyond.

### Closing Reflection: The Legacy You Create

As we usher in a new era of data-driven business, the most successful organizations will be those that marry analytical rigor with narrative clarity. They will be led by professionals who understand that behind every data point is a human story, and behind every visualization, an opportunity to connect.

Let your data stories be the spark that ignites change—within your team, your company, and the world at large. The future of business belongs to those who can not only interpret the numbers, but also move hearts and minds with the stories they tell.

Go forth, and make your insights unforgettable. Your story—and your impact—awaits.

Made in United States
Troutdale, OR
11/03/2026

56845381R00173